So, What Am I Doing Here, Anyway?

Astrological and Philosophical Essays

Also by Ray Grasse

The Waking Dream: Unlocking the Symbolic Language of Our Lives

Signs of the Times: Unlocking the Symbolic Language of World Events

Under a Sacred Sky: Essays on the Philosophy and Practice of Astrology

An Infinity of Gods: Conversations with an Unconventional Mystic

Urban Mystic: Recollections of Goswami Kriyananda

StarGates: Essays on Astrology, Symbolism and the Synchronistic Universe

The Sky Stretched Out Before Me: Encounters with Mystics, Anomalies, and Waking Dreams

When the Stars Align: Reflections on Astrology, Life, Death, and Other Mysteries

So, What Am I Doing Here, Anyway?

Astrological and Philosophical Essays

Ray Grasse

THE WESSEX ASTROLOGER

Published in 2024 by
The Wessex Astrologer Ltd
PO Box 9307
Swanage
BH19 9BF

For a full list of our titles go to www.wessexastrologer.com

© Ray Grasse 2024
Ray Grasse asserts his moral right to be recognised as
the author of this work

eISBN 9781916625136

Cover design by Fiona Bowring at Bowring Creative
Typeset by Kevin Moore
Astrology charts created using Solar Fire v9.0.29 Astrolabe Inc (alabe.com)

All pictures are the author's unless otherwise indicated
Line illustrations by Thomas Tiernan and Ray Grasse

A catalogue record for this book is available at The British Library

No part of this book may be reproduced or used in any form or by any
means without the written permission of the publisher.
A reviewer may quote brief passages..

Table of Contents

Introduction		1
Chapter 1	A Few Words About Sun Sign Astrology	3
Chapter 2	Does the Horoscope Continue Working After Someone's Death?	5
Chapter 3	The Challenge of Vastly Different Astrologies	10
Chapter 4	A Rich Landscape of Meaningfulness	14
Chapter 5	No, We Aren't in Kansas Anymore: A Personal Look Back at the Sixties	17
Chapter 6	Sensitivities	35
Chapter 7	Some Simple Tips from a Long-Time Astrologer	42
Chapter 8	The Surreal Genius of Salvador Dali	58
Chapter 9	You Are the World: The Deep Truth Contained Within Astrology's Twelve-Fold House Structure	71
Chapter 10	Leaving Hell Behind	75
Chapter 11	Toward a Grand Unified Theory of Synchronicity	77
Chapter 12	On the Pleasures of Existence	92
Chapter 13	Can One's Horoscope Indicate a Sense of "Mission"?	101
Chapter 14	Neptune and the Cross of Obligation	107
Chapter 15	The Meal (A Short Story)	117
Chapter 16	The Star Wars Man	119
Chapter 17	So, What Am I Doing Here, Anyway?	123
Chapter 18	Are We "Pattern-Seeking" Creatures?	128
Chapter 19	Whatever Saturn Touches…	131
Chapter 20	My Astrological Guessing Game and the "Late Bloomer" Dynamic	138

So, What Am I Doing Here, Anyway?

Chapter 21 What is "Mother"?	146
Chapter 22 Thinking Outside the Box: A Closer Look at Uranus-Mercury Aspects	151
Chapter 23 What the Movie Barbie Has to Teach Us About Planetary Retrogrades	163
Chapter 24 When the Planets Change Their Clothing: Ten Examples of Planetary Ingresses	166
Chapter 25 The Great Pyramid as a Cipher to Existence	177
Chapter 26 Fritz Lang's Metropolis and the Challenge of A.I.	185
Chapter 27 Stage Fright: Confronting Fears and Transmuting the Horoscope	191
Chapter 28 The Jazz Band Principle and the Aquarian Age	197
Chapter 29 Planting Seeds: Seeing the Long-Term Effects of Transiting Conjunctions	202
Chapter 30 One More Thing About the Sixties: Bigfoot and the Patterson-Gimlin Footage	213
Chapter 31 A Mystical Look at War and Suffering	220
Chapter 32 Arnold, Madonna, and Tom: Three Exemplars of "Manifestation"?	223
Chapter 33 Teaching	229
Chapter 34 Are the "Great Ages" Even Real? (And Does it Even Matter?)	232
Chapter 35 Science and Imagination: A Psychoanalysis of Scientific Discovery	236
Chapter 36 A Synchro-Historic Meditation on the Discovery of the Coelacanth	248
Chapter 37 The Divine Scale: Searching for a Skeleton Key to the Universal Mind	254
Chapter 38 At the Still Point of the Turning World	268
Chapter 39 Legends of the Fall	271
Acknowledgements	283
About the Author	284

"Few men have imagination enough for the truth of reality."

—Goethe

INTRODUCTION

As a writer, perhaps the most meaningful feedback I've received from a reader was hearing them say a book I'd written changed how they see the world, *their* world. That's certainly what I'd say about those writers whose works impacted me in significant ways. *Moby Dick* was one such work, Yogananda's *Autobiography of a Yogi* was another—and there have been many others. We all have our own picks.

Having one's imagination stretched to new boundaries—is there anything more important? It's through the imagination that we can understand other lives and cultures, past or present. It's our imagination that allows us to conceive new futures, step into other dimensions, and open up to possibilities never before considered. Whether they realize it or not, this is actually the implicit goal of all writers, whether fiction or non-fiction—to impact and engage the imagination of readers in some manner.

As with my last two anthologies, this collection of essays explores a diverse range of subjects that sometimes requires ways of imagining you may not have entertained before. Besides astrology, we'll be navigating through such topics as pop culture, synchronicity, art, science, war, sacred geometry, meditation, historical cycles, along with a few autobiographical side-trips that may help shed some light on my own imaginal roots. You may be familiar with many or most of the topics themselves, but it's possible the perspectives we'll be bringing to them will be new to you.

So, What Am I Doing Here, Anyway?

The vast majority of these essays are original to this book, but a small number are from older sources. While the astrological essays included here presume at least a beginner's familiarity with the subject, I've attempted to write them in such a way that hopefully even novices will draw something useful from them, or at least be stimulated enough to explore those themes further.

Regardless of your own background, it's my hope that these essays will stimulate your imagination as well.

— R.G. July, 2023

CHAPTER 1

A Few Words About Sun-Sign Astrology

Like many astrologers, I'm sometimes asked what I think about the sort of popular astrology columns found in newspapers and online sources.

"After all," one fellow said to me, "roughly one-twelfth of the world's population was born under any given zodiacal sign. So how could something as general as a zodiacal sign possibly tell you anything useful about someone?"

My answer to that is similar to what most other astrologers generally say when asked that question—namely, that the Sun sign is really just one facet of the overall horoscope. To truly understand a given horoscope you have to take into account *all* its facets, including the other planets and bodies, their house placements and "aspects," and still other things.

Having said that, though, the Sun sign is hardly unimportant! In a sense, you could think of it as the "ground zero" of a horoscope, as far as revealing a person's core perspective which in turn influences many other factors in their psychology and life. I'll never forget reading Linda Goodman's best-seller book *Sun-Signs* when I was just a teenager, and how startled I was by her detailed descriptions of the different signs and how accurately those seemed to match not only my own personality but those of family members and friends—all based just on Sun signs!

Here is an analogy I've sometimes found useful for conveying that point. Suppose you encounter someone born and raised in Italy.

So, What Am I Doing Here, Anyway?

That by itself actually tells you quite a bit about them. How is that possible when you consider there are so many millions of Italians, all with their own personal character traits and idiosyncrasies?

The reason is that—despite all those individual differences—Italians will generally share certain attitudes and traits intrinsic to their culture, which will be quite different from those experienced by individuals born and raised in Japan, say. Yes, there are a multitude of nuances unique to each individual Italian, just as there are to each individual Japanese, but as a *general* perspective, simply knowing the country someone is from automatically gives you certain basic information about them and how they've been "trained" by their culture. *On average*, an Italian will respond to situations differently than your average Japanese—or for that matter your average Brazilian, American, German, or Iranian person. If you've spent any amount of time in countries besides your own, you will know what I am talking about.

I regard Sun sign astrology as a bit similar to that. Knowing someone's Sun sign is akin to knowing what country or culture someone is from. Yes, there are many millions of people born under any given sign, but you'll find they do share certain broad similarities and traits. Beyond that starting point, of course, there will be a host of unique differences with each person, as revealed by all the other factors in all those individual horoscopes.

In short, while it's a mistake to place *too* much emphasis solely on someone's Sun-sign, it would be a mistake to underestimate its role as well. It may be only one piece of the larger horoscopic puzzle but it's a vitally important one.

In previous books I've explored other pieces of that astrological puzzle; in the following chapters we'll be looking at several more, and perhaps even brush up against a few completely different puzzles along the way.

CHAPTER 2

Does The Horoscope Continue Working After Someone's Death?

In a discipline replete with unusual features, one of the most unusual in astrology is the fact that transits or progressions of planets to someone's horoscope seem to continue working long after that person has passed on.

It's often the case that a famous celebrity or politician will die, then years later they'll experience a huge resurgence of popularity or notoriety: a major film, TV show, or written biography about the person will appear—and lo and behold, you'll see strong indications in their chart of some newfound prominence or attention happening for them right then. Or a person will die and their body will be exhumed years later as part of some investigation, and it takes place precisely when some "resurrectional" transits are firing in their horoscope, like Pluto crossing their Ascendant or a Saturn return. In earlier writings I've mentioned the life and death of mythologist Joseph Campbell as an example of this post-mortem principle in astrology, but here are a few others.

Having received my degree in film, for years I closely followed the work of filmmaker Orson Welles, so I was delighted when the United States Post Office announced in

1999 they were issuing a commemorative stamp honoring him and his film *Citizen Kane*.

I couldn't help but notice that Welles' legacy was being touted on several other fronts during that same time as well, with the release of TV shows like HBO's *RKO 281* and the Tim Robbins' film *Cradle Will Rock*. Suddenly, Welles and his work were extremely "hot" again. I was intrigued by the convergence of all these factors, and looked at his horoscope to see if something might explain it. Among other things, I saw he was precisely in the midst of his posthumous Uranus return. Appropriate? You bet, not only because it shows his life coming full-circle in a way but due to the symbolic connection between Uranus and the media, which this confluence of developments showcased in particular.

Here's another example. In 2011, an imposing statue commemorating the legacy of Martin Luther King Jr. was unveiled in Washington, D.C., as part of a larger memorial to the man. His face and legacy were suddenly so omnipresent in the media, I thought there must surely be something triggering in his horoscope right then—and indeed, there was. The unveiling of his memorial occurred within just *a few days* of his Uranus return, but also close to his Jupiter return and his Neptune half-return as well. By any standards, that was a tectonic year for MLK, even if his spirit wasn't around in physical form to appreciate it!

My astrological colleague Karen Christino recently called attention on social media to another example of this phenomenon associated with a statue, but this one portraying a decidedly different figure: the leader of the Confederate army during the U.S. Civil War, General Robert E. Lee. A statue of the general has stood in Charlottesville, Virginia since 1924, but in the wake of controversy over Lee's past connection with slavery and racism, the statue was melted down and rendered into bronze during the fall of 2022. Lee died in 1870, so it naturally prompts the question: was this development indicated by any modern activations to

Lee's horoscope? Indeed it was, and in a particularly striking way: exactly as this literal melt-down occurred, transformational and alchemical Pluto was transiting over Lee's natal Sun, the symbol of ego and public reputation. One would be hard-pressed to come up with a more fitting transit for this event than this.

Nor does this sort of thing only just happen with the benefit of 20/20 hindsight—the lazy fallback of some astrologers, alas. (I'm reminded of a comedian on late-night TV years ago who played a psychic with the catch phrase, "*I predict the past!*") Some 15 years ago I examined the horoscope of artist Vincent van Gogh and noticed that his Neptune return would be coming up in 2017, give or take twelve months on either side. That was when this distant planet would be making a complete return to where it was at his birth in 1853. I marked down that upcoming time in my computer's calendar, mentioned it to a few friends on social media, and kept my eyes peeled for any significant attention being paid to him during that time. My best guess was it would most likely take the form of some major film or TV series based on his life and work.

As it turned out, that's when the artist cropped up in a number of places, but especially via a highly celebrated film about his life, *At Eternity's Gate*. Directed by Julian Schnabel, it starred actor Willem Dafoe in the lead, and was filmed in 2017 but released in 2018. It not only came out during van Gogh's Neptune return but within days of a Neptune station, thus amplifying the influence of that return exponentially. (The movie went into wide release on November 16, Neptune changed direction on November 24.) On top of that, Pluto was crossing over his Descendant/Ascendant axis at the time, suggesting a bringing forward of old themes and energies from his past into the present day.

We could cite many examples of this phenomenon, drawing on the lives of other well-known figures from history—Abraham Lincoln, Walt Disney, Madame Blavatsky, and countless others—and I'm sure many of my colleagues could cite examples as well.

So, What Am I Doing Here, Anyway?

The question is, *what does a phenomenon like this really say about astrology?*

To my mind, examples like these clearly undercut any simplistic mechanistic or "force-based" theories as to how astrology really works. Why? Because how could celestial energies coming down from the heavens affect someone when that "someone" is no longer even alive? Who or what is being affected in those cases, exactly?

My own take is this. The explanation here is almost certainly spiritual or metaphysical in nature. A chart continues working in this way *because it is an imprint in the cosmic mind*. Whereas the physical body comes and goes, the horoscope has a life of its own. Unlike a purely physical entity or phenomenon, the chart is essentially a mental phenomenon in the mind of—dare I say it?—God, Allah, Brahma, or as Plotinus called it, *the One*.

Your horoscope "works" in these ways not because of some tangible energy like electromagnetism or gravity affecting your body and brain, but because your personality is a living entity in the cosmic imagination, not unlike Hamlet existed in the mind of Shakespeare or Ahab in Melville's imagination. That's not to say there are no physical energies involved with astrology at all, simply that they represent a comparatively small facet of its workings. In the case of post-mortem astrology especially, it's as though the planets continue to affect the *legacy* and *reputation* of that individual over time, beyond just that person's physical presence.

The horoscope doesn't abide by strictly mechanical laws any more than an idea in your mind does, or a figure in a playwright's imagination; it abides by the "laws" of the universal imagination. This explains not only how a horoscope continues working after death but illumines such otherwise mysterious workings of astrology such as "day for a year" progressions, the theory of correspondences, horary astrology, and the division of both the zodiac and horoscope into twelve parts—none of which quite make sense from a purely materialistic standpoint but which are quite sensible in a universe based on laws of the mind.

In short, one's horoscope lingers because our presence continues to exist as a living meme in the fabric of reality itself. As a spirit, you may well move on from this world, casting the body and all its works behind, but the *idea* of your personality, and all it's done, remains forever imprinted on existence, and along with it the horoscope and its celestial signature. *That* remains.

CHAPTER 3

The Challenge of Vastly Different Astrologies

Many of those reading this piece are probably ensconced in the Western astrological tradition, working primarily with techniques handed down through European and Middle Eastern cultures, with some others working in the Hindu astrological tradition, perhaps.

But there are many astrological traditions born of other historical streams radically different from these, such as the Mayan, Tibetan, Aztec, Chinese, Egyptian, Navaho, and many others.

It's true, there are certain commonalities linking many of these systems with our own, and those usually involve the qualities of the planets, or sometimes the 12-fold division of the zodiac and houses. But for the most part there can be profound differences amongst all of these—sometimes even when it comes to the planets or that 12-fold chart division. All of which leaves us with some fairly challenging questions to ponder.

For example, do we simply relegate all those other systems to history's dustbin of made-up beliefs about the cosmos, with no intrinsic validity of their own? I've read critiques exactly like that from skeptics over the years—namely, the fact that so many different cultures have projected such different conceptual maps onto the sky clearly demonstrates just how subjective and imaginary they all really are. Or so the critics say.

From that standpoint, the fact that those belief systems survived as long as they did was simply the result of "confirmation bias" on

The Challenge of Vastly Different Astrologies

a more collective level—that is, we essentially find the results that affirm what we're looking for and conveniently ignore those which don't. An analogy would be the way European and early American doctors saw bloodletting as a cure for many ailments for centuries, fully believing in its value. How was that possible, if not due to bias-confirming delusions?

On the other hand, it could be that each of these astrological traditions has its own relative validity for its own time and place, despite how radically different it may be from other systems that aim to "decode the stars." After all, most of these traditions enjoyed a long history; can we really conclude that all the individuals employing them *never* obtained valid info by means of them, and *never* made accurate predictions using those techniques?

Another Perspective on the Problem

While I don't doubt that the sort of mass "confirmation bias" mentioned earlier explains some of what sustained these traditions, there are a couple of ways to account for their persistence and how it's possible they could have indeed produced valid results for users.

One of those is the fact that there are many different ways to "slice the cosmic pie," as it were, with each of these cultures coming up with its own unique methods for extracting information from the cosmos.

By analogy, think of the way several different literary scholars might look at Herman Melville's *Moby Dick* and come away with uniquely different interpretations, yet all of them might be valid. How is that possible?

It's because a symbolic text can be read on different levels, with different readers or scholars looking for (and finding) different things, using their very different perspectives, backgrounds, and objectives. One of those scholars might focus on the sociological

So, What Am I Doing Here, Anyway?

level, another on a more Freudian level, another on a more Jungian level, and so on.

In much the same way, I'd suggest that the cosmos is itself a "symbolic text" of sorts, and can be read on different levels using different perspectives, backgrounds, and objectives.

As a result, one astrological system might choose to divvy up the year into 260 days and 20 zodiacal signs, as did the Aztecs, and with that approach uncover symbolic patterns not available to someone employing a system divvying up the year into 365 days and 12 months, like most of us in the West do. Likewise, another system might focus its attention on the rising or setting of stars throughout the year, as did the ancient Egyptians, and develop a detailed body of symbolic information we might not pay nearly as much attention to in our own tradition.

Is There a "Synchronistic Zeitgeist"?

Which brings me to the following thought. Is it possible a given civilization comes up with precisely the sky-maps and belief systems symbolically appropriate to that culture at that time?

Said a little differently, maybe it's conceivable that a society historically unfolds within its own symbolic "mind-field," its own *synchronistic zeitgeist* that informs all its beliefs, rituals, and perhaps even historic events. As such, their chosen astrological practices—however "weird" by other standards—might actually be perfectly suited to their spiritual and emotional needs at the time.

In the end, I suspect the reality may lie in some combination of these factors, with many of these traditions—including our own—representing a blend of genuinely effective techniques alongside genuinely fantastical notions. After all, just as certain medical procedures of the past have fallen by the wayside, so there may well be astrological notions we currently use that will eventually be left behind by future astrologers.

Whatever the truth of the matter, these are worthwhile questions to ponder when weighing the relative value of astrological systems and techniques around the world, and their sometimes dramatic differences from our own.

CHAPTER 4

A Rich Landscape of Meaningfulness

When the tragedy of 9/11 unfolded in New York City back in 2001, most astrologers looked to the opposition between Saturn and Pluto taking place at the time as being the most likely explanation for what had just occurred. This is a planetary combo known to often accompany turbulent or "dark" developments in history. Well in advance of 9/11 astrologers had been fearing something of that sort might transpire this time as well.

We all know what happened that day.

While looking through the ephemeris during the days which followed the tragedy, I happened to notice that Mars in Pisces would soon be forming a stressful t-square to that opposition, in late December. Would that volatile t-square trigger another act of terrorism, I wondered?

What happened when that Mars t-square fired came to be known as the notorious "shoe bomber" incident that made headlines throughout the holiday season. On December 22, 2001, Islamic sympathizer Richard Reid attempted to detonate explosives hidden in his sneakers on board American Airlines flight 63 from Paris to Miami, carrying 197 people. Fortunately, he was restrained by both passengers and crew members after trying to light a fuse that was connected to explosives in his shoes.

The symbolism of the act was truly uncanny—yet that could only be fully understood (or appreciated) by someone with an eye for symbolism. Consider: Mars is both explosive and "fiery," while

Pisces is the zodiacal sign symbolically associated with the feet—and the major news story of the time proved to be a man trying to set fire to his feet!

As the saying goes, you can't make this stuff up.

I mention this event as a good example of why I think trying to explain astrology solely through scientific or materialistic means may essentially be doomed from the get-go. Think about it: what possible connection could there be between a pattern in the stars and this event down here on the plane? Did the shoe bomber act the way he did because of some mysterious "burning feet" rays emanating down from the sky?

No, the relationship between these phenomenon, celestial and worldly, was one of *symbolism*, involving something known in esoteric circles as the "theory of correspondences." This is a traditional doctrine holding that our visible reality is undergirded by a hidden network of symbolic relationships, which in turn operates on principles of meaning rather than mechanistic cause-and-effect. Objects or phenomena which to the casual eye have no relationship at all may be integrally connected on deeper levels of affinity, interacting more like themes weaving through a great novel than discrete billiard balls on a game table.

It calls to mind a favorite line of mine from Muriel Rukeyser's poem, *The Speed of Darkness*: "The universe is composed of stories, not atoms."

The attempted terrorist act on that plane and the angular relationship of those planets in space were joint expressions of a common field of meaning, tied together by what Carl Jung famously called *synchronicity*, an acausal correspondence of disparate phenomena. Or as the ancients put it simply, *As above, so below*.

But precisely because astrology *is* a symbolic language, its core principles can manifest in a wide range of ways, rather than just one. As a result, that planetary configuration in 2001 made its presence felt for many others in vastly different ways, all of them "volatile" in their own way.

Take the case of my client for whom the Martian focus of that same t-square landed precisely on her Ascendant, the segment of the horoscope relating to one's physical body. What happened to her? As she related the incident, she was working in her kitchen when a pot on her stove exploded, sending boiling hot water across her body and resulting in third-degree burns. In her case that fiery Mars manifested through the watery sign Pisces through *actual water*, rather than in the form of someone's feet.

In my own life, the symbolism of that same configuration manifested differently from either of those two incidents. The Mars in Pisces t-square was hitting my chart closely, but it crystallized with me becoming embroiled in a heated discussion with a Christian fundamentalist about politics. How does that fit in here, symbolically? Well, Pisces, like its kindred sign Sagittarius, is a very ideological sign (while also being strongly associated with Christianity, most astrologers would agree). So with a Piscean Mars stressfully aspecting my horoscope, it wasn't too surprising to find myself drawn into an argument over religion and ideology. The same archetypal dynamics were at work, but expressing themselves through very different symbols.

We live our lives within vast interlocking fields of meaning, with each of our personal dramas fitting in to the larger "story" of the cosmos itself.

Astrology, I'd suggest, provides us with a useful tool for both understanding and navigating our way through this rich landscape of meaningfulness, while simultaneously shining a light on the profound interconnectedness between our inner and outer worlds.

CHAPTER 5

No, We're Not in Kansas Anymore: A Personal Look Back at the Sixties

Like most children, I experienced my own share of "magical" moments growing up, and one of those involved a TV set.

My family owned a simple black-and-white one, which I watched far too often throughout my childhood. (On those occasions when I find myself casting a judgmental eye on some younger person glued to their smart phone, I stop myself to remember just how addicted to media technology I was as a kid. Sad to say, I'd probably be no different growing up in this present age of digital realities.)

One day a friend mentioned to me that his parents bought an impressive new color set and invited me over to watch a presentation of *The Wizard of Oz* that coming weekend. This was a pretty big deal, since none of us had really seen a color TV before, not up close and personal anyway. I'd watched *The Wizard of Oz* once before on TV, but that was in black and white. I liked the movie, of course—what kid doesn't?—but I didn't really have any idea what this would be like, seeing it in color this way. I was eager to find out, though.

What I saw that night was surprising in a way I didn't expect. There was something magical about how those techno-colors glowed electronically off the screen, in a way that branded itself onto my retinas, as well as my imagination. That was especially true of that pivotal early scene where Dorothy steps out of her monochromatic world into one of vivid color, with all of the little people tittering

So, What Am I Doing Here, Anyway?

and coming out of hiding to greet her. A certain stroke of genius, that was—going from black-and-white to color like that.

A good deal of what I felt that night was no doubt due to the beautiful tones of the original movie itself, which was an indisputably gorgeous production that will probably outlast many others rolled out on the Hollywood assembly line. Even my high-minded film professor in college years later, Stan Brakhage, said, "You know, I've seen that film now probably 30 times, and it continues to enchant. I can't really explain it."

But it's not just the original film itself I'm talking about here, important as that was. Rather, I'm referring to the *electronic* nature of those images filtering through that new TV set. It's something we take for granted now, but that vivid self-illumination of the color screen was distinctly different from anything many of us had seen before, not just on television but in movie theaters, illustrations in magazines, let alone paintings on museum walls. Not necessarily better or worse, mind you, just *different*. These electronically-mediated images were in some strange way alive for me in a way that felt dramatically new, as though I was stealing a glimpse into a different world.

My experience that night with that color TV has become something of a metaphor in my memory for the entire 1960s. In a curious way, it was as if *everything* changed from black and white to color during those years, as though everything became "electrified."

But to really grasp what I mean, you need to first understand something about the decade which immediately preceded it—namely, the 1950s.

The "Black-and-White" Years

Me, I was born in 1952. While there were some fairly magical or otherworldly moments in my life in the years building up to the 60s—like going to the movies with my parents to watch *The Seventh*

Voyage of Sinbad in 1958, or the equally mind-blowing *Journey to the Center of the Earth* in 1959, or standing in the backyard with Mom and Dad one night and seeing the first satellite slowly streaming overhead—for the most part, that previous decade really *does* seem to me now like it was all in black and white.

I'm not just talking about the TV shows either, but the fashions, societal values, the humor, the music—all of it. They were all kind of black-and-whitish to me. What color *does* linger in my memory from the 1950s now seems largely pastel in nature, far more muted, certainly in comparison to what would come later. Musically, the songs on the radio were muted in their own way too, along the lines of "I love you, you love me," and so on. While certain iconic recordings stand out for me from that time—like Henry Mancini's "Peter Gunn" theme, or his timeless "Moon River," and quite a few Elvis songs, of course—they didn't quite compare with what awaited us on the road ahead.

Me and my two key loves, age 11—dinosaurs and the piano.

With the unfoldment of the 1960s, it was as if a bomb went off, as I watched our familiar cultural landscape explode into a million little kaleidoscopic pieces. Almost overnight, things went from black-and-white to color—electrified color at that. There were other colors, too, like the trippy day-glo posters lit by black lights in the popular "hippie" shops up on Chicago's near-north side, or the colorful experimental photos Richard Avedon snapped of the Beatles in the late 1960s, or the surrealistically infrared images on the cover of numerous rock albums.

And while I didn't dabble in them myself until 1970, psychedelics were obviously a major catalyst in that consciousness revolution. Directly or indirectly, they impacted advertisers, fashion designers, budding mystics, and most of all, almost everyone in the arts. While watching a rerun of *The Twilight Zone* from the early 1960s recently, I was haunted by those classic opening lines uttered by host Rod Serling:

"You're traveling through another dimension, a dimension not only of sight and sound but of mind; a journey into a wondrous land whose boundaries are that of imagination."

That iconic statement now seems almost like a preview—an omen, even—of what was ahead in the decade to come. It really was as though we'd stepped through some kind of portal into another dimension, politically, psychedelically, and artistically.

The Pop Explosion

For many of us kids at the time, the emotional epicenter of all that change was music. The 1960s were thrilling beyond words for teens like myself, and the rush of great new bands and performers seemed nearly endless. One week there'd be a new recording by the Rolling Stones or Bob Dylan, the next week by the Jefferson Airplane, or the Kinks, Animals, Cream, Joni Mitchell, Jimi Hendrix, Procol Harum, King Crimson, Aretha Franklin, Jimmy Webb, Mamas and the Papas, Steppenwolf, Gordon Lightfoot, Simon and Garfunkle,

No, We're Not in Kansas Anymore: A Personal Look Back at the Sixties

Leonard Cohen, Yardbirds, Smokey Robinson, the Byrds, Stevie Wonder, The Band, Donovan, Laura Nyro, Otis Redding, Led Zeppelin, Small Faces, the Four Tops, Miles Davis, the Who, the Mothers of Invention, the Doors—and countless others, week after week, month after month. I doubt there will ever be anything quite like it again.

One of the great pleasures of following musical trends is hearing a new sound or musical style for the first time, when it's still fresh and unfamiliar; it's dramatically different from hearing something that's been marinating in the cultural psyche for years or even decades. I've been fortunate to experience that sensation quite a few times over the years, but the 1960s were *overflowing* with such moments. Like hearing Jimi Hendrix's cover of "All Along the Watchtower"; Jeff Beck's "Beck's Bolero"; Pink Floyd's "See Emily Play," the Cream's "White Room," the Yardbirds' "Shapes of Things"; the Byrds' "Eight Miles High"; Jefferson Airplane's "White Rabbit," The Beach Boys' "God Only Knows," Dylan's "Desolation Row"; David Bowie's "Space Oddity"; Frank Zappa's "Peaches en Regalia," or the lush atmospherics of the Moody Blues' "Tuesday Afternoon." These, and others, were startling new sounds at the time, utterly different from anything we'd heard on the radio before.

At the heart of that tidal wave of pop music, though, were the Beatles. True, Elvis shook things up in previous years, along with Chuck Berry, Little Richard, Jerry Lee Lewis, Bill Haley, and others. But none quite compared to what the Beatles ushered onto the world stage in terms of originality and diversity. I remember sitting on the floor of my cousins' apartment over on Waller Avenue in Chicago's Austin district on February 9, 1964, to watch the Beatles on the Ed Sullivan Show that very first time. I look back now and wonder what affected us so much about that song then, since it sounds quite tame now. But back then, their sound was new and riveting, like nothing else I'd heard, though perhaps how the Everly Brothers might have sounded had they been doing acid.

But if that appearance on the Ed Sullivan show hit like an atomic explosion, the movie release of *A Hard Day's Night* a few months later was more like a 50-kiloton hydrogen bomb being dropped. This wasn't just because of the movie's music, impactful as that was, but because of the movie's freewheeling style coupled with those four distinctive personalities. Together, they exuded an attitude of freedom, humor, and joy that felt liberating to watch, and gave us all permission to be free and funny and creative ourselves, or at least try to.

There was something magical—dare I say archetypal?—in the way John, Paul, George and Ringo came together in that moment of time. They were constantly reinventing themselves, and it was fascinating to hear the unique sounds and arrangements they came up with on each new album—which was all the more impressive considering the limited technology of the time. Most of their early songs—recordings like "When I Get Home," "I Don't Want to Spoil the Party," or "No Reply"—have extremely simple arrangements consisting of just vocals and three or four instruments, yet many of those recordings pack a greater musical punch than more elaborate productions of that or later years. Even more surprising was the fact they came up with all that music in such an incredibly short time, eight years—a span of time in which many bands now release just two or three albums. How was *that* possible? I still wonder about it.

Dark Undercurrents

Yet beneath all the excitement and joyful exuberance of the time swirled a host of ominous undercurrents that hinted of danger or even impending doom. I had my first clear sense of that with the Cuban Missile Crisis in 1962, when I was just ten and seriously wondered whether we might all burn alive in a nuclear holocaust. "Duck and cover" sounds silly now but it was scary stuff to us kids at the time. Right on the heels of that came the JFK assassination, which pried open the floodgates to the underworld just a bit further, unleashing a variety of strange new energies into the collective mindstream. The murders of Robert F. Kennedy and Martin Luther King Jr. were the final gut punches for many, and I clearly remember the sense that society was now sailing into completely uncharted waters.[1]

A tangible sense of rebellion and anti-authoritarianism took hold as the decade progressed, and along with that a growing thirst for social reform. Civil Rights became a burning issue in the U.S., quite literally at times, leading to riots on many city streets. This was a decidedly double-edged change taking place throughout the time: the same decade that gave us the Beatles also ushered in Charles Manson and Kent State, while the same year that gave us Woodstock also gave us the concert tragedy at Altamont. Along with all of the light came all of the dark.

I was probably more politically aware than most kids my age simply because of the fact my brother Greg was shipped off to Vietnam, which brought the war much too close to home for my family. I was strongly against the war, and wrote letters to the Chicago newspapers to voice my protest numerous times. Greg returned home in one piece, more or less, but his tour of duty during that year nearly gave my mother a nervous breakdown.

Before he first shipped out from California, though, he encountered an odd little newspaper called the Los Angeles Free Press and purchased a gift subscription for me. Though Greg was a staunch conservative at the time, the L.A. Free Press was a far-left newspaper with incendiary articles, scathing political cartoons, and explicit sexual advertisements that shocked my mother senseless when she stopped to actually page through a copy one day.

The upshot was, publications like that made me politically more aware than I would have been otherwise. I recall when news broke out that Black Panther activist Fred Hampton had been killed in a police raid in Chicago, it became a hot topic amongst some of us in civics class that morning. "The police assassinated him!"

my classmate next to me blurted out, as our teacher looked on in puzzlement.

Even apart from all the anxieties triggered by developments in the outside world, the 1960s were turbulent for me in emotional ways, too. The teen years are difficult for most everyone, of course, but I sometimes wonder whether the same energies that made that decade so volatile for society-at-large bled over into our personal lives as well, making it an especially disorienting time for hyper-sensitive teens like myself.

My own high school years extended from the fall of 1966 to the spring of 1970. I was a socially awkward kid—"on the spectrum," some would probably say now—with a particular difficulty deciphering social cues of all types. I didn't have as much of a problem making friends since I could generally camouflage my discomfort with an ability to make conversation, though that often crashed and burned in spectacular ways. I was especially scared to death of girls, I never dated, and certainly didn't take part in such alien rituals as prom or homecoming.

Sometimes the discomfort and pain of that period became distinctly physical for me. I suffered two serious injuries during those four years, the first of those involving a severe concussion during sophomore year followed two years later by a back injury that left me in a partial body cast for five months.

While suburban Oak Park wasn't the hotbed of violence typically associated with the inner city, my town certainly had its share of problems. There were a few especially vicious bullies and malcontents in the neighborhood who moved on after graduation to illustrious careers in crime and even homicide. One especially surprising case was my relatively quiet (and very non-bullying) classmate, Carlos Torres. To everyone's surprise, he managed a few years later to reach the number one slot on the FBI's "Most Wanted" list, as a result of his involvement with a Puerto Rican radical group known as FALN. It just goes to show that, well, you just never know.

The most problematic encounter I experienced was totally unexpected, since it involved one of my closest friends, a fellow named Harmon. One night while his parents were gone, I was at his house with a couple of mutual friends when he called me up to his bedroom. "What's up?" I said on reaching the top of the stairs, at which point he stuck a loaded revolver against my forehead and pulled the trigger back. Fortunately, I was able to grab the gun away from him in a moment of distraction and talk him down from his ledge of rage. It was all over a misunderstanding involving his girlfriend, but a nearly fatal one. He was a charismatic but deeply troubled kid, and as fate would have it, he'd be dead from spinal meningitis less than a year later.

The Brighter Side

Yet amidst all the turbulence and insanity were those glimmers of that extraordinary spirit of creativity which suffused the decade, and served as a life-saving escape for me and no doubt many others. I've written before about the phenomenon of the *zeitgeist* and how certain periods seem noticeably richer with possibilities than others, when unique ideas and powerful feelings are more accessible like low-hanging fruit.[2]

For astrologers, one of the hallmarks of such times are major configurations involving the outer planets, such as the alignment of Pluto and Neptune during the 1890s or the conjunction of Uranus and Neptune throughout the 1990s. That's because astrology doesn't just affect individuals, but vast collectives as well.

When it comes to the 1960s, the planetary energy in question was an alignment of Uranus and Pluto—two powerhouse bodies that typically stir things up whenever they meet. The last time they'd aligned this closely was a hundred years earlier, during the mid-

1800s. With the rise of global culture, though, it was stirring things up even more powerfully this time.

Throughout that decade a sense of new possibilities opened up on a number of fronts, but especially the arts. For me personally, it felt a bit like sitting atop a creative volcano as I became increasingly obsessed with playing music, painting pictures, and making little 8mm films with the camera I bought with money made from my paper route. Ideas were bursting from my head, and I saw much the same thing happening not just with friends but well-known figures like Dylan, the Beatles, and Brian Wilson.

The alignment of Uranus and Pluto became exact in 1965 and 1966 but exerted an influence quite a few years on either side—precisely when these performers reached their creative peaks. I certainly felt it in my own bones, even if I didn't understand that's what was responsible for it. I've sometimes wondered what I might have come up with had I been older and my skills more developed to better take advantage of that celestial window in time. Regardless, the sense of exploration I felt with those creative experiments made it an exciting time for me. Here are a few from that period.

A pencil portrait I did of my father reading the newspaper, January 16, 1962, when I was nine. It was only decades later I realized I drew this picture close to the historic line-up of planets in Aquarius that occurred in early February 1962, which formed a "grand trine" to the Gemini and Libra planets in my own chart.

No, We're Not in Kansas Anymore: A Personal Look Back at the Sixties

An ink drawing done during my short-lived "Andrew Wyeth" phase, 1967, when I was fifteen. Years later, my father told me about the suffering he experienced in childhood on the farm in Wisconsin, when his mother died suddenly during the 1918 pandemic. Was I somehow picking up on the memory of that experience, through epigenetic memories, perhaps? I still wonder about that.

Ink drawing of Bob Dylan, done in the weeks after his album Blonde on Blonde was released, 1966.

So, What Am I Doing Here, Anyway?

Surrealistic landscape, 1967 (oil on canvas).

Surrealistic landscape, 1968 (oil on wood).

No, We're Not in Kansas Anymore: A Personal Look Back at the Sixties

Portrait of my father, 1969 (oil on canvas). This was this painting that gained me entry into the School of the Art Institute of Chicago in 1970.

So, What Am I Doing Here, Anyway?

My artistic experiments of the 1960s culminated in this painting that I finished in 1970, titled "Reunion of Elements" (oil on canvas).

On a more intellectual plane, unusual new ideas were filtering into the collective mindstream as well. There was a massive surge of interest in anomalies and "fringe" subjects like UFOs, lost civilizations, magic, ESP, and anomalous creatures like Bigfoot and even the "Minnesota Iceman." TV shows like *Star Trek, One Step Beyond, Twilight Zone, The Invaders,* and others, pushed the media envelope in imaginative ways, and I lapped it all up eagerly. I even had a few real-life UFO sightings and possible ghost encounters myself during this period, so the sense that something was "breaking through from the other side" at the time was a palpable one to me.

Eastern religions became a white-hot topic when the Beatles traveled to India to study with Maharishi, as books on Edgar Cayce started exploding in popularity, all of which further ignited my interest in Atlantis, reincarnation, and psychic phenomena. The subject of Egypt played a big role in all this for me, too, so that when my parents bought me a copy of Peter Tomkins' lavishly illustrated book *The Complete Pyramids* for Christmas one year, I was in seventh heaven for months.

But a particular turning point for me came as a result of a book that opened my eyes in unexpected ways, yet strangely enough I can't even be sure now if it's the book I thought it was, or if the passage in question even existed. Let me explain what I mean.

One of the iconic publications of the 1960s was a book titled *Morning of the Magicians*, by Louis Pauwels and Jacques Bergier. It was a synthesizing work that drew together assorted esoteric and occult threads which included parallel universes, telepathy, alchemy, extraterrestrials, pyramidology, and quite a few others.

Yet the one idea from the book which had the biggest impact on me was a passage that explained the notion of "waking up" and becoming fully present. I was 16 at the time, and I recall reading that passage and experiencing a startling sense of "I AM!" It was the first time in my life I really felt as though I knew that I *existed*. It was as if a bright light suddenly turned on, and the page in front of me—along with everything else—lit up, brightly.

Yet when I went back decades later and tried to find that passage, I couldn't. I combed through the book's pages several times, but try as I might, it simply wasn't there, not that I could see. So where did I read it? Could it have been an earlier edition that was changed later on, perhaps? Or another book entirely? I have no idea. Whatever the source, that sense of "awakening" was real enough in itself, and served as a pivotal moment of awakening in my early life.

The Window Closes

Whereas in the 1960s I felt like artistic ideas were bursting from my head, during the seventies what previously seemed like low-hanging fruit felt more and more out of reach. In my book *When the Stars Align*, I described a dream I had during the 1970s where a well I'd been drawing water from gradually began to run dry. That seemed a fairly obvious symbol for what I felt was happening in creative ways for me throughout that period. Particularly in art, I simply couldn't seem to find the ideas that flowed so easily for me before. Here, too, I saw much the same thing happening with many of the creative artists I'd admired so much that previous decade, like John Lennon, Paul McCartney, and Bob Dylan. These and others seemed to be struggling to keep their own creative fires alive after having them blaze so brightly just a few years earlier. For years I struggled to understand the reasons for my own creative drought and came up any number of theories, in the end just chalking it up to my own creative failings, plain and simple.

Looking back with the benefit of astro-hindsight, however, I came to believe a key factor in that shift was likely the waning influence of the Uranus-Pluto conjunction. Under its influence, the creative veil had been stretched wide open, but afterwards it began closing off, the result being that inspired ideas seemed harder and harder to come by. In the case of world-class geniuses like Lennon or Dylan, they were able to drill down occasionally and draw up masterpieces from the collective water table, including "Blood on the Tracks" or "Double Fantasy"; but for the most part, those were the rarity. It really did feel to me like an important moment in time had come and gone.[3]

Yet I've also come to believe that creative drought was part of a longer-range unfolding taking place for me personally. I say that because the same lessening of energy I experienced in artistic ways made possible my eventual shift into writing—culminating in this book you're reading now. Had that lessening not happened, I surely would have remained one-pointed in my artistic pursuits. I continued to tinker over the years in the arts, particularly photography and music, but not with the same urgency. I no longer felt that was the path I was meant to walk, not exclusively.

Assessing the Legacy

The seeds planted during that decade have continued unfolding throughout the world up to the present time—for both better and worse.

On the one hand, the 1960s ushered in an awakening of social conscience like never before, and brought with it a trend towards self-empowerment and a certain democratizing of creativity. From my vantage point, it felt like an explosive awakening of the collective imagination taking place, not just in the arts but in our openness to what was possible in reality itself. The sense I personally had of "waking up" from books like *Morning of the Magicians* (or whatever book that was) now strikes me as something of a microcosm for what was happening for many others throughout that time.

Yet that decade also inaugurated a sense of hyper-individualistic "Me first!" narcissism—probably one of the effects of the Pluto-in-Leo generation coming up through the ranks at the time. While that decade saw a casting aside of many outdated social norms, especially in areas of race, drugs, and sexuality, those changes sometimes left ripple effects that became increasingly problematic in later decades, with the AIDs crisis being one example.

Perhaps most insidious of all, that decade brought about a refinement of mass manipulation techniques by both commercial and governmental interests that grew more sophisticated over ensuing years. The same technological genius that put Neil Armstrong on the Moon also created the tools for what Noam Chomsky called the "manufacturing of consent," with the public almost never realizing how it was being shaped and manipulated in its tastes and opinions.

In the end, we'll have to leave it to future historians and philosophers to decide just what the legacy of the 1960s will ultimately be.

So, What Am I Doing Here, Anyway?

Personally, though, I'm glad to have lived through it—problems and all.

Notes

1. For anyone looking for a fuller picture of those complicated currents in the 1960s, I highly recommend my friend Gary Lachman's brilliant book *Turn Off Your Mind: The Mystic Sixties and the Dark Side of the Age of Aquarius* (revised edition, Daedalus Books, 2022), which explores the more turbulent occult and socio-political aspects of that decade.

2. For more on the zeitgeist and its astrological influences, see my essay "StarGates: Planetary Portals and Windows in Time," in my book *StarGates: Essays on Astrology, Symbolism, and the Synchronistic Universe* (Inner Eye Publications, Chicago, 2020). Also, see my chapter "Tuning into the Zeitgeist," in *Under a Sacred Sky: Essays on the Philosophy and Practice of Astrology*" (The Wessex Astrologer, 2015).

3. While the Uranus-Pluto alignment of the 1960s came and went, there was one more outer-planet alignment yet to come before the century was finished, that being the conjunction of Uranus with Neptune during the 1990s. Though it wasn't quite the same for me as before, I experienced yet another burst of ideas during that period which included the publication of my first book in 1996, *The Waking Dream*, as well as the first artworks I'd done in decades (including the photocollage for the cover of that book). The creative window of the 1990s was a productive one for many others as well, this being a decade which not only ushered in an explosion of interest in "World Music" and "Grunge," but TV shows like *Twin Peaks* and films like *The Matrix, The Truman Show, Pulp Fiction, Fargo, Fight Club, Exotica, Raise the Red Lantern,* and *Shawshank Redemption,* among others. This was also the decade of the Hubble Telescope and the rise of the Internet, both of which changed our world—one cosmological, the other social. All in all, it may not have been quite as explosive a decade as the 1960s but it nonetheless made a huge mark of its own. Those of us who have been around since the 1950s and 1960s, or earlier, should consider ourselves lucky to have lived through two such outer planet alignments. Humanity won't experience another one until after the present century is completely over—that being the Uranus-Pluto conjunction of 2103. (Book your reservations now!)

CHAPTER 6

Sensitivities

I was talking recently with a colleague about the so-called "power of prayer," especially when directed towards the benefit of others. Does it *really* make a difference in those recipients' lives?

My colleague expressed some skepticism about the matter—something I understand, since that's a doubt I've entertained myself more than a few times. But it so happened that exactly one day earlier I'd received an email from someone touching on this very subject, and that offered some anecdotal evidence which I found fascinating.

After I published *An Infinity of Gods* about the Kriya Yoga mystic and astrologer Shelly Trimmer, a fellow named Jeffrey Bruce Gold got in touch with me to say he read my book, and actually knew Shelly Trimmer quite well himself, having visited him and wife Deborah quite a few times at their home in Bradenton, Florida. We shared some of our own anecdotes about Shelly (who passed away in 1996), but one of Jeffrey's stories was particularly interesting to me. I asked Jeffrey for his permission to share it here:

> *I probably visited Shelly and Deborah about 10-12 times. One time—and one time only—I arrived on Longboat Key hours early. It was summer so it was very warm. I was hanging out on a beach near their house with nothing to do.*
>
> *So I waded in the water. I didn't get far and sat down in the Gulf with the water reaching up to my chest. I decided to meditate (breathe kriya) while sitting on the sandy floor there. I reached a far more balanced state than I usually reach, so I sent Shelly and*

> *Deborah warm thoughts, wishes, vibrations, or whatever one might want to call them. As I said, this is the only time I ever did that prior to a visit with them.*
>
> *Eventually, I arrived at their house. Early in the conversation, Shelly said: "Thanks for the kind wishes you sent this morning."*
>
> *My mind was completely blown. I should add that he never said that any other time when I didn't send the vibrations.*

A fascinating story, but not altogether surprising, since Shelly struck me as an extraordinarily sensitive being. The fact that he may have picked up on Jeffrey's intentions that morning hardly strikes me as impossible. As I mentioned in my book, there were times when he seemed to know things about me and *my* life there was no practical way for him to have known. Some of those were quite personal, some even embarrassing, but here's one I feel comfortable sharing and that I've not published before.

Shelly Trimmer, 1977.

Sensitivities

It was around 1981 that I hit a particularly rough patch in my life. My long-term relationship with my first girlfriend had fallen apart, and on top of that were several other disappointments, which all seemed to come to a head around the same time.

Literally on the same day my depression reached its lowest point, I was surprised to find a letter from Shelly in my mailbox. That was unusual in itself, not only because he wasn't a prolific letter writer but because he normally didn't reach out to students in an unsolicited fashion like that.

Even more surprising was the fact that this letter was extremely complimentary, filled with encouraging words about my work and future, all very upbeat in tone. That was especially unexpected, since he was normally pretty tough on me—not in a mean or callous way but simply in the way most good teachers tend to be, almost like drill instructors. I'd certainly never received anything upbeat like that from him before. The end result was that I felt like I was being thrown a life preserver in the midst of drowning, and I couldn't help but be struck by how uncanny his timing was.

I had similar experiences around Goswami Kriyananda as well, who I wrote about in my book *Urban Mystic*. What follows is one particularly striking experience from the early 1980s, which I quote here from that book:

Throughout much of the time I studied with him, I struggled with meditation, often feeling as though I was simply spinning my wheels in the backwaters of conventional mind. I saw others sitting quietly and motionless during their meditations, but I usually felt frustrated by my own restlessness and inability to go very deep in my meditations.

But for one short but unusually fruitful stretch of time, I seemed to "strike gold" with one Kriya technique known as the *Hong Sau* mantra. This is a silent, strictly internal mantra that is coupled with one's breathing patterns.

So, What Am I Doing Here, Anyway?

For that relatively brief span of time, things came together for me in a powerful way, to where I felt as though I finally "got" what the technique was about—or at least one aspect of what it was about (since a given technique doesn't necessarily have a single intended outcome). Each time I engaged this technique I experienced a heightening of awareness along with a welling up of blissful energy that was dramatic, and deeply pleasurable.

During one of Kriyananda's talks during that period, I was sitting in the back of the dimly lit room and began practicing the Hong Sau technique. My eyes were closed, and I was completely silent, with nothing externally to indicate what I was doing internally. Then, shortly after I began feeling that surge of blissful energy in me, I heard Kriyananda stop lecturing in mid-sentence and go completely silent for about 15 seconds. That wasn't at all normal for him during a talk, so I opened my eyes to see what was going on—only to see him peering through the darkness directly at me, as everyone else in the room now turned to see what he was looking at. Embarrassed by the sudden attention, with all eyes now directed

Goswami Kriyananda, 1983.

Sensitivities

at me, I stopped the technique, and Kriyananda resumed his lecture as if nothing had happened.

Exactly one week later, a friend of mine who didn't know I was using that technique happened to walk into Kriyananda's office to ask if he would teach him the Hong-Sau mantra. Kriyananda replied, "Why don't you ask Ray to teach it to you? He seems to be having some pretty good luck with it."

When my friend told me of that exchange, I was shocked, not only because it indicated Kriyananda knew I was having a powerful meditation that day but even pinpointed the exact technique I was using. *That* was impressive, I thought.

I've only had a handful of experiences during my life where I felt like *I* was the one sensing things about others in apparently psychic ways. While not nearly as dramatic as those displayed by Shelly or Kriyananda, they were compelling to me.

One of those took place in July of 2012, while I was drifting in and out of sleep late one night. Suddenly, around 1:35 in the morning (central time) I heard the sound of screams. It was so distinct and real that I immediately woke up, sensing something violent must have happened. I could tell I wasn't hearing it with my physical ears but in a more intuitive way, as if from inside my head. The overall impression was so striking I decided to look at the clock beside my bed and make a mental note of the time, so as to check news reports later that morning and see if anything corresponded to when I heard those screams.

On awakening several hours later, I turned on the TV and saw breaking news that a 24-year-old man had walked into a movie theater in Aurora, Colorado, during a midnight screening of *The Dark Knight Rises*. He set off tear gas grenades then shot into the audience, using multiple firearms. Twelve people were killed, 70 others were injured. The time when the carnage occurred? Precisely when I heard those screams—12:35 Colorado time.

Finally, I'll close with an anecdote from my book *The Sky Stretched Out Before Me* about an incident involving the Dalai Lama from the time I was working on the staff of Quest Magazine for the Theosophical Society:

A few of us on the staff were involved with helping to organize the Parliament of World Religions held in Chicago in 1993, a mammoth undertaking that involved coordinating religious figures and groups from around the world. Like its predecessor a century earlier in 1893, the aim was to stimulate a dialogue amongst the world's various faiths, hopefully culminating in a joint statement by the various speakers promoting greater political and religious harmony throughout the world.

There was a sense of electricity in the air amongst attendees, since this was a chance to mingle with others of like mind and possibly encounter well-known teachers like Swami Satchitananda or Amma, the "hugging saint." The main activities of the Parliament were held at Chicago's Palmer House hotel. While I attended as many talks as possible, the one I was drawn to was a press conference convened by the Dalai Lama.

As usual, His Holiness's comments were inspiring and noble, concerning the need for harmony amongst countries and peoples, and all that. But frankly, most people don't usually go to hear the Dalai Lama for his words as much as for his non-judgmental, compassionate presence.

The modest ballroom where he spoke was packed, standing room only, with roughly 300 people in attendance, many of them from the media. My boss at the magazine, Bill Metzger, was seated in the front row while I stood off to the side several feet away. It had been a rough week for Bill, since his wife was in the last stages of cancer and given only weeks to live. He was able to break away for just a few hours to attend this gathering, and it was obvious he felt relieved to have a little time off from his caretaking responsibilities.

Sensitivities

The moment the press conference ended, the Dalai Lama darted from his podium and rushed over to Bill, clasping Bill's hands fervently and uttering something to him (which neither of us later recalled)—then, just as quickly, throngs of admiring men and women rushed in to touch the proverbial hem of the holy man, as the Dalai Lama disappeared into a sea of outstretched arms.

I was struck by the fact that out of the hundreds of people in the room, the Dalai Lama zeroed in on Bill, who was going through such a terrible time. Nor was Bill the nearest audience member to him at the time, not at all. It may have been just a coincidence, but one hears stories like that in association with spiritual teachers quite often, in terms of their seemingly heightened awareness of others' suffering.

So what are we to make of incidents like these? Is it really possible for us to be aware of the thoughts, feelings and intentions of others, even when those others are far away?

Far as I'm concerned, it's not a problem at all—presuming you don't buy into the myth that your consciousness is limited strictly to your body and brain.

Which I don't.

CHAPTER 7

Some Simple Tips from a Long-Time Astrologer

One of the advantages of having practiced astrology for a number of decades—in my case, five in all—is the knowledge and insight one hopefully gains from studying a large number of case histories and the planetary patterns accompanying them.

It's with that in mind I thought I'd share some of the basic interpretive and counseling tips I've found useful when dealing with clients, both in terms of natal and predictive work. While nothing can really replace one's own long years of experience, I've found that simple tips gathered from fellow astrologers can sometimes shave years off that slow and sometimes arduous process of trial-and-error experienced constructing and reading charts. So in no particular order, here are some of my own thoughts about this discipline that I'd like to share.

* * * * *

Be Positive

An early teacher of mine made an especially important point once that stuck with me to the present day, which is this: *the first thing you say to a client about their horoscope should be positive, because your initial comments will tend to make a profound and lasting impression.* As one example of that, I remember an early consult where the vast majority of comments to my client were positive in nature. However, the very first thing I said to them had been in a slightly negative vein, about a challenging pattern I saw in their horoscope. After moving on and talking for almost an hour about other things in their chart, almost all of them upbeat, the client said to me in a dejected tone, "Well...don't you see anything *positive* in my chart?" I was stunned, but I'd learned my lesson not to make that mistake again.

* * * * *

Check What's Going On

Which brings me to another step I always take when working with clients, which is to check their transits or progressions on the day I'll be speaking with them. Is Saturn squaring their Mercury? If so, then I know I'd better measure my statements more carefully with them, since they could easily take what I say more negatively than intended. On the plus side, precisely *because* what I say could have a longer-lasting impact than normal, I'll try to work with that energy toward leaving a more *positive* lasting impression, by focusing on constructive suggestions as to how they might redirect, discipline, or reframe the difficult energies in their chart.

* * * * *

Know What Your Client is Looking For

Back when I first started doing readings, I'd generally launch right into describing what I saw in their horoscope, only to sometimes discover at the end I hadn't addressed what they came to me for in the first place. Whereas I may have focused primarily on career, say, what they *really* wanted to know was about romance, or health, or family life. For that reason, when I speak to a client these days one of the first things I ask is, "What are you hoping to learn from our talk today?" That simple question has improved the quality of my readings dramatically, and certainly leaves the client far more satisfied at the reading's conclusion than otherwise.

So, What Am I Doing Here, Anyway?

* * * * *

Speak their (astro) language

I find it helpful asking clients beforehand what their knowledge of astrology is, if any. That way I know if I can include the astrological rationale for what I'm saying. Besides giving them some hopefully useful education into the workings of astrology, not to mention my own thinking processes, I've found that including the technical reasons can help them better understand the points I'm making, by backing those interpretations with the astrological reasons familiar to them. To be clear, I *never* present it just at the level of jargon or technical terminology, and always make sure to present an in-depth interpretation of what those patterns mean. But for clients with even a beginner's understanding of astrology, coupling my interpretations with some explanation for the reasons behind them seems to add a useful dimension of information for them.

* * * * *

Zoom in on closest aspects

As far as my own approach to interpretation goes, one of the first things I do when preparing a reading (besides looking at someone's Sun, Moon, and Rising signs, or checking their elemental make-up) is to look for *the closest planetary aspects in their chart, especially stressful ones.* To some extent, the closest aspect or aspects in anyone's horoscope can indicate the most urgent and powerful karmas and lessons in a life, and may even be a central driving force for the entire chart—a point I'll be coming back to in a later chapter.

One of my first astrology teachers, Goswami Kriyananda, once remarked, "If you ever have difficulty interpreting a chart, just look for the closest approaching square or opposition and talk about that. At the end, the client will probably walk away thinking,

'What an incredibly accurate reading!'" While I personally don't limit it solely to stressful approaching aspects, as he did, I certainly understand his thinking there.

While squares or oppositions can definitely indicate serious challenges, it's important to remember there is always the potential for those energies to be redirected or transmuted in some way. For example, some of the greatest writers I've come into contact with have particularly "afflicted" Mercurys. Likewise, the greatest martial artists sometimes have extremely challenged Mars, while the greatest spiritual teachers sometimes have the very challenged Neptunes or Jupiters, and on it goes. What does that tell you? Simply, the fact that a planet is stressfully aspected essentially forces a person's awareness onto a given area to such an extent that it can—ideally—lead to greatness. I see one of our jobs as astrologers to help them better understand those possibilities, and redirect their difficult potentials in ways that can be more fulfilling and constructive for them.

* * * * *

Note the late bloomers

In my own work, I've found it especially helpful when speaking to clients to look for what I call the "late bloomer" dynamic, whenever that may be applicable. A culinary analogy would be how some foods are perfect right from the start, such as an apple, a Caesar salad, or a glass of milk; but certain other foods—like gourmet cheese or a fine wine—age more slowly and reveal their greatest virtues over longer spans of time. Horoscopes can be like that sometimes, and it's suggested by various factors.

The most obvious of those are Saturn aspects, such as trines to personal planets, Saturn on the angles, or sign placements including planets in Capricorn. The late singer Tina Turner had a particularly conflicted horoscope when it came to relationships, as shown by a t-square to Mars in the 7th house; that suggested a combative energy around partnerships (although that pattern also accounted for much of her dynamic and assertive energy as a performer). But she also had a tight Saturn-trine-Venus, which strongly suggested that things would become much better for her in later years both romantically and financially, which is exactly what happened.

While this late bloomer process unfolds more smoothly in the case of trines or sextiles, even hard aspects from Saturn can evolve in this way. As mentioned previously, hard aspects like squares or oppositions bring an even greater urgency towards working on whatever areas are affected, although the "ripening" will tend to be accompanied by more delays and frustration. Consider the example of architect Frank Lloyd Wright, who was born with a close Saturn-oppose-Venus (on the Ascendant/Descendant angle, no less). While both his career and love life experienced enormous ups and downs, he had his most productive creative period between the ages of 69 and 90!

Needless to say, when evaluating this "late bloomer" dynamic one needs to consider the entire chart as well as the attitude and resilience of the individual. That said, I've found this "late bloomer" dynamic to be one of the most helpful—and reassuring—elements for certain clients, to the extent that some have told me it was the most valuable insight they carried away with from our consultation. Learning that there is a light at the end of the tunnel—especially when it comes to younger clients struggling with a hard life—can provide a major boost to their morale and hopefully provide some much-needed direction.[1]

* * * * *

Differentiate solar & lunar responses

A particularly useful concept gathered from my early teachers was the notion that the Sun is an "objective amplifier" whereas the Moon is a "subjective amplifier." What does that mean? Simply put, planetary aspects to the Sun indicate events or energies that tend to be more out in the open for everyone to see, objectively, whereas aspects to the Moon tend to be experienced more internally and subjectively, often through relationships or in a largely private way.

For example, Uranus squaring the Moon in a chart can indicate intense emotional restlessness and a need for freedom in relationships, sometimes with a rebellious streak thrown in. That may not be quite so obvious to casual acquaintances, but it certainly will be clear to the individual with that aspect. By contrast, Uranus squaring the *Sun* in someone's chart indicates a concern with freedom and independence in ways that are more obvious to others, especially in professional contexts. In many cases it can cause someone to be more entrepreneurial, or at least want a longer leash in work situations.

* * * * *

Exalt the most elevated planet

As I've written about in earlier books, I pay enormous attention to the most elevated body in any chart, especially if it happens to be close to the Midheaven. Why is that significant? In my experience, the highest horoscopic body is intimately related not only to reputation but to one's *primary aspirations*. By contrast, whereas the 1st house tends to indicate who you *are,* in terms of your everyday personality, planets or bodies near the top of your chart indicate what you're *aspiring to become*. (Much the same applies to the zodiacal sign on the MC.)

Case in point: someone with Mercury as their highest planet will tend to have a powerful desire to teach, write, or communicate; someone with Venus high in their chart may be driven to be an artist, fashion designer, or project beauty to the world in some way; in the case of Saturn, the native may be driven to business, politics, architecture, or science—and so on. In line with the "late bloomer" dynamic mentioned previously, I've also found that planets near the top of the chart often unfold more fully later on in life, usually from the 40s onward.[2]

* * * * *

Don't disrespect dignities or debilities

Though I've found the traditional doctrine of debilities and dignities to be useful in some contexts, such as horary astrology, in certain contexts I feel it may have done more harm than good. Here's an example of what I mean.

I recently saw someone on a social media page bemoan the fact he was born with his Mercury in Pisces. Why? Because he learned from an older book that it was in its "fall" there. He obviously regarded this placement as a true negative in his life, a horoscopic liability he simply had to live with. Sad to say, I've come across that attitude more times than I can remember, and it's obviously a destructive one for those who subscribe to it, since it dramatically limits their sense of those planets' potentials.

My own opinion has always been this: *there is no aspect or placement that doesn't have* some *constructive application somewhere, somehow.* For example, Mercury in Pisces may be difficult for certain things, admittedly, but it's actually a *perfect* placement for a poet, fiction writer, mystic, astrologer, musician, singer, mythologist, or priest/priestess. Just consider some of the famous natives born with Mercury in that so-called "fall": Abraham Lincoln, Lady Gaga, Kurt Cobain, Edgar Cayce, Justin Timberlake, Elton John, Victor

Hugo, J.S. Bach, Tony Robbins, Copernicus, Eckhart Tolle, Billie Holiday, Baudelaire, Aretha Franklin, Rudolf Steiner, and others. In that same spirit, I approach all placements and aspects with that attitude, in terms of not just discussing their negative potentials but their positive ones as well.[3]

* * * * *

Empower clients to make their own decisions

As many of us in the field know all too well, there are some clients who come to us hoping we'll make their important life decisions for them. Should I marry this person? Should I have babies? Should I get plastic surgery? Personally, I don't see major life decisions like that as our responsibility. In the spirit of *Star Trek*'s "prime directive" of non-interference, I don't believe we should be interfering heavily in the destinies of others, beyond what advice may be appropriate and wise to offer. We're there to help them better understand the perils and pitfalls of their horoscopes, and carefully help them plot out possibilities as best we can, I am always careful never to say "You *should* do this!"

Here's an example. When I was 21 and had just started doing horoscopes, I became friends with a young woman whose chart showed an incredibly challenged 5th house (romance, children, creativity, and pleasures). Not only was Saturn in Scorpio perched there but it was at the focal point of a t-square involving the Moon and Venus. Talk about difficult! She didn't ask me about children, and had no interest in astrology at all to begin with and so wouldn't have cared one way or another what I had to say on the matter; but I remember thinking how problematic it could be if she ever decided to have them, as far as raising kids or even dealing with the physical challenges of childbirth.

As it turned out, I lost contact with her over the years but got back in touch with her decades later on social media. When I asked her if she ever wound up having a family, she said she endured no less than *five* miscarriages before finally giving birth to a healthy son, and with whom she now enjoyed a fantastic relationship. Having that one son "made all the earlier sufferings worthwhile," she said. Thinking back about the old days, I honestly suspect that had she asked me whether or not to have kids, I may well have steered her away from it, citing all the potential problems. Yet that shouldn't be the job of an astrologer! Having that t-square to Saturn didn't necessarily mean she *shouldn't* have children, it simply indicated the struggles she might have encountered if she did. Knowing what I know now, if someone like her were to ask me that question these days I would offer my best insights and information, including both positive and negative possibilities, but I would ultimately leave the decision up to them. For both ethical and karmic reasons, that's where I choose to draw the line—even if some clients would prefer me to cross over it and make their major life-decisions for them.[4]

* * * * *

Foster the growth of a 'difficult Moon'

I've found that one of the trickiest—but also most important—areas to deal with when talking to clients is the so-called "afflicted Moon" problem. This is when a client's horoscope displays a particularly challenged Moon, due to intense squares, oppositions, or conjunctions, with few or no supporting aspects to help balance things out. In simple terms, that can indicate an especially difficult challenge for that person in emotional ways, especially (but not strictly) during childhood. It's not only a complicated situation for the astrologer in terms of how to provide a fully nuanced interpretation, but because of how easily the client can misread any comments and thus amplify an already existing challenge.

Suppose a client has their Moon in a tight conjunction to Saturn—arguably one of the most difficult and frustrating combinations anyone can experience (as I well know, having my Moon-Saturn conjunction in the 1st house). I've sometimes had clients with a pattern like that refer casually to their "bad Moon"—as though that's all there is to it, seemingly with no idea as to the positive potentials of that combo. But consider some of the notable luminaries born with that celestial duo, like David Bowie, Elvis Presley, Bob Dylan, Sophia Loren, Miles Davis, William Burroughs, and many others.

I do feel it's our job as astrologers to make our clients aware of the serious challenges their charts may indicate, but not without underscoring the positive potentials of those energies. In fact, as the above mentioned celebrities illustrate, those difficult energies can actually turn out to be the key to their greatest accomplishments. Focusing solely on just the negative potentials of those patterns runs the risk of providing a misleading impression of their horoscopes, and in turn, their entire lives.[5]

* * * * *

Establish a context

When someone comes to me wanting to know about the period ahead for them, one of the most important things I can do is ask what's been happening for them during the *previous* few months, for better or worse. That not only gives me a far better sense of context, in terms of how their current transits and progressions may already be manifesting, but also how those energies will likely *continue* unfolding for them in the months ahead.

Suppose I look at someone's chart and see a progressed Saturn squaring their Venus coming to a head nine months away. If while talking to them beforehand they inform me they've been having marital problems over money, I'll have a much better idea of what to think regarding that upcoming aspect—i.e., it could very well involve money. True, there are times when someone's transits and progressions are *so* clear-cut in their meanings and potentials that

I won't feel a need to gather any further backstory from them, but aside from those exceptions, I've found that posing a few carefully articulated questions beforehand can provide an especially useful springboard when discussing their upcoming energies.

* * * * *

Place the big stones first

When preparing a more predictively-oriented reading, my very first priority is understanding the "big picture" of what's going on in that person's life, in terms of the grasping the larger patterns and cycles happening in their chart. By comparison, when I first started doing chart readings I simply worked from a planetary "hit-list" that displayed all of their transits and progressions over the coming year, in strict sequence. Armed with that, I might have said, "On January 1, you have Mars squaring your Moon; on the January 7 you have Uranus squaring your natal Uranus; while on January 20 you have progressed Jupiter sextiling your Venus," etc., etc.

Yet that can be an extremely simplistic (and inefficient) way to discuss transits and progressions. Why? Because it doesn't give either the client or myself a true sense of the bigger picture at work, in terms of understanding those aspects in their proper context, and their relative priority and magnitude. For instance, take one of those transits I mentioned—Uranus squaring a client's natal Uranus. An energy like that actually applies to a much broader phase or chapter in someone's life, not just a passing moment in time lasting for a few days, and will set the stage for other shorter-term transits happening during that period. For that reason, I generally begin my forecast readings by carefully describing those larger "chapters" happening in a person's life and working my way down to the shorter-term transits and trigger points unfolding against the backdrop of those larger cycles.

Just like I do when forecasting for personal clients, when studying historic developments on a more mundane (global, socio-political) level, I always focus on the "big picture" first. For many astrologers, the initial instinct when a major event happens is to immediately draw up a horoscope for the specific moment it happened. The problem with that microscopic "in the moment" approach is it can cause one to miss the forest for the trees—i.e., the larger macroscopic picture, since the historic event may be a reflection of a much larger cycle.

Consider the attack on the U.S. capitol that happened on January 6, 2020. The vast majority of astrologers drew up horoscopes for the particular day and time when the mob breeched the police barriers. Yet such a microscopic approach misses the fact that this development was symptomatic of the U.S. Pluto return taking place at the time, a cycle indicating a spirit of upheaval in the national body politic. That's decidedly *not* something which would be shown by any microscopic look at a single moment in time, without a sense of the larger historic context involved.

Or consider the abortion debate. Even if one could find a specific moment to erect a horoscope for that controversy (which is highly unlikely, considering that debate has been around for centuries), I don't feel any single horoscope could explain the broader significance of this development. For that, I think it's far better explained as a symptom of the broader cycle of the "Great Ages"—specifically the shift between the Piscean and Aquarian Ages. On the one hand, we have the largely Christian pro-life forces defending the values of the fading Piscean Age with its heavily religious concern for the helpless unborn; on the other hand, we have the pro-choice forces defending the more Aquarian, independent and secular values of individuals. To be clear, I'm not suggesting that either side is right or wrong, simply that there are archetypal dynamics involved. In some situations, taking a broader approach like this can provide a depth of understanding that no one horoscope for a single moment in time can really match.

So, What Am I Doing Here, Anyway?

* * * * *

Keep an eye on mundane themes

As for my own choice of predictive methods, I typically focus on four things particularly: a) *transiting aspects to natal planets or angles: b) secondary progressions to natal planets or angles; c) secondary progressions to secondary progressed planets or angles; and finally, d) solar arc progressions to natal planets and angles.* Other astrologers may of course choose to work with other factors besides those, but these are the ones I've found most useful in my work.

I should add that I also consider, when applicable, the "world transits" taking place at the time—that is, what's happening astrologically for the *world at large.* Suppose someone comes in asking me about starting a new business. Their personal transits or progressions might be relatively uneventful at the time, but on the day they're scheduled to open up that business, I see that Neptune is squaring Mercury! That wouldn't necessarily ruin their chances with the new business, but I would definitely make them aware of that energy and what it could portend for their business, in both positive and negative ways.

Or suppose a woman has her Sun in late degrees of Pisces. When Saturn first moves into that sign, she will likely feel that energy as a certain seriousness of purpose, or a desire to work hard towards something—even though it's nowhere close yet to actually *conjuncting* her Sun. As one astrologer I knew once put it, "You don't have to touch the stove to start feeling the heat from it." That goes for major planets moving into the vicinity of your personal planets as well. Like I said, always focus on the big picture.

* * * * *

Underline the station points

When looking at someone's chart, whether in terms of natal patterns or upcoming transits and progressions, I pay particular attention to *station points*, which is when a planet slows down and stands relatively still while changing directions. As Goswami Kriyananda once expressed it, station points have a "branding iron" effect which amplifies that planet's energy considerably.

As a result, in natal charts you'll sometimes find a stationing planet assuming an oversize influence in someone's life in ways that aren't easily explained by other methods. My early teacher Shelly Trimmer was an exceptionally "Uranian" character in many respects—independent, unconventional, inventive—yet the only thing which really indicated those qualities in his birth chart was having been born precisely on a Uranus station point. In my predictive work I likewise place enormous emphasis on whether a stationing planet happens to be forming any close aspects to that person's natal planets or angles at the time, since the aspect then becomes amplified. Indeed, those stationing points can be the times when those transiting aspects are felt the strongest! [6]

* * * * *

Tie progressive events to radical themes

There's a familiar astrological saying: *Only that can happen which is written in the birth chart.* For the most part, I've found that to be true. The result is that whenever I look at the key transits or progressions coming up for someone, I always look to see the condition of those planets in their birth chart, since those natal patterns will color the outcome of those transiting aspects enormously.

Suppose someone has an exact natal Saturn-Sun trine in their birth chart. When transiting Saturn comes along to *square* their natal Sun, it will probably be difficult in some ways but the eventual outcome will almost certainly be constructive. Due to those natal patterns, the effects of transiting or progressed aspects will be heavily modified.

On the other hand, consider someone born with a tight Neptune-Mercury square in their birth chart, but has transiting Neptune coming up to form a *trine* to their natal Mercury; the resultant developments may *initially* seem positive on their surface, yet can easily degrade into something more problematic, presuming they aren't careful. (What do I mean by "careful"? Simply, watch their speech more carefully, read the fine print on any documents being signed, and think twice before sending texts or emails!)

* * * * *

Find ways to make your input help

Finally, if I had to sum up my philosophy of astrological consulting as simply as possible, I would put it like this: *How can I help my clients best take advantage of their horoscopic patterns, whether those be natal or predictive, while helping them avoid or redirect their more difficult potentials?"*

Imagine someone has a hard Neptune-Moon aspect in their natal chart. I'll make them aware of the negative potentials there, but as hinted at earlier I'll go out of my way to point out the positive potentials, too. While it's true that an energy like that can produce a certain amount of confusion, addictive behaviors, or co-dependency, it can also indicate extreme sensitivity, artistic talents, psychic abilities, and compassion for others.

Or suppose they have transiting Pluto coming up to square or oppose their natal Sun. This will probably trigger an assortment of issues in their life, such as power struggles with authorities or colleagues, or contending with unresolved anger from the past; but it can also indicate a period of personal empowerment, career reassessment, deep investigation into some subject, or even an activist involvement with social causes. Covering *both* the positive and negative potentials of horoscope patterns is an immensely important part of this work, I believe, and represents one of the most helpful gifts we as astrologers can present to the world.

Notes

1. See my essay "Saturn the Late Bloomer," in my book *Under a Sacred Sky* (The Wessex Astrologer, 2016). I might add that I've experienced the late-bloomer dynamic in a very up close and personal way. One example is my natal Saturn-trine-Mercury. I came to writing relatively late, having started out in the arts, with my first book not being published until my mid-forties. Of the eight books I've published prior to this present volume, six of those were published in my 60s!

2. See my essay "Decoding the Most Elevated Planet in the Horoscope," in my book *StarGates* (Inner Eye Press, 2020).

3. See my essay "Rethinking Traditional Concepts of Dignities and Debilities," in my book *When the Stars Align* (Inner Eye, 2022).

4. See my essay "On the Perils of Telling People What to Do," included in *Under a Sacred Sky*.

5. See my essay "Why Your 'Bad Moon' May Actually Be Your Best Friend," in *StarGates*.

6. See my essay "Tectonic Triggers: The Hidden Power of Station Points," included in *Under a Sacred Sky*.

CHAPTER 8

The Surreal Genius of Salvador Dali

It was sometime during junior year in high school, very close to the time Jupiter was conjunct Uranus in Libra, when a classmate of mine tapped me on the arm to show me something.

I turned to my right to see Demetrius open a book on his desk to a page displaying a reproduction of a painting I'd never seen before. Mostly in shades of blue, it was a surrealistic, dream-like mystic vision of a man astride a marble-like horse against a background resembling a cathedral vault, but with the sky visible through its webbed arches.

The painting was titled "Santiago el Grande", and the artist's name was Salvador Dali. Upon taking a moment to gaze at this image, I felt my soul explode wide open.

Mimi proceeded to show me more pages from that book, authored by writer Robert Descharnes, and my excitement only grew. With each new painting, it was as if some mysterious depth charge of beauty had detonated in my spine.

I had been trying my hand at painting for several years by that point, including surrealistic landscapes, but nothing prepared me for what I saw in this book. Well, almost nothing; I had seen Dali's inspired sequence for Alfred Hitchcock's film *Spellbound* when I was 12. As I wrote in *The Sky Stretched Out Before Me*, that short section of film was a revelation to me and influenced my visual style for years. But actually seeing his artwork more directly like

The Surreal Genius of Salvador Dali

"Santiago el Grande," © 2023 Salvador Dali, Fundació Gala-Salvador Dali, Artists Rights Society.

this, in all its forms, felt as though "all the tumblers had fallen into place" once and for all.

From that day forward, I wanted to get my hands on everything he did. I was driven by the sort of fevered enthusiasm only the young truly understand. It inspired my own artistic ambitions deeply, and I quietly set as my goal to become an artist like Dali! My hopes were high.

So when I finally attended college classes at the Art Institute of Chicago, I was taken aback to discover that Dali was widely considered by many in the art community to be "kitschy," "gimmicky," or even "crass." I didn't embrace all of Dali's work myself, but I couldn't quite understand the intensity of all the criticism. By contrast, the contemporary artworks championed by my professors struck me as unimaginative and little more than conceptual "tricks," and nothing particularly inspired.

The result was that the fevered passion I felt for surrealism was being torn in two directions. Though I was still greatly enamored of surrealism—a feeling kept on life support for me by the brilliance of younger artists I came across like Ernst Fuchs, Abdul Mati Klarwein, and De Es Schwertberger—I even started to question my own tastes.

That wasn't helped any by the fact I was myself turned off to certain aspects of Dali's own personality and opinions. Apart from his ostensible obsession with money, there was his bizarre support of fascism—something completely at odds with my own political sentiments. His best works had an undeniable touch of the spiritual, so how could he be so off-base in his personal life and opinions? Or was all that surface brou-ha-ha just done for publicity?

The Mystery of Multiple Imagery

Despite concerns like that, I continued to study Dali's works, and continued to uncover new levels of meaning and nuance in many of them. Paradoxically, his work was otherworldly yet grounded in a crystal-clear and highly disciplined technique. For a period of about ten years starting when I was 18 and extending through my late 20s, I experimented with LSD and during that time carefully contemplated paintings of his like "Tuna Fishing," "Last Supper," or his "Hallucinogenic Toreador." It was this last work that proved pivotal in my understanding of Dali's work.

I'm referring to his talent for multiple imagery—that is, creating images that could be seen or understood on several levels simultaneously. We've all seen images like that before, such as the familiar drawing of a beautiful young women who appears from a slightly different perspective to be a grim elderly woman of some sort.

But Dali took that conceit and explored it further than anyone else had—and in so doing, touched on a profound esoteric truth, I came to believe. To my mind, the best example of that was his aforementioned work, "Hallucinogenic Toreador." Its subject is ostensibly that of a bullfighter, but as you look more closely at it you realize it is actually a combination of several different images that overlap and intersect with one another.

In the lower left-hand corner of that canvas, most dramatically, Dali actually combined *four distinct* overlapping images, the most obvious of which is the toreador's right shoulder. But that overlaps onto an image of a mountainside or hillside which adjoins a lake; in turn, that combines with a much harder-to-see image of a wounded bull, and finally, there is a relatively abstract image of carefully arranged circles forming an atomistic pattern. All of these blend together. This wasn't just an example of double imagery, but of *quadruple* imagery—something I'd not seen anyone else attempt before or since.

The more I reflected on this, the more I came to see that Dali was, consciously or unconsciously, touching on a great insight—namely, *the mystery of symbolism itself.*

A true symbol always combines multiple meanings simultaneously. My old friend Alice O. Howell once explained this point by asking listeners to consider a common cup. On one level, it has its most literal and obvious meaning, that of a drinking vessel. But it also embodies the archetypal principle of *receptivity*, what astrologers might call a "lunar" significance. That cup also has mythic and historic associations like those of the Holy Grail and the Last Supper—and there are still other inferences besides these. The essential point is, within that singular object you can find several interpenetrating levels of meaning simultaneously.

In turn, that capacity of symbolism to encapsulate so many meanings and ideas hints at an esoteric truth about *reality itself,* which is simply this: our cosmos and reality is itself a cross-section of interpenetrating dimensions, reflecting multiple levels and worlds of meaning in all their forms and phenomenon. In other words, what we see in our world is actually a congealing of multiple dimensions and meanings, a thin slice from a far more complex reality.

So besides just being an entertaining visual "trick," I felt that Dali's experiments with multiple imagery touched on a particularly mysterious aspect of our existence.

The Tour Guide

At some point I heard about a museum in Cleveland, Ohio that housed a large collection of paintings and drawings by Dali, compiled through the decades by multi-millionaires Reynolds and Eleanor Morse. It wasn't exactly a short drive from Chicago, but when I learned the museum was going to shut down for at least two years so the collection could be relocated to St. Petersburg, Florida, I finally decided I'd make the effort to head out to Cleveland before it closed.

My plan was to drive from Chicago to Beachwood, Ohio, and arrive on the very last day the museum would be open to the public. Just to make sure everything would go without a hitch, I called the museum the day before leaving, in order to confirm the museum would indeed be open when I arrived. The person answering the phone said, yes, everything is going according to plan, so you can come in tomorrow and still see the exhibit, not to worry.

I convinced my girlfriend at the time, Irene, to come along for the ride, along with her young child, David. We spent the night in a motel midway to Cleveland, and arrived at the museum around noon that next day. Surprisingly, the parking lot before the museum was almost devoid of cars, which struck me as odd, considering this was the last day.

When we walked up to the front entrance, I saw a sign on the front door saying that the museum was closed—permanently. "But be sure to come and see us when we reopen in St. Petersburg, Florida," it said.

That felt like a kick in the gut. I pushed the button on the intercom to learn what happened, and an older woman's voice came on the other end saying, in very business-like tones, they had to close the museum doors earlier than expected, but "Thanks for coming!" When I explained my plight and how we'd just driven 600 miles to see the collection, she clearly wasn't up for debating the issue. So, there we stood on the front steps of the building, terribly disappointed, and definitely feeling quite sorry for ourselves.

Just then, a woman in her mid-30s happened to walk up behind us, and seeing the obvious look of gloom on our faces—as well as the presence of Irene's four-year old child—asked me what happened.

So, What Am I Doing Here, Anyway?

I related our plight, milking it for every ounce of pity I could, at which point she said, "Wait here a second, I'll see what I can do." She buzzed the intercom and identified herself to the woman on the other end, at which point the proverbial drawbridge was lowered and in she went without further delay.

One minute later, the same voice we heard earlier came back on the intercom and invited us into the building. As we passed through the doors we were greeted by a distinguished-looking older woman, very upper-crusty and exuding an aura of money. She extended her hand and said quite formally, "Hello, I'm Mrs. Morse, and my husband and I are owners of this collection. My friend told me what happened and I want to apologize for that. We wound up having more work to do with the collection than we expected so we closed up shop early, but I'll be happy to take you around and show you our collection."

I knew a little about Eleanor already from the articles I'd read. She was a highly cultured woman with a background in music, and had translated several books about Dali into English. She and her husband, Reynold, started collecting Dali artwork decades earlier, and in the process amassed a vast collection of oil paintings and drawings worth untold millions. Over the next hour and a half she proceeded to take Irene, her son David, and me on a guided tour of their entire collection, personally relating the story behind each and every artwork in the collection, sounding for all the world like she'd done this a thousand times before yet somehow not seeming the slightest bit bored doing so one last time.

Her manner softened considerably as we moved through the collection. When I first sauntered through that front door, she seemed slightly taken aback by my long hair and casual outfit. But as we continued walking and talking about the paintings, she seemed impressed by my knowledge of Dali and his work—especially when we stopped before that massive "Hallucinogenic Toreador" canvas, as I proceeded to explain to her my theory about multiple imagery. Whether she truly understood what I said to her or not, she seemed genuinely intrigued.

By the time we'd finished and said our goodbyes, she was extremely friendly and remarked, "I'll have you know that you're the last visitors to see the collection in this location before it moves, so I hope you've enjoyed it!" We certainly did.

The Letter

On returning home, I sat down to write her a letter, simply to thank her for the personalized tour she gave us. One week later, I received a nice letter back from her, which read as follows:

July 19, 1980
Mr. Ray Grasse
738 Belleforte
Oak Park, Illinois 60302

Dear Ray,

How nice of you to take the time to write to thank me for doing what was really my pleasure. I have shown enough visitors through the museum by now (we have been open for 9 years) to know when someone is truly interested. Although I did not know it at first, I felt by the way you scrutinized the works that you must be a painter yourself. It was the same manner used by my husband's friend from Denver who is a painter and wanted the collection there (Bruce Dines). However, the Director of the Denver Museum of Arts walked through quickly and said to me at the end of the tour "You have a nice collection, "Mrs. Morse." I knew immediately that Denver was not the place for Dali whether it was my husband's birthplace or not... and he agreed with me.

Believe me we are delighted with our reception in St. Petersburg. Everyone is so enthusiastic and young. You might think about moving down there as you might find people more avid for art than in the more sophisticated atmosphere of the mid-west.

Whatever you do, remember to work hard. Dali says he is only now learning to paint! Your being able to see the museum was something Dali likes to call "objective chance" – the object – to see the works of Dali - the chance – that I was about to show them to my friends. Fortuitous for us all as I felt a sympathy towards you and your wife and darling child.

Good luck, Ray.
Sincerely yours,
Eleanor R. Morse

Final Thoughts

Since those early years, it's clear that Dali's reputation in the art community has improved since his death, with respected art critics like Robert Hughes weighing in favorably on the artist's legacy, suggesting that his importance in the annals of 20th century art matched or possibly exceeded that of Picasso's.

While I'm no longer obsessed with Dali's work to the degree I was back then, I continue being moved by it, and am even more impressed in some ways than before, especially in terms of the sheer volume of what he achieved. Looking through a comprehensive catalog of his entire life's work recently, I was stunned at how he managed to accomplish so much during his life—not just paintings and drawings but jewelry, set designs for theater, film work, books, sculptures, and others.

In 2015 I attended a large retrospective of his work at the Philadelphia Museum of Art, and the overall impression of those works over the decades was deeply moving to me. It seemed obvious to me that that was the reaction of many others in attendance that day as well.

The Surreal Genius of Salvador Dali

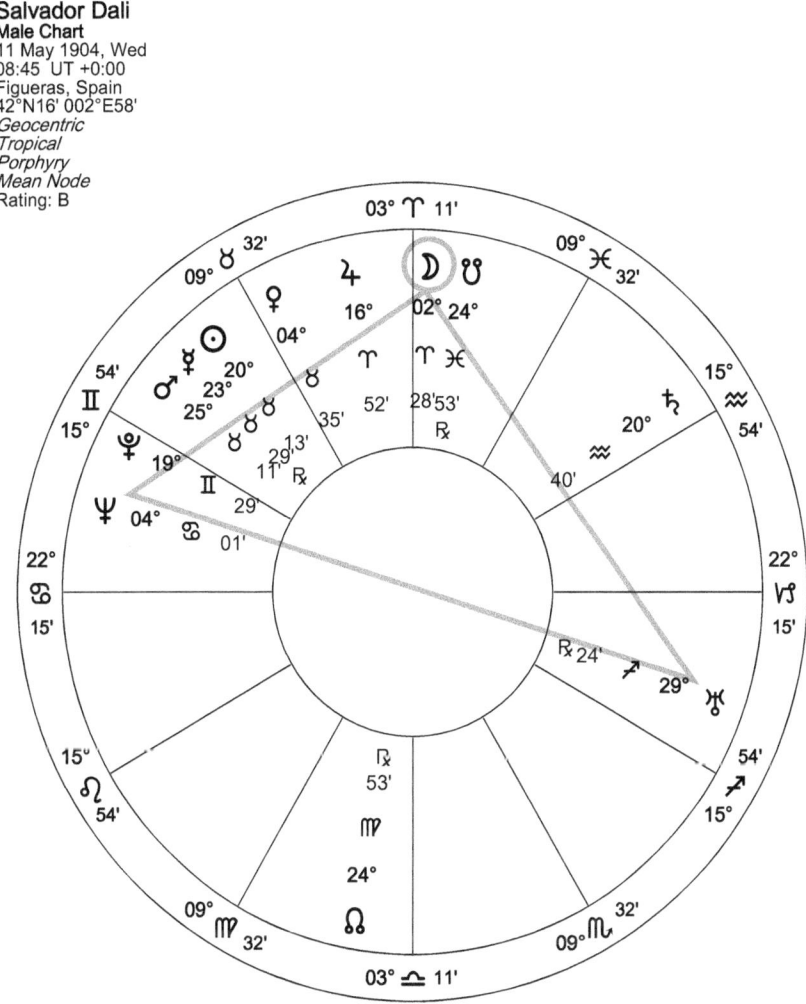

So how will posterity look back and judge his works? I have no doubt it will be an increasingly positive one. But as for his personality—well, that could prove to be a considerably more complicated affair. Maybe his horoscope can give us a few clues about that. (born May 11, 1904, 8:45 AM, Figueras, Spain.) While I'm not convinced that "genius" can be shown solely through the horoscope, we can certainly single out some of the contributing factors. The following are a few of those I found particularly interesting about Dali's case.

The heavy emphasis on Taurus (where the Sun, Mars, Mercury, and Venus are located) clearly indicate his affinity for art, beauty, and yes, money. The tight sextile of Neptune to the ruler of Taurus, Venus, shows a relatively refined aesthetic sense.

What about the fact that Saturn forms such an intense fixed square to his Sun, as well as his Mercury and Mars? Aside from the troubles that caused him with his father—and perhaps even his fondness for "strongman" figures like Hitler and Franco—it was a blessing for his artistic career. Why? Because those Saturn squares gave him an extraordinary capacity for discipline in devoting untold hours not only to his highly detailed and complex canvases but to all his other projects. And since Saturn is the planet of "crystallization," it also gave him the ability to put into concrete form ideals and concepts that might otherwise be too ethereal and diaphanous for human eyes.

But perhaps the real key to his extraordinary artistry was his Moon—the most elevated planet in his chart, and one of several key factors in any horoscope relating to the imagination and mind. In Dali's case, that Moon is positioned at the focal point of a t-square between the distant planets Neptune and Uranus—two planetary bodies largely invisible to the naked eye (and therefore symbols relating to the deep unconscious). The influence of any planet positioned at the focal point of a t-square tends to be amplified many times over, for better or worse. It's technically considered a very stressful configuration, but it also has huge potentials if approached constructively.

With those distant planets involved, this triad clearly ties in to his propensity for surrealism, not to mention unconventionality, eccentricity, and all around weirdness.[1] Especially with his Neptune positioned in the 12th house (the unconscious mind), Dali had a unique ability to tap into the depths of the collective unconscious, in both its beautiful and disturbing aspects, along with a disciplined talent for bringing these into concrete form.

Strictly on the personality level, however, his chart paints a very different picture from what his public persona suggested. His Moon in Aries squared by Neptune showed considerable sensitivity, yes, but also considerable insecurity. The fact that the Moon is so close to the top of his chart—in Aries, no less—is surely a key factor in explaining why he was compelled to seek public attention so aggressively throughout his life. The fact that the Moon also rules his 1st house—anatomically, the head—may also shed light on why his upturned mustache wound up becoming one of the most iconic "trademarks" of 20th century pop culture.

In turn, that lunar insecurity was further reinforced by his Saturn-square-Sun, which can show considerable self-doubt about one's own worth, although that can fuel a considerable drive toward succeeding on a professional level. I remember watching a handwriting analyst on TV years ago talk about Dali's handwriting and how intrigued she was by the fact he always wrote his "I's—as in *"I am the greatest artist in the world!"*—in lower case script, thus becoming *"i am the greatest artist in the world!"* Why is that significant? "Because it often indicates a small ego," she explained.

In the end, whatever his personal foibles or insecurities may have been, it's ultimately his stunning body of work that he'll be remembered for, and for that, I'm grateful.[2]

Bravo, Dali!

Notes

1. I have a similar triad of energies in my own chart, with my Moon-Neptune conjunction squared out by Uranus. No doubt that partly explains the reason for my own attraction to Dali's work, and to surrealism generally.

2. Though I very much hoped to meet Dali in person back then, I never did, though it wasn't for lack of trying. I knew he came to New York City

So, What Am I Doing Here, Anyway?

every year and stayed at the St. Regis Hotel while there, and thought maybe I could find a way of connecting to him that way. So when I was 19, I made a long-distance call to the hotel and asked to be put through to "Salvador Dali's room." To my surprise, the operator did just that, and a man on the other end picked up the phone saying, "Peter Moore here" (who I already knew to be Dali's manager, from articles about the two of them). I very nervously said, "Uh, hello… is this the Salvador Dali… entourage"? There was a mild chuckle on the other end, as I heard Moore then turn to the others in his room and loudly ask, "Say… is this the Salvador Dali *entourage?*" (extending out "entourage" for comic effect). I could hear others laugh in response (perhaps including Dali himself?). Moore then asked why I wanted to know. I said I was a big fan of Dali's and would like to speak to the artist himself. Not very surprisingly, he said, "I'm sorry, that's not possible"—and that was that. Well, you win some, you lose some.

CHAPTER 9

You Are The World:
The Deep Truth Contained Within Astrology's Twelve-Fold House Structure

Astrology holds a great many secrets for the esoterically-inclined, from the deeper meanings of the planets and signs to the aspects, elements and polarities, and many others besides these.

What I'd like to focus on here instead is a subtle but particularly intriguing facet of astrology implied by the horoscope's twelve-fold house division. (Note: what I'll be saying here applies to whichever house system you may personally prefer to use.)

Take an ordinary horoscope—say, your own—with its twelve-fold division of houses (or, as some traditionalists prefer to call them, *places*). Now, suppose I were to ask you which of those houses most represents "you," in terms of your personality and identity. What would you say?

I suspect most astrologers would agree that would be the 1st house—that segment of the horoscope representing the everyday personality, the individual body-mind.

But that's really just an illusion. Why do I say that?

Because you are not just a single horoscopic house; the *entire horoscope* is "you," truly. Your possessions, siblings, home, children, work, spouse, friends, and so on—all these things indicated by the

So, What Am I Doing Here, Anyway?

twelve houses of your horoscope represent different *facets* of who and what you are, acted out through the seeming external world.

Think about that. When a difficult planet fires in your 4th house, something might happen in your external home or family; or when something fires in your 10th house, you may experience developments with the authority figures in the workplace; or when planets in your 11th house fire, events may transpire with your friends—and on it goes, through all the different houses, with the energies in your chart being played out through your surrounding environment.

But how could all that really happen if the seemingly "external" world around you wasn't intimately connected to your own life and consciousness? Must not there be some deeply symbiotic and synchronistic relationship between your subjective experience "in here" and the external world "out there"?

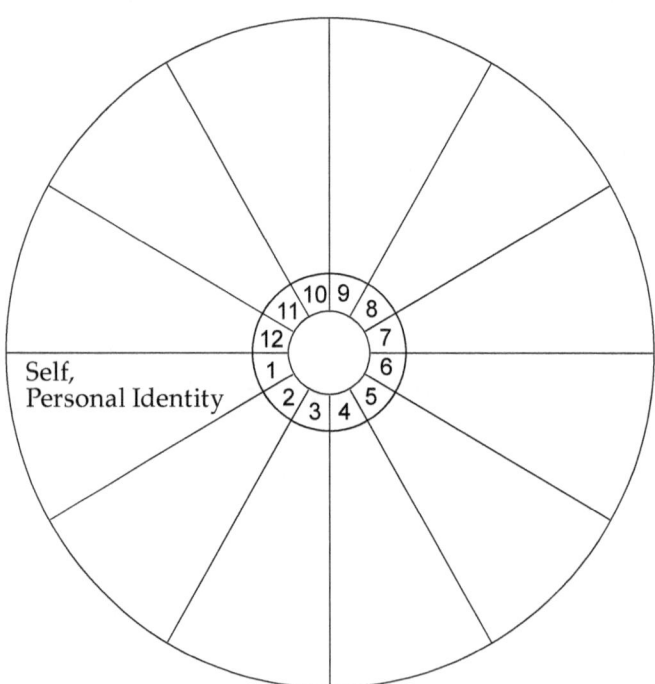

72

The Deep Truth Contained Within Astrology's Twelve-Fold House Structure

Said another way, the whole world is you. Or, more precisely, *your* whole world is you. I say it that way because the whole world *as experienced* by you is unique and specific to your consciousness, and no one else. My early teacher Goswami Kriyananda made a particularly cryptic comment one day that continues to haunt me, and which may well offer a deeper clue into the mystery here:

"You can look down from the vantage point of the Ajna chakra (the "third eye") and see everybody else's material and mental realms. From that vantage point you see an infinite number of universes, and that *surrounding each spark of God is built a universe.*" [1]

I'll restate it this way: You may well think of yourself as being just this individual personality—represented by the 1st house—but in fact you are much bigger than that, you are far greater than any one compartment or any one house. You are *all of it,* the entire reality-bubble of experience you find yourself immersed within. This includes all the phenomena of the world around you: your neighbors, family, finances, co-workers, bosses, partners, domestic space, and so on—all of these are really acting out the energies of your own unfolding nature.

This, then, is the great secret implied by the horoscope and its twelve houses.

Simply put, *you are the world.*

Notes

1. *Urban Mystic: The Teachings of Goswami Kriyananda* (Inner Eye Publications), 2019, p.26.

CHAPTER 10

Leaving Hell Behind

While watching a TV show recently, I heard a definition of hell that someone came up with, which I found clever:

"'Hell' is being on your deathbed and meeting the person you could have become."

Like I say, clever. And ten or twenty years ago, it would have been my idea of hell, too. Throughout much of my life I've judged myself harshly based not just on mistakes I've made but even more on what I know I *could* have done, had I been just a bit wiser or hardworking.

I'm glad to say that's not the case anymore.

That's because one of the advantages of growing older can be learning to become more accepting and less judgmental toward oneself. I'm all too aware of how completely I've fallen short in so many areas of life—I'd need a pocket calculator to tally them all up—and that's all right. Because at least now I'm able to accept myself with all those imperfections more than when I was younger, back when self-judgment was pretty much a full-time job.

So now if I were on my deathbed meeting that person who embodied all I could have become, I'd probably laugh and think to myself, "Wow, would you look at that…Very impressive! Well, maybe I'll do better next time."

And then I'd move on, to wherever life takes me next.

CHAPTER 11

Toward a Grand Unified Theory of Synchronicity

Introduction: This paper is the culmination of a decades-long process of investigation into Carl Jung's theory of synchronicity, which first began with the writing and publication of my book The Waking Dream *in 1996. That's where I first hinted at the possibility of a broader meta-theory that might help us better understand the significance of "meaningful coincidence," not only as it occurs within our own lives but in the world at large. This essay lays out a tentative framework for that approach.*

"Symbolist thinking regards the world as a kind of language, with the people, animals, and events representing elements of a living vocabulary..."

—The Waking Dream

So, What Am I Doing Here, Anyway?

In the early 1950s, psychologist Carl Jung published his seminal work on a phenomenon he termed *synchronicity*, which can be simply defined as the experience of "meaningful coincidence."[1] While most coincidences in our lives can be easily explained as nothing more than the result of pure chance, some coincidences are so striking that we're compelled to wonder if there isn't some deeper purpose or process at work underlying those events.

A famous example from Jung's own files was that of the patient who described a dream she had involving an Egyptian scarab beetle. She'd been resistant in her therapy up to that point and firmly entrenched in a rigidly rational mindset towards life. While listening to her describe that dream, Jung heard a tapping at the window of the therapy room. It turned out to be from a beetle—the closest approximation to a scarab in those northern Swiss latitudes. Taking this as a cue, he went and grabbed the beetle from the window and handed it to her, saying, "Here is your scarab." The fact that this occurred at a key moment in the woman's therapy struck Jung as significant, and her receiving it seemed to have the effect of triggering a breakthrough in her otherwise rationalistic mindset.

Jung regarded experiences like these as *eruptions of meaning*—that is, significant events in our psychological or spiritual growth, issuing from that mysterious divide between our inner and outer worlds. Importantly, the appearance of the beetle wasn't "causal"—that is, it didn't happen directly because of anything either the woman or Jung said; rather, it arose simultaneously through a deeper connectedness of meaning. This was an example of what Jung called *acausal connectedness*.

Since its publication, Jung's theory has spawned a virtual tsunami of books, articles, and media discussions, all attempting to understand its nature and importance. So how best shall we grasp what meaningful coincidence really says about our world?

In Search of the Big Picture

What I'd like to propose here is the possibility of a "grand unified theory" which aims to place synchronicity into its broader context. Just as some scientists have been searching for a unifying model that ties together the disparate forces of nature, so we can envision a theoretical framework that not only reveals fundamental insights into synchronicity's workings but illumines its connection to various other concepts and symbolic systems. As we'll see, this necessarily requires a more philosophical approach than a scientific one, as only that can truly unravel the deeper mysteries of this phenomenon, I'd suggest. By focusing our attention just on isolated coincidences, I believe we run the risk of missing the true significance—and magnitude—of the synchronistic phenomenon.

As an analogy, I'd invite you to recall the classic tale of the five blind men and the elephant. Each of them examines a different part of this creature's body, as a result obtaining a completely different sense of what the animal is like. For instance, the man feeling only the elephant's tail naturally concludes that this creature is similar to a snake or perhaps a length of rope; but he'd obviously have a woefully incomplete picture of what the whole elephant is like. Because his perspective is so narrow, he'd be missing the full reality and significance of the elephant.

In much the same way, I'd suggest that trying to understand synchronicity solely by focusing on isolated coincidences is akin to the predicament of the blind man who examines only the elephant's tail (or ears, tusk, trunk, or legs). By limiting our focus strictly on individual instances of synchronicity, we're missing the broader worldview of which coincidences are just a part.

In short, *understanding the true significance of synchronicity requires nothing less than a dramatically different cosmology than what we are generally familiar with in our modern materialistic culture.*

But what exactly *is* that "dramatically different cosmology"?

So, What Am I Doing Here, Anyway?

The Five Blind Men and the Elephant (Public Domain, illustrator unknown)

The Symbolist Worldview

This is what I (and certain other colleagues, like John Anthony West) have called the "symbolist" worldview.

Simply put, this is a way of thinking that regards the cosmos as akin to a great dream—and, like our own dreams, written in the language of symbols. "The symbolist standpoint considers life to be a living book of symbols, a sacred text that can be decoded." [2] The manifest world mirrors an underlying consciousness, much in the same way that our nightly dreams reflect the workings of our own consciousness, but on a vastly different scale. The world is not only suffused with mind, it's *saturated with meaning*. In *The Waking Dream*, I boiled down the symbolist worldview to a few essential points, including these:

The world reflects the presence of a greater regulating intelligence, or Divine Mind, that both permeates and transcends material reality.

All things partake in a greater continuum of order and design; consequently, there are no coincidences or truly random events. In turn, any seemingly chance event or process can divulge greater patterns of meaningfulness within the life of an individual or society.

Reality is multi-leveled in character, involving phenomena and experiences across a wide range of frequencies or vibrations.

The world is interwoven by a complex web of subtle correspondences, secret connections that link seemingly diverse phenomena through a deeper resonance of meaning.

All phenomena can be reduced to a basic set of universal principles or archetypes. Described in various ways by different traditions, these principles constitute the underlying language of both outer and inner experience.

While all of those points play an important role in a broader meta-framework of synchronicity, I'd like to focus our attention here on one of those in particular—the so-called "doctrine of correspondences."

The Doctrine of Correspondences

Virtually every esoteric or magical tradition has subscribed to this concept in one form or another, which can be broadly described as a sense that all things are connected in ways beyond the immediately obvious, involving a subterranean network of deeper qualities or *metaphoric essences*. As Ralph Waldo Emerson put it,

"Secret analogies tie together the remotest parts of Nature, as the atmosphere of a summer morning is filled with innumerable gossamer threads running in every direction, revealed by the beams of the rising sun."[3]

So, What Am I Doing Here, Anyway?

For instance, suppose you were to ask a scientist to explain what the planet Mars really *is*. They would likely fall back on describing it in terms of that planet's most obvious and observable properties—i.e., its chemical or elemental composition, its physical dimensions, weather patterns and energy fields, cosmic history, orbital dynamics, and so on. Furthermore, were the scientist to try and classify it in relation to all other phenomena in the universe, they would likely think in terms of readily observable relationships such as the fact Mars belongs to a particular class of celestial bodies and interacts with other bodies in measurable ways that include gravity, magnetism, and so on. Simply put, the scientific perspective would provide us with a *quantitative* approach toward understanding the planet Mars.

But for the symbolically-minded student, Mars can also be understood in terms of its essential *qualities* or *symbolic meanings*—a perspective that requires a very different mode of perception, and one that affords access to a very different order of information within the universe's phenomena.

Seen through a more symbolic lens, Mars can be linked to such qualities as *force, energy,* or *assertiveness*. These, in turn, link via a subtle network of qualities to such other phenomena as warfare, the metal iron, anger, energy, sharp objects, fire, and still others. From this perspective, a certain event might happen over *here*, just as the planet Mars is engaged in a planetary dance *over there*, and though the two may not seem connected in any obvious way, they can be related via subtle tendrils of meaning, through subtle patterns of archetypal resonance. While the purely literal eye would regard such meanings and connections as nonsensical and entirely imaginary, to the esoteric eye they are actually quite real, albeit subtle.

Said another way, this is a mode of thinking that regards the world as consisting of verbs and living processes, rather than solely as nouns or dead "things." Indeed, *all* phenomena can be viewed on either of these two levels—literal or symbolic, as nouns or as verbs. Each level has its own validity and relevance, but it's on this more symbolic level that we uncover that otherwise hidden network of acausal connections that links all phenomenon in our lives, and in turn to the cosmos.

The essential point is this: when seen on that subtler level, we discover that our lives are *permeated* with coincidences of one sort or another, but some are simply more obvious than others. As such, the rare and dramatic "meaningful coincidence" described by Jung is only the tip of a far greater iceberg of interconnectedness that spans our entire lives.

Jung hinted at this himself when he spoke of individual synchronicities being just "a particular instance of general acausal orderedness"; yet in the end, he chose to narrow his focus almost exclusively on the rare and unusual coincidence. Why? Presumably to make an already difficult subject less difficult and more digestible to both colleagues and general readers.

Whatever his reasoning, the key toward embracing that broader vision of synchronicity lies within a cognitive or epistemological shift. Seen through a purely literal eye, synchronicity indeed appears to be a rare and infrequent phenomenon; but when perceived through the eye of metaphor, one's vision opens up to a far broader universe of meanings and acausal connections, similar to how donning a pair of night vision goggles allows someone to behold a previously hidden landscape of subtle patterns not visible before.

Astrology – the Celestial Skeleton Key

Admittedly a controversial inclusion to the discussion, astrology is a subject even Jung himself felt important to include in this study. He believed that the correlation of planetary movements to an individual's life experience provided a real-world illustration of synchronicity-in-action. As an example, he found that an analysis of certain Sun/Moon configurations between married couples offered statistical evidence for the presence of a synchronistic connection between heavenly patterns and personal experience.

While I largely agree with all of that, my own reasons for including it here are somewhat different, and broader. Because astrology essentially represents the art and science of correspondences, it provides an especially helpful tool for approaching that otherwise hidden network of meanings we're discussing here.

Due to its elaborate network of symbolic "rulerships," whereby each planet or zodiacal sign is assigned a host of subtle connections throughout the world, one quickly discovers that our lives are *populated* by countless acausal associations that are otherwise invisible to the purely literal eye. One of the values of astrology is that it gives us the ability to examine those subtle connections more quickly, and far more comprehensively. Let me give a simple example.

Suppose someone finds themselves in the midst of a disruptive period in life where no obvious synchronicities or coincidences are visible. Apply the lens of astrological symbolism to their life, however, and you may well discover that the planet Uranus is firing strongly in their horoscope right then—at which point a host of acausal connections and subtle coincidences suddenly become clear, all related to the overarching principle of "Uranus." This might include such Uranian correspondences and symbols as technical or mechanical problems, delays in catching a flight, issues of personal freedom in a relationship, or even an ankle injury (that being the body part associated with Uranus). Yet this particular matrix of "secret analogies" would be completely invisible to the strict materialist, since it requires a heightened sensitivity to metaphoric essences rather than purely obvious appearances.

In that way, astrology provides us with an especially useful tool for helping us become more familiar with this subtle language of correspondences and, in turn, the deeply synchronistic language of daily life.

Envisioning a More Holistic Model

So where do we go from here? Picking up from where I left off in *The Waking Dream*, I'd suggest a few possible directions for continued research and exploration.

A more holistic and integral approach to synchronicity might be envisioned in the form of a pyramid, with the narrowest aspects of this research symbolized by the pyramid's peak and expanding downward to include progressively broader aspects of synchronicity closer to the bottom, as follows:

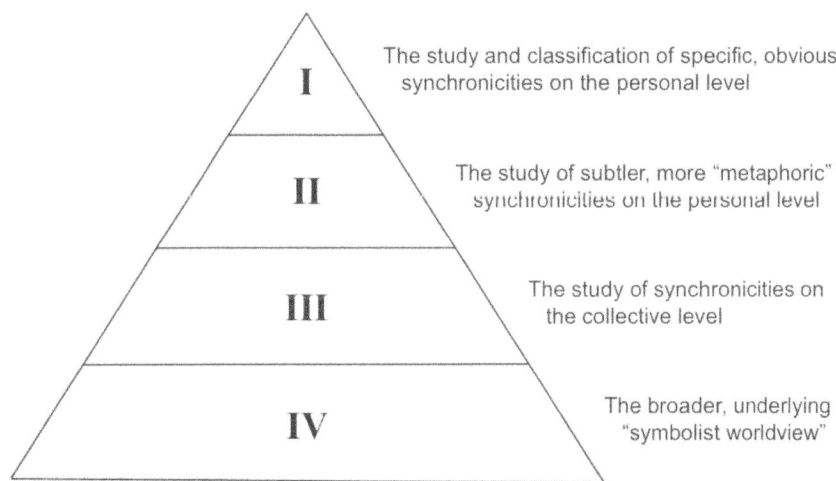

A PROSPECTIVE MODEL FOR A 'UNIFIED FIELD' APPROACH TO THE STUDY OF SYNCHRONICITY

I. At the peak of the pyramid, akin to the most visible portion of an iceberg, a systematic approach to synchronicity would focus on the study and classification of meaningful coincidences of the most obvious and literal types—e.g., a woman talking about her dream of a beetle at the precise moment one appears at the window to that room.

II. At the next level down, our focus would broaden out to include meaningful coincidences of a more symbolic and subtle nature, where the emphasis is less on the form of the event and more on the underlying meaning. A simple example of that would be the time I was biking over a footbridge in a local forest preserve and unexpectedly saw a deer swimming across a river, something I'd never seen before in all my years of hiking or biking. I later discovered that this sighting occurred at the very moment a close friend of mine passed away following a lingering illness. (In fact, I'd even been thinking about that friend just moments before encountering the deer.) Strictly on its surface, there is no obvious coincidence between a deer crossing a river and news of someone's death; yet to someone employing an analogical or metaphoric eye, the synchronistic connection is clear enough, and even echoes back to classical notions of death being likened to the "crossing of a river." At this level of our pyramid, we could also include the wide range of symbolic "messages" described in various omenological and divinational traditions known by such names as pyromancy, kledonism, ornithomancy, geomancy, bibliomancy, and many others—all of which involve meaningful or anomalous events and connections but which may not take the form of obvious, readily recognizable coincidences.

III. Moving further down the pyramid, our study widens out to focus on more *collective* synchronicities and symbolic events, both obvious and subtle, involving groups of people rather than solitary individuals. One example of this would be the outbreak of revolutionary fervor that sometimes occurs across the world in seemingly unrelated contexts, at the same time. In his book *Cosmos and Psyche*, my colleague Richard Tarnas points out how the famed mutiny that took place on the English ship *Bounty* in 1789 happened at the same time as the French Revolution—two iconic historic events involving rebellious uprisings, yet without there being any direct connection between the two.[4] In turn, Tarnas notes, this took place during a powerful relationship happening between the planets Uranus and Pluto. This could obviously be considered a "synchronicity," yet it certainly wasn't one that affected just one lone individual.

IV. Finally, we come to the base of our proverbial pyramid, where we find the study of the synchronistic worldview at its broadest—that is, *what is the symbolist cosmology underlying all these levels?* This level of inquiry would include such topics as the doctrine of correspondences, the law of cycles, the nature of archetypes, and even the doctrines of karma, reincarnation and teleology (purpose) in relation to the more personal side of this phenomenon. These are all interconnected elements informing the unfoldment of "meaning" on the personal, collective, and universal levels. Last but not least, a truly integral approach to synchronicity would involve a deeper look into the potential theological dimensions of this phenomenon—i.e., is the universe the dream-like expression of a great being or some cosmic principle? That's not a possibility we should overlook too casually. As I've written before,

"…in order for the diverse events of our lives to be interwoven as intricately and artfully as synchronicity implies, and as systems like astrology empirically demonstrate, there would seem to be a regulating intelligence underlying our world, a central principle organizing all of its elements like notes in a grand symphony of meaning."[5]

Revisioning Jung's Synchronicity

To recap, I've suggested that the phenomenon of synchronicity can be best understood in the framework of a cosmology that regards the entire world as dream-like in nature, and which is as symbolic in its own way as our own nightly dreams, likewise encoded in the language of symbols and subtle correspondences. Nested within that cosmic dream are the smaller dreams of both groups and individuals, with all of these seamlessly intertwined like threads in a vast quilt. As a result, a single, isolated coincidence occurring for any one individual actually takes place within the context of this larger infrastructure of meaning that suffuses all these different levels.

So how would such a broad vision specifically alter our understanding of Jung's model of synchronicity? I think it can be boiled down to a few essential points:

* Most obvious of all is the matter of *frequency*—that is, how often does synchronicity really occur? On the one hand, Jung spoke of synchronicity as involving an acausal connection between an outer event and an inner psychological state, or between two external events. In either case, he described it as a "relatively rare" phenomenon, a decidedly infrequent eruption of meaning in our lives. Employing the symbolist approach, however, we find there are actually *many* "eruptions of meaning" in our lives, occurring in a wide variety of contexts. Taking a hint from the esoteric traditions, we could include such seemingly common developments as the births of children, chance encounters with strangers or animals, life-tragedies, changes in the workplace, travel experiences, health problems, nightly dreams, and anomalous events of any sort. All of these—and many more—are "meaningful eruptions" with deep acausal connections to broader patterns of significance in our lives, all playing their own role in the phenomenological drama of everyday experience.

But considering how all-pervasive synchronicity then becomes, how shall we begin to sort out the proverbial "signal from the noise" in unearthing meaning from ordinary experience? In *The Waking Dream* I suggested a simple rule of thumb—namely, to focus attention particularly on those events which are *most* unusual or out of the ordinary. If you have a subscription to a daily newspaper, say, finding a copy on your doorstep is nothing particularly significant. But suppose you have *never* subscribed to any newspaper and one day find a copy at your front door—*that* suddenly takes on significance, with the meaning perhaps being revealed by the symbolism of the headline that day, or perhaps even the subject of a phone conversation you were having at the moment you found it.

* In formulating his theory of synchronicity, Carl Jung focused his attention strictly on coincidences of a simultaneous sort—that is, those which specifically take place *in the same moment in time*. Jung's story about the scarab is one example of this; another would be receiving a phone call from a childhood friend at the same moment an old letter from them falls out of a book you just pulled off the shelf. Such events synchronize in time—hence Jung's term *synchronicity*.

Prior to Jung, though, the Austrian biologist Paul Kammerer undertook his own study of coincidences but focused his attention instead on coincidences of a *sequential* sort, those which happen consecutively. For example, an obscure old song might pop up numerous times over the course of a single day, one after the other, in completely different contexts. Looking at such events, Kammerer termed his own theory *seriality*, emphasizing the consecutive rather than simultaneous character of coincidences.[6] What the symbolist worldview at its broadest does is dispense with any strict emphasis on simultaneity *or* sequentiality, instead opening up to acausal connections of *all* types—sequential or simultaneous, obvious or subtle. As the symbolist perspective suggested by astrology illustrates in particular, the synchronistic tapestry of correspondences extends in *all* directions, through both time and space.

* Whereas Jung saw synchronicity strictly as a personal phenomenon, related to the psychodynamics of individuals, the symbolist world view sees acausal connections or synchronicities taking place on at least three distinct levels: *personal, collective, and universal*. I mentioned the coincidence between the Mutiny on the Bounty and the French Revolution as a synchronicity involving groups rather than just individuals. Another example would be the curious way similar inventions or theories sometimes arise simultaneously in different parts of the world, seemingly disconnected to one another. A famous instance of that was the development of the telephone by both Alexander Graham Bell and Elisha Gray, both inventors having filed notices with the Patent Office in Washington, D.C. on the very same day, February 14, 1876.

In turn, it's even possible to talk about synchronicity in contexts where *neither* individuals or groups are involved. For instance, astrologers might examine how a volcanic eruption on a remote Pacific island coincided with a celestial pattern involving the distant planets Uranus and Pluto, say. Such a connection would constitute a truly "synchronistic" development, in that it's a truly acausal connection of events, yet it's one that didn't involve individuals or even collectives in any direct way. Likewise, there are astrologers who study the relationship of planetary configurations to weather patterns throughout the world, whether humans are directly involved or not. In contrast with Jung's model, in other words, *individual human psychologies needn't even be present or involved for "synchronicities" to occur.*

Conclusion

To borrow William Irwin Thompson's classic analogy, we are like flies crawling across the ceiling of the Sistine Chapel, unaware of the archetypal drama spread out before us. What the infrequent and dramatic coincidence does is simply pull back the curtain on *one small portion* of that tableau which encompasses not just our personal lives but our society, and indeed the entire universe.

As such, synchronicity is the key to a dramatically different cosmology than what is suggested by conventional science. Beyond simply implying an intimate relationship between one's outer and inner world, or a subtle "entanglement" between distant phenomena, it describes a worldview that is both multi-leveled in its meanings and levels, and interconnected in ways far beyond what the literal eye can possibly perceive.

While it's within our grasp to understand that broader worldview, it won't be had through any purely literal mindset or mechanistic methodology, let alone through the study of individual coincidences in themselves. Rather, it will need to unfold in partnership with a broader philosophical inquiry into the symbolic and archetypal dimensions of existence itself. That, and nothing less, will allow us to finally perceive the "whole elephant" of synchronicity.[7]

Notes

1. Jung, Carl. "Synchronicity: An Acausal Connecting Principle," in *The Structure and Dynamics of the Psyche*, Vol. 8, Collected Works. Princeton, NJ: Bollingen Series, Princeton University Press.

2. Grasse, Ray. *The Waking Dream: Unlocking the Symbolic Language of Our Lives*. Wheaton, IL: Quest Books, 1996, p.6.

3. Emerson, Ralph Waldo. From his essay "Demonology," in *The Complete Writings*, Vol. II. New York: William H. Wise, 1929, p.949.

4. Richard Tarnas, *Cosmos and Psyche*, New York, Penguin Group, 2006, pp.50-60.

5. www.theosophical.org/publications/quest-magazine/1441-synchronicity-and-the-mind-of-god

6. As described by Arthur Koestler in his book *The Case of the Midwife Toad*. London: Hutchinson and Co., and New York: Random House, 1971.

7. For a deeper dive into correspondence theory and the dynamics of symbolism, see chapters 10 and 11 of my book *The Waking Dream*, as well as chapter 36 of *StarGates: Essays on the Philosophy and Practice of Astrology*.

CHAPTER 12

On the Pleasures of Existence

A while back I had lunch with an old friend who had been going through a depressing time, feeling discouraged and deflated, especially over his non-existent love life.

"What's especially frustrating," he said, "is the fact that there's just no pleasure in my life anymore—none. It's been 15 years since I've had sex. With someone other than myself, that is."

I could empathize, especially since my own romantic life hadn't exactly been something to write home about. Reflecting for a moment on his comments, I didn't want to simply suggest ways he could distract himself or paper over those heavy feelings, since I know there can be value in learning from those, too.

But I couldn't help but notice that, for him, pleasure equated almost exclusively with *sex*—and that was that. What was ironic about all of that for me was the fact that as we sat in that nice restaurant, he was eating what seemed to be a delicious meal—a meal that any starving person in the world would have probably given their eye teeth for. So I asked him, "What about that meal you're eating right now? Do you find any pleasure in that?"

He seemed slightly caught off guard by the question, and said, "Well yeah…there's *that*."

Not to compare a great meal with great sex, let alone a great, sustained relationship, but I do think there's a useful point to be made here. In the process of associating "pleasure" so exclusively with just one or two activities in life, I think it's easy to overlook the

On the Pleasures of Existence

many avenues of pleasure we move through daily, often without even knowing it.

This is something I've struggled with throughout much of my own life, since I know I have the tendency to take much for granted in my daily experience—that is, until something comes along which points that out for me. Like unexpectedly being deprived of an ordinary luxury like running water or indoor plumbing; or seeing someone else do without those simple things I casually take for granted. It's led me to make a more concerted effort to turn this around and look at things in my world a bit more closely. With that in mind, I thought I'd share a list of some of the "tricks" I sometimes employ for doing just that.

The pleasure of eating

A few years ago, I watched a film about the life of critic Roger Ebert and the struggles he faced in the wake of throat and mouth cancer. Because of his condition, he had to take in nourishment through a tube in his throat. That was a sobering thought for me. Try to imagine never being able to taste a simple meal with your mouth or tongue again. I can't speak for anyone else, but food has probably been the key source of comfort and pleasure throughout my entire life (as a result, fasting has never come very easy for me); I frankly don't know how well I'd deal with it were I to find myself in Ebert's shoes for any period of time. Though I may be less aware in these respects than I'd really like, I try to never take for granted even the smallest bites of food I consume during an ordinary day.

The pleasure of breathing

As mentioned previously, during high school I sustained a back injury that put me in a cast for several months. The first night after the doctors applied the plaster strips, the cast constricted as it dried and the effect left me feeling like I was gradually suffocating, bit by bit. It was a terrifying experience (offset somewhat by the heavy-duty painkillers the nurse administered late that night). By the next day I was considerably better, but that first evening was akin to torture, and made me appreciate oxygen more than any book or lecture could ever have. Since then, I make a point of taking a few moments now and then throughout the day to slow down and savor the experience of every breath, if not every molecule of oxygen.

The pleasure of drinking water

Have you ever spent hours or even days in a hot, dry climate with no access to water, even to the point where you grew concerned about your survival? If so, then you'll likely recall what an amazing sensation it was when you finally had access to that first drink of water. I've had that experience a few times over the years, and since then whenever I turn on the tap I make a point of feeling gratitude for the extraordinary gift of running water—while also taking a moment to appreciate the remarkable taste of water itself. Did I say "taste of water"? Indeed. Strange, really; water supposedly has "no taste" and yet it has the most remarkable taste of all—when you're truly thirsty!

The pleasure of seeing

My mother went blind during the last years of her life, as a result of a medical mistake made during surgery. The tragic irony was, she went in to the clinic for a routine cataract procedure specifically designed to improve her eyesight for the sake of her painting, a hobby she had picked up in her later years. Taking care of her during that period made me realize more than before what an amazing gift it was just to *see*—to take in the sights of nature, appreciating works of art, beholding the night sky, reading the expressions on peoples' faces, simply maneuvering through the world every day, and just generally appreciating the beauty and extraordinary complexity of life brought about by those trillions of photons swirling through my eyes and brain at every moment.

On the Pleasures of Existence

The pleasure of music

Parallel to my mother's situation, I had a friend in childhood who was deaf, and it allowed me to see first-hand how painful and isolating that was for him not only in social situations but because of how he could never enjoy the music that was so important to many of us at that age. He was never able to experience the incredible thrill we had on hearing each new album by the Beatles, Rolling Stones, or Dylan; nor could he ever enjoy the transcendent strains of Debussy or Ravel I personally grew to love during those years, among others.

So, What Am I Doing Here, Anyway?

Despite how absolutely pervasive it is, from songs on the radio to jingles on TV commercials, music is a genuinely mysterious phenomenon in the strange way that sonic proportions are able to evoke such deep and complex emotional states in us, and seemingly transporting us to different worlds. Yet it's a phenomenon completely denied those without the miraculous gift of hearing.

The pleasure of walking

I remember being deeply touched by an interview with a paraplegic once, in which the fellow said, "Before my accident I never dreamt there might come a day when I'd actually feel jealous just watching someone else walk across the room." That was his Mount Everest, apparently—simply being able to stand up and walk a few feet. He knew better than anyone else how walking is one of life's greatest pleasures, whether it be for hiking across a majestic landscape or simply traveling from one room to the next.

The pleasure of being outdoors

During the mid-1980s, I was asked to give a talk to some prisoners at (the now-decommissioned) Joliet Penitentiary in Illinois. I was initially nervous, since I'd never been inside of a prison before; yet it turned out to be a great experience for me in several ways. One of those was the fact that the group of the 70 or so prisoners I spoke to seemed deeply appreciative having someone from the outside come in to talk with them. But it was also meaningful for me because of how the experience made me more appreciative of the ordinary freedoms I take for granted, not just in having control over my time and actions but in being able to simply go outdoors and just walk around. I should elaborate.

At one point the prison employee who hosted my talk took me out for a walk around the prison grounds, where I saw various prisoners milling around, generally in various groups. I didn't think too much about the situation until we came upon a particular handful of tattooed men walking towards us from the other direction. As we passed them by, my host whispered, "Don't look 'em in the eye—*look down*..." I did as he suggested, and afterward he explained that the one thing you don't want to do on these grounds was make eye contact with prisoners you're not directly allied with. Needless to say, I don't have to worry about such things when I leave my own home and walk around my neighborhood, or go to the store, and I would imagine the majority of my readers don't either. Either way, it's a freedom and a pleasure I've grown to appreciate particularly these last few years, in the wake of dealing with certain health challenges that have made long walks a somewhat more infrequent one for me.

The pleasure of sleeping in a bed

I've been fortunate to have only experienced "homelessness" for two days out of my entire life, when I found myself stranded in a foreign country with no money or shelter, after having my wallet stolen. Which is to say I've never *really* been "homeless"—not in the way genuinely homeless people experience. But what surprised me, even for that very short time, was how vulnerable and even depressed the experience made me feel. It was just long enough to make me empathize with those forced to resort to sleeping on the ground or on cold cement, park benches, or in makeshift cardboard boxes, be they refugees or just men or women down on their luck. It certainly led me to appreciate simply having a bed to sleep in, one that's housed in a secure space where I didn't have to worry about extremes of temperature, vermin, or violent attacks in the middle of the night.

Then there is the experience of *sleep itself*—easily one of life's greatest pleasures. I remember driving cross country with my friend Bill Hogan while in college, from Chicago to San Francisco. Because of a deadline my friend had to meet, we had to reach our destination in no more than 48 hours, but because I didn't know how to drive my friend's stick shift back then, I had to stay awake in order to keep *him* awake that entire time. Including the time

So, What Am I Doing Here, Anyway?

spent getting ready before the trip to meet up with him, by the end of the trip I'd been awake a total of almost 60 hours. It's impossible for me to describe how blissful it was when I finally had the chance to lie down on a bed in a seedy motel room and fall asleep.

The pleasure of emotions

What do I mean by that? I no longer recall the title, but I remember seeing a science fiction movie or TV show once where a mechanical robot wanted badly to know what it felt like to experience human emotions—even the seemingly unpleasant ones, since even that was a realm of experience the robot was unable to know. We take our emotions for granted, and sometimes even wish we didn't have them. Yet how dry and empty would our lives be without them? While the mystical traditions enjoin us to control our emotions and lift our states of consciousness, that doesn't mean the goal is to become robots! I often think back to a comment Goswami Kriyananda once made: "Everyone is trying to find God when they haven't even found their humanness yet." There is value in aspiring to the spiritual heights, it's true, but that shouldn't come at the expense of completely bypassing the value—and beauty—of our everyday existence, in *all* its facets.

The pleasure of thinking

One of my childhood friends, Steve, had a serious motorcycle accident in his mid-20s, which left him seriously brain damaged. For years afterwards, he was unable to string words together to form even simple sentences. He struggled mightily to communicate, but eventually would just explode with primal sounds at the top of his lungs, out of sheer frustration. For most of us, our brains run like reasonably well-oiled machines; but if you've ever watched someone like my friend Steve, or experienced mental or brain issues yourself, you'll know what an extraordinary thing it is to simply think and communicate your thoughts clearly, or understand those conveyed to you by others.

Above and beyond ordinary thought, there is that extraordinary faculty of thinking we call *imagination*. By means of it, we can create entire worlds in our minds, travel to distant lands or dimensions, reimagine our future self, conceive beautiful works of art or music, or call up or reconfigure memories from our past. These, too, are gifts afforded us by those entities we so casually refer to as "thoughts."

Last but not least, the simple pleasure of existence itself

When I was in my 20s, I happened to watch a documentary on public television about capital punishment, and it included a brief sequence showing the execution of a well-dressed man somewhere in the Middle East. He was led to the scaffold, and when they tried to place the noose around his neck, he repeatedly—and desperately—kept moving his head around in hope of dodging the rope. It was a deeply sad thing to see, because he obviously knew he couldn't forestall his fate forever, yet was fighting to grab even just a few more seconds of life. The sequence cut off right before it showed his demise, fortunately, but it was just enough to illustrate just how much most of us really want to *live*—however messed up our lives may seem on their surface. We may not normally think of simply existing as something inherently "pleasurable" in itself, yet to a person ascending the scaffold, or to almost anyone facing their possible demise, whatever the reason, it rapidly becomes apparent just how meaningful and wonderful this simple fact is.

I'll take it one critical step farther and invite you to consider the following thought experiment. Imagine you had divine powers and could have offered that man on the scaffold a choice: on the one hand, he could have access to the greatest pleasures in the world, including the greatest food, sex, and beautiful stimuli of all types possible, but it would be on the condition that it would last for just one week, after which his life would end. The other choice would be to *not* have any of those extraordinary pleasures to enjoy, but he could go free at the end of that week, he'd be granted a reprieve to live out the rest of his natural life as he pleased.

Which of those options do you suppose he would go for? I think it's safe to say it would be the latter one. That's simply because as great as all those other pleasures may be, they're completely outstripped by what may be the greatest pleasure of all: simply existing.

CHAPTER 13

Can One's Horoscope Indicate a Sense of "Mission"?

Occasionally we come across someone who expresses a sense that they've come into this world for a purpose, a "mission." It's a feeling that they came here to *do* something, even if they aren't always 100% sure what that is exactly. Who knows; perhaps you're one of those individuals yourself.

As an astrologer, I've long wondered whether the horoscope can indicate this sort of thing. What kind of aspects, signs, or house placements would indicate that kind of intimation?

Having looked at countless charts over a number of decades, I've come to believe there are indeed certain indicators which strongly suggest a condition like that. I'd like to look here at two or three of those which strike me as significant.

I. First and foremost, I look for any planets or luminaries near the MC (especially if they are the ruler of the Sun sign, Ascendant, or the MC itself). As I've discussed in earlier books,[1] there is something about the most elevated bodies in a chart which suggests a trait or goal one is *aspiring towards*—and along with that often comes a sense of "mission," where the person feels drawn to fulfill some purpose or calling. In the case of Mars, that might involve athletics, the military, physical activity, social activism, sexuality, or general risk-taking; in the case of Venus, that might be the arts, fashion, or something aesthetic; with Neptune, it may be artistic or spiritual in nature; if the Sun, it's most likely leadership—and so on.

So, What Am I Doing Here, Anyway?

To a lesser extent, I've even found this sense of mission can apply to any planet closely aligned with *any* of the horoscope's four angles—such as when a musician has Neptune aligned with the IC, or a writer has Mercury closely conjunct the Ascendant, or a fashion designer has Venus on the Descendant. But based on what I've seen, this sense of being on a "mission" does seem considerably more pronounced when the planet is elevated near the top of the horoscope, especially when aligned closely with the MC.

II. The other factor I've comes across involves any particularly *close* aspect between two or more planets in a chart. That's because there is something about extremely tight aspects—especially stressful ones (squares, oppositions, certain conjunctions, or even inconjuncts)—which indicates areas where an individual feels compulsively drawn to *do* something, possibly as a problem to be solved or managed. The closer the aspect, the more that compulsion can feel nearly unavoidable in its urgency.

A classic example of this would be architect Frank Lloyd Wright, who was born with a tight opposition between Saturn and Venus—astrologically, a classic significator for architecture and sculpture. Or consider filmmaker, actor, and radio announcer, Orson Welles, who was born with several tight aspects, including a close square between the Sun and Uranus. From a young age he became famous for his need to "shock" the world, with media projects like his "War of the Worlds" broadcast of 1938 or his rule-breaking film *Citizen Kane* in 1941. Judging from his various biographies, it's clear that that desire to shock was there from an early age.

What I've found particularly noteworthy is when these previous two factors I've mentioned *converge* in a chart—that is, when a very close aspect also happens to be aligned with an angle, especially (but not exclusively) the MC. In those cases, that compulsive sense of "mission" becomes amplified by leaps and bounds.

A classic example would be evangelist Billy Graham, born with a Mars-Moon conjunction in Sagittarius near the MC, which in turn

Can One's Horoscope Indicate a Sense of "Mission"?

is cemented by a trine to Saturn. This is a configuration strongly suggesting an urge to assert or "preach" a philosophy or dogma, and doing so with considerable authority. (Mars is also the ruler of Graham's Ascendant, adding more power and personal charisma to this configuration.) Graham was drawn from a young age to a life of evangelizing, in a way that only gained more momentum and success as he became older.

Another illustration would be singer-songwriter Sting, who was born with a close conjunction in Libra between the Moon and Neptune (less than one degree). That's an aspect frequently found in musicians, mystics or actors, and in his case it's *closely* aligned with the IC/MC axis. Along with his Leo rising and Jupiter near the top of his chart, it's safe to say that attraction to music was a powerful seed in his psyche long before he set foot on any stage.

One of the best examples I've come across in my own practice was a client I spoke with not long ago, whose chart I've displayed here (with permission). There is much of interest in this horoscope, but take note of one configuration in particular: the nearly exact trine from Saturn down on the lower right (Uranus and Venus are also involved, but more indirectly) to his elevated Jupiter up in the 10th house—keeping in mind that Jupiter is the ruler of his Sun sign, Sagittarius. While not exactly conjunct the MC, Jupiter is nonetheless the closest body to that angle, and conspicuously placed.

My first impression on looking at this horoscope, and its tight Saturn-Jupiter trine in particular, was one of considerable "good karma" for success, with that potential symbolically reinforced by the placement of Jupiter being so elevated. The fact that this man's Sun is in the same sign as his Saturn also suggested a certain potential for leadership and achievement, not to mention ambition and capacity for hard work. Finally, the heavy 6th house emphasis implied some involvement possibly with health or health care.

So, What Am I Doing Here, Anyway?

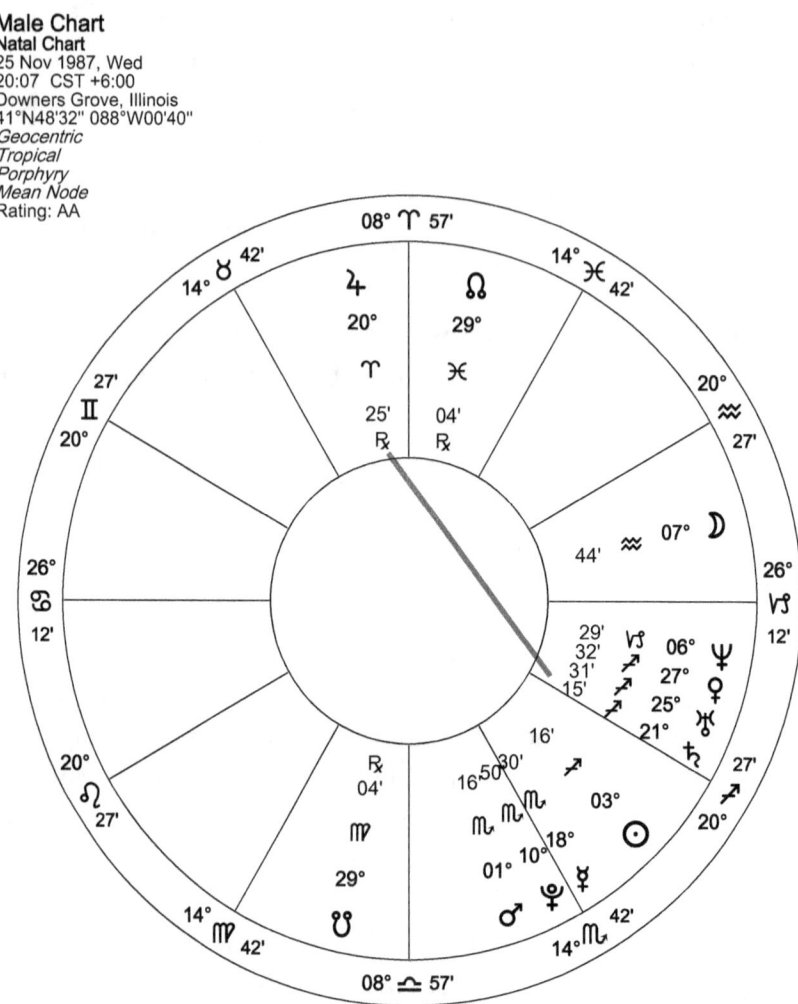

As it turned out, this young man became involved with a major media project involving health care that gained him considerable attention, even a little fame, with him winding up as boss to roughly 200 employees—all while still just in his mid-30s! The key point here is that he had a confident sense of his potential and life-direction from a young age.

Some Difficult Questions

I'd be remiss not to also mention that this sense of "mission" isn't necessarily always a positive or constructive one! There are numerous instances from history where someone is drawn from a young age to make their mark on the world because they feel it's their "calling"—but they turn out to be a dictator, religious zealot, or criminal mastermind!

In horoscopes like those, we generally find some of the same indicators I've been laying out here but leading to a decidedly more unfortunate outcome. It naturally raises a number of thorny ethical and interpretive questions, such as: If we see those potential problems in a horoscope, should we say anything about it, and if so, how? More to the point, is there any way to *really* tell from the horoscope when that sense of "mission" is constructive or destructive, or perhaps just motivated by delusions?

I wish it were as simple as looking for squares from Neptune or Jupiter, or from a problematic Mars, say. Personally, though, I haven't found it to be that easy. There's also the dicey question as to who decides what is really "constructive" or "destructive," "positive" or "negative." While this may be more clear-cut in the case of someone like Hitler, who obviously was driven by a more nefarious sense of "destiny" in life than most, in the case of someone like Billy Graham, it's far more subjective how to judge the impact and value of spreading Christianity throughout the world. Positive or negative? I'll have to let the reader decide that one.

In the end, I'm left to conclude that this sense of "mission" is, in itself, essentially a *neutral* factor, and can be redirected in either positive or negative ways by the individual.

One last thing. In some cases, the sense of mission I've describing here can evolve or morph considerably over the course of a single lifetime. I'm reminded of the client I've discussed in earlier books who was born with Neptune near his Midheaven. Growing up in the inner city, he was drawn as a young man to emulate the neighborhood drug dealer and that character's flashy clothes and attractive "girlfriends." In later years, he wound up transmuting his Neptunian "mission" into one of counseling drug addicts and otherwise directionless teenagers. The archetype remained the same, but the form it assumed changed dramatically. The upshot is, the chart can indeed provide hints of a person's "mission," but it's ultimately up to the individual what to make of that.[2]

These, then, are just a few examples of what I've suggested here. I'd encourage you to take some time to examine these indicators in the charts you come across to see if they shed any further light on their dynamics.

Notes

1. See "Decoding the Most Elevated in the Horoscope" in my book *StarGates: Essays on Astrology, Symbolism, and the Synchronistic Universe* (2020).

2. I think it's useful to point out that, while there can be horoscopic indicators indicating a sense of "mission" in someone's life, that doesn't mean a chart should necessarily be limited to a single theme. A client recently asked me, "What does my chart say is the karmic reason I came here for this time around?" My answer was that while there may be a dominant theme guiding someone's life, each of us may actually be coming here for *several different* reasons, karmically. For instance, Mahatma Gandhi obviously had a certain destiny in terms of his involvement with politics and spirituality, but probably had any number of other challenges or issues to work on in this life, from personal relationships to money matters or health concerns. In short, our lives can be complex tapestries involving a variety of challenges and lessons, rather than just one.

CHAPTER 14

Neptune and the Cross of Obligation

After its discovery in 1846, astrologers debated intensely over the possible meanings of Neptune in horoscopes, and over time eventually settled onto a few basic qualities for this planet, which included such keywords as *spiritual, nebulous, illusions, sensitivity, otherworldly, artistic, addictive, empathic, and escapist*—and that's for starters.

But there is one aspect of its influence that's been too often overlooked by astrologers, and that's proven indispensable in my own analysis of charts over the years. What is that, exactly?

In a word, *obligation*.

It's an association I first learned from an early astrology teacher of mine, Goswami Kriyananda of Chicago, who made a comment in class one day how, under certain circumstances, Neptune relates to feelings of obligation towards others. Look up the word in any dictionary and you'll find a description along the lines of "the sense of feeling morally or emotionally bound to do something." When it comes to obligation, there's usually an implicit sense of "Well, I guess I ought to do this…"

First, though, it's helpful to draw a distinction here between what I'd call "positive" obligation and "negative" obligation.

Simply stated, obligation of a more positive sort is when one does something that involves an element of sacrifice or helping others but performed relatively effortlessly, perhaps even happily. Having to attend a child's baseball game may be an obligation, but generally one is glad to do it. Like I say, generally. A good example of this, astrologically, would be my close friend who was born with a tight Neptune-Venus trine, who happily devotes his time and energies to helping his spouse in a wide variety of ways. He doesn't do any of this as a "burden" but out of true love and a spirit of selflessness. Back in the 60s there was a popular song titled "He Ain't Heavy, He's My Brother"; that pretty well sums up the essence of Neptunian obligation at its best.

On the other hand, obligation of a more negative kind is where one does something for others more grudgingly and foot-draggingly, like "Okay, okay, *I'll do it*..." In this case, the sense of burden is quite real, maybe with a touch of the "woe is me" syndrome thrown in to the mix, where one might even liken oneself to Jesus bearing his cross on the fateful road to Golgatha. Margaret Cahill came up with the term "compassion fatigue" to describe some of the effects of Saturn moving into Pisces, but that's actually quite similar to the more problematic side of Neptune we're looking at here.

Here's an example. I had a client who spent her days as a social worker, who was born with Neptune closely squaring her Sun. Over time she experienced a growing sense of burnout from the extra-heavy caseload she'd taken on, and from dealing with so many suffering people who depended on her. She believed in the importance of the work itself, yes, but the sense of "burden" became so intense that she confessed to me at one point that she felt like a lifeguard who had jumped into the water to save drowning swimmers only to be pulled under and start drowning herself. In cases like that, Neptune is experienced as the sense of having to rescue others—or sometimes even as the need to be rescued oneself!

A Tale of Opposites

Sometimes a helpful way to understand any planetary principle is through contrasting it with a very different energy—in this case, I'll choose Uranus. Consider how these two planets respond

Neptune and the Cross of Obligation

differently when they come into contact with another body in the chart, say, like the Moon.

To begin with, the Moon concerns one's ability to relate to others and bond with them emotionally, as well as the capacity for expressing *or* receiving nurturance. Uranus is an *extremely* independent energy, so when it forms any hard aspect to the Moon, the native generally has no problem at all establishing sharp boundaries, to the extent that one client with this pattern joked that her theme song should be "Don't fence me in." In extreme cases, an individual like this might even be considered selfish or cold by those near and dear to them.

On the other hand, *Neptune* in hard aspect to the Moon is completely different, since it has the tendency to *dissolve* personal boundaries. On the plus side, that can lead to compassion, empathy, and sometimes even psychic abilities. More negatively, though, that great sensitivity and dissolution of boundaries can lead to becoming emotionally enmeshed or co-dependent with others. Along with that usually comes a heavy sense of obligation—"Sigh, I *have* to take care of them," or, "I *need* to rescue them…" In cases like those, the emotional bond with others can feel less like love and more like glue.

To help illustrate the effects I'm describing here, let's briefly look at some of the ways this sense of obligation may be experienced when Neptune is prominent in the horoscope. I've chosen to focus here mainly on the effects of Neptune as positioned on or near the four primary angles, since that's where I've generally found its influence to be strongest. (I specify "on or near" the angles, by the way, since I've found that Neptune's effects apply even when it's just in the general vicinity of the angles rather than just perched specifically on those exact degrees.) To be clear, there are *many* different ways Neptune can manifest; what I'll be describing here is primarily in relation to that felt sense of obligation.

Neptune On or Near the Descendant

Neptune in the vicinity of the Descending degree can definitely show extreme sensitivity to others, an attraction to artistic or spiritual partners, or an involvement with the health and healing professions. But it can also indicate a sense of obligation over having to "rescue" others, as when dealing with a sick or injured spouse, lover or friend, or others who are alcoholics or substance abusers. As with the social worker I mentioned, the heavy weight of obligation can also center around the public, as when dealing with needy customers, patients, or students. For similar reasons, I've found this placement to be fairly common in the charts of celebrities, actors, or musicians, who often feel the weight of dealing with the public in ways that are problematic or exhausting at times.

Neptune On or Near the IC

When Neptune is near the bottom of the horoscope, especially when close to the I.C., it can indicate a pronounced spiritual, religious or artistic influence in the family or home environment. Actress Uma Thurman has Neptune located here, for instance, and her father, Robert Thurman, is a respected religious scholar. For some, this placement shows one might see their home as a spiritual or artistic sanctuary. On a much more prosaic level, I've had a surprising number of clients with Neptune low in the chart who lived near or even *on* bodies of water. One radio announcer I've spoken to who was born with Neptune on the I.C. lived for much of his adult life on houseboats!

When more negatively expressed, however, this placement can point to a strong sense of obligation around caretaking or "rescuing" a family member or relative, possibly in connection with alcoholism, mental illness, or some physical infirmity. Sometimes, it's simply family responsibilities of a powerful kind, as in the case of my single mother client who admitted to feeling exhausted by the responsibilities of supporting a family all by herself. Or, that sense of obligation may be towards upholding a family *tradition*, as when a child is expected to carry on a family business begun by a parent or grandparent. In a few cases, I've had clients with this placement who became involved with helping the homeless, where that obligatory drive to help or rescue others seems to have extended to matters of "home" and "domesticity" in a broader and more social sense, to the public at large.

Neptune On or Near the MC

When Neptune is positioned near the top of the horoscope, that sense of obligation can be directed towards a parent or authority figure—or perhaps even the entire world. For example, this can take the form of a desire to heal, harmonize, or inspire others, whether that as a healer, minister, or artist. Princess Diana had Neptune as the planet closest to her MC, and that energy was especially obvious in her work with charitable and philanthropic causes. It's fascinating how many musicians or performing artists have Neptune placed high, like Jimi Hendrix, Patti Smith, Elvis Presley, and Bob Dylan. Walt Disney is rightfully known as the "king of fantasy," and with good reason: he was born with Neptune near the MC.

But more problematically, Neptune near the top of the chart can indicate considerable difficulty dealing with that same sense of obligation towards the public. For example, the desire to inspire and heal that drove Walt Whitman in his poetry also weighed heavily on him while working with wounded or dying soldiers during the Civil War. For all of her positive work, Princess Diana felt extremely constrained by the obligation to maintain a certain "royal" image for the public and the paparazzi.

So, What Am I Doing Here, Anyway?

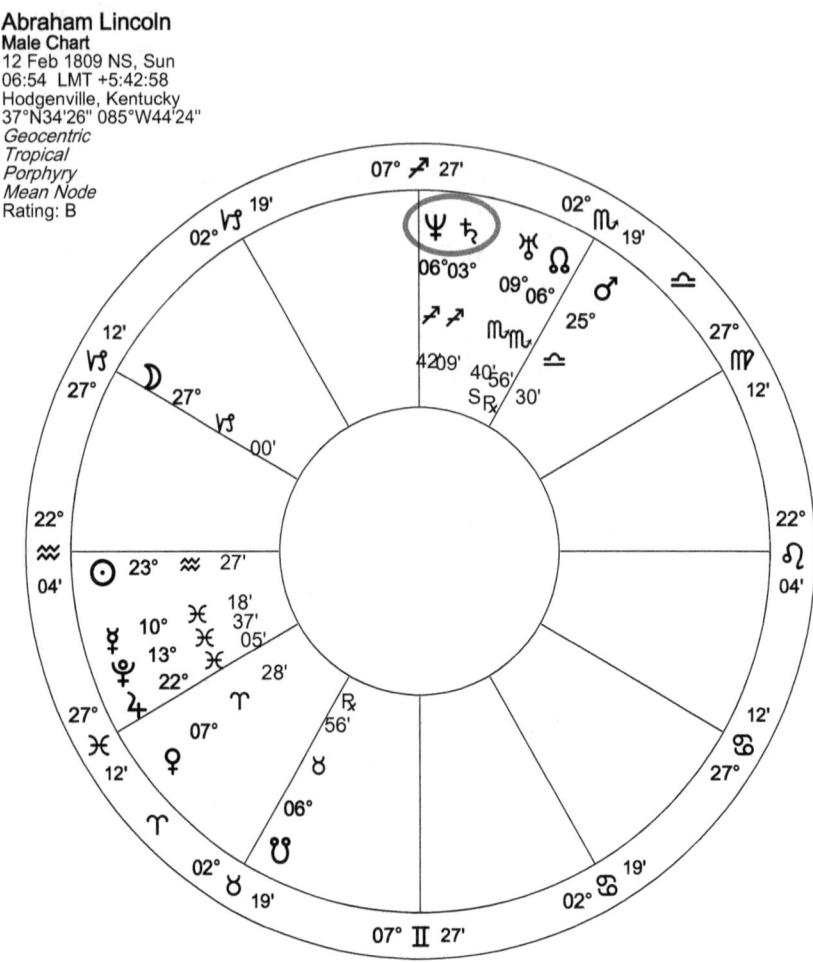

Abraham Lincoln had Neptune aligned with Saturn near the MC, and he clearly felt like he was bearing a heavy cross in his role as "emancipator" and restorer of the Union. For some individuals, this Neptunian impulse can metastasize into a full-blown messiah complex, where one entertains delusions about one's own spiritual importance and divine "mission" to help or save the world. At its most problematic, it can even trigger an impulse towards martyrdom, leading to what one client referred to as a "pound another nail in me, guys" attitude. Fortunately, those cases have been far fewer in my experience.

Neptune On or Near the Ascendant

Finally, we come to what I find is the most subtle and enigmatic placement of Neptune: when it's located on or near the Ascendant. In positive ways, this placement shows extreme sensitivity, and can even point to a pronounced spiritual or artistic streak in the personality.

But in this case that sense of Neptunian "obligation" may be directed towards one's own *self*, in terms of caretaking one's body, health, or personality.

Consider my client born with Neptune exactly on her Ascendant who struggled much of her life with a series of chronic health problems; for her, the "cross to bear" manifested primarily as the need to attend to *her own body*, as far as diet, exercise, or medical treatment goes. This can also take the form of some physical impairment or disability one feels "obligated" to contend with. In extreme cases, this placement can lead to feeling obligated to caretaking the proverbial "monkey on one's back" in the form of addiction to substances like alcohol, heroin, opiates, or sugar. One may not consciously *want* to feed that addiction but may feel nearly helpless in the face of it, almost like an obligation to the addiction itself—i.e., "I've *got* to have that drink…"

Similar to Neptune near the top of the horoscope, Neptune on or near the Ascendant can manifest as an obligation to maintain a certain persona or "mask" before the public. The classic example of this is actress Marilyn Monroe, who was born with Neptune in her 1st house. She struggled during her professional career with maintaining that sexy and glamorous image from films even while offscreen. As she once said, "My problem with men is that they all want to go to bed with Marilyn, but they wake up with Norma Jean" (her given name prior to show business).

While Neptune near the Ascendant is potentially the most spiritual and sensitive indicator of all Neptunian placements, those born with this pattern need to be especially careful of falling into the "woe is me," self-pitying trap mentioned earlier. In instances like those, one's great sensitivity can make dealing with the harsh realities of the world a major challenge. And whereas Neptune on the Descendant can feel like *others* around you are "needy," Neptune on or near the Ascendant can sometimes manifest as *you* being the needy one!

One other point. Because the Ascending degree is one-half of the 1st/7th "relationship axis," Neptune near the Ascendant can trigger relationship concerns almost as much as when positioned on the Descendant. On countless occasions I've read for clients or associates born with Neptune near the Ascendant who describe the weight of obligation felt having to caretake or "rescue" a spouse, friend, or partner in need. (Much of that same dual dynamic applies to the MC/IC axis, incidentally—i.e., any major planet perched on one end of that angle will exert a huge influence on the opposite point as well.)

Final thoughts

Whichever horoscopic angle Neptune may be aligned to in an individual's chart—or for that matter, whichever *personal planet* it may be closely aspecting—one needs to pay especially close attention to maintaining healthy boundaries with others. A strongly emphasized Neptune diffuses that dividing line between self and other, and with that comes a variety of huge potentials but also vexing challenges. What makes it especially tricky in the case of Neptune is how inherently slippery and nebulous that effect can be sometimes. Like the physical planet itself, Neptune's effects can be invisible to the naked eye sometimes and thus more difficult to get a firm handle on.

If properly balanced and grounded, though, those diaphanous boundaries can give rise to a profound empathy that knows its proper limits, and may even confer a genius for creativity that's able to access realities and ideas far beyond the normal limits of the senses.

Postscript: it's worth mentioning that much of what I've written here about Neptune also applies to the influence of Pisces in the chart. For instance, Pisces on the Descendant can have much the same effect as having Neptune on that angle. The Dalai Lama was born with Pisces at the top of his chart, for instance (with Saturn there too, no less) and has likely felt the weight of obligation to his fellow Tibetans and refugees in a way similar to having Neptune near the MC. If you have Pisces on any of the angular houses, look closely to see if any of the points covered in this essay apply to you as well.

CHAPTER 15

The Meal
(A Short Story)

Once upon a time there was a man who enjoyed life and all of its pleasures, but loved food more than anything else.

Over time he grew to have nagging concerns about death, not just because he enjoyed life so much but because he wondered whether he had actually lived a good life or a bad one. Would he go to heaven when he died, he wondered? Or instead to hell?

Eventually, the man passed away and entered the afterlife—and was very pleasantly surprised to find himself escorted to a beautiful dining area with the most delicious meal he could have possibly imagined laid out before him. He sat down and began to eat, and swooned in ecstasy over how delicious the food was.

At that point he realized, beyond any shadow of a doubt, he truly was in heaven.

The next day—as far as "days" can really be counted in heaven—he found himself treated to the same meal as before. And so it was on the next day, and then the day after that—and on it went like this, for hundreds, thousands, and eventually millions of years, the exact same meal, without the slightest difference, throughout all of eternity.

At which point he came to realize that, beyond any shadow of a doubt, he had truly entered hell.

CHAPTER 16

The Star Wars Man

In my book *When the Stars Align*, I wrote about the disappointment I felt on failing to land a job on the post-production crew of the film *Apocalypse Now* back in 1979. After graduating from film school at the Art Institute of Chicago in the early Seventies, I tried several times to break into the film industry, but with no luck. That was one of them.

Several years earlier, another setback had taken place around a project I was working on with a fellow by the name of Dan Agnew. Together, we developed a simple special-effects technique known to some at the time as the "slit-scan" method, originally devised by Douglas Trumpbull for the closing "stargate" sequence in Stanley Kubrick's *2001: A Space Odyssey*. It involved taking moving light sources and filming them with time-lapse methods, the end result being a fascinating play of color and form not readily obtainable back in those pre-computer days. What we did with this technology was a variation on what Trumpbull had come up with but taken in a slightly different direction.

Right after the first *Star Wars* film came out in 1977, I wrote to director George Lucas, telling him about our work and asking if we could have an audience with him to present it to him. Ideally, we were hoping to find employment on the projected sequel to *Star Wars* that was being talked about at the time (and which later turned into *The Empire Strikes Back*). We assumed he was busy and heavily in demand, and expected that if he responded at all, it might be quite a while.

So, What Am I Doing Here, Anyway?

December 15, 1977

Mr. Ray Grasse
Belleforte
Oak Park, Illinois 60302

Dear Mr. Grasse:

Thank you for your letter regarding the special developments that you've been working on with the Slit-Scan device.

At the moment, it's not something that I can use, however, I will keep your letter in the event that I might want to use it in the future.

I appreciate your bringing this to my attention.

Sincerely,

George Lucas

GL/jb

The Star Wars Corporation, P.O. Box 186, San Anselmo, California 94960, Telephone 415—457-5282

The Star Wars Man

To our surprise, I got a reply from him just seven days later. He declined our offer, but was gracious in doing so. While it was a thrill having heard from him personally, both Dan and I were terribly disappointed. We had naively set our expectations too high.

Yet looking back with the benefit of 20/20 hindsight all these years later, I see things very differently. That's because I now realize if those situations with the film industry had worked out as I originally hoped, my life would have likely gone in a very different direction than it did. As a result of those and other disappointments, I repeatedly found myself drawn back to the Midwest, flailing for direction and unsure of where to go next.

It was essentially out of desperation that I finally decided to look for work at the Theosophical Society outside of Chicago. I'd attended lectures and workshops there years earlier, but because the organization was so low-paying I didn't seriously consider working for them. It was only after my graveyard shift at UPS in a nearby suburb became so intolerable that I decided to take the plunge in 1989 and apply for a job, starting work for just five dollars an hour. I certainly didn't get rich there monetarily, but during those subsequent ten years I acquired a fortune in writing, editing, and publishing experience that eventually proved invaluable in my writing pursuits.

The upshot is, I've come to believe there was a certain element of destiny in the way my life unfolded—including all those early disappointments and setbacks. Looking back, I now believe that writing is much closer to my own "life-plan" than working in the film or entertainment industry would have been—however fun, glamorous, and creatively interesting that might well have become.

Someone once asked me: do I really believe in destiny? Well, yes, but maybe not in the way some others think about it. I don't subscribe to the notion of destiny in the sense that the universe or "God" has appointed me to do this or that in my life, for the good of humanity and all that; that smacks a bit too much of grandiosity and self-importance for my taste. However, I do believe in "destiny" in the sense that *you yourself* have chosen to come into this world to achieve certain things or live out certain experiences—that makes much more sense to me. If in turn that life-plan of yours happens to align with the life-plans of thousands or even millions of others, well, so be it. But it's not because you've been picked out by the Divine because you're somehow more special or important than others. It's simply because of some personal karmic pattern you're wanting—or needing—to fulfill that involves others. That's my take on it.

In the next chapter, I'll share some thoughts as to why I may have been drawn back to this part of the U.S. so many times, while also touching briefly on an intriguing aspect of George Lucas's own horoscope.

CHAPTER 17

"So, What Am I Doing Here, Anyway?" Exploring the Synastry of Self and City

For a long time now, I've found it somewhat perplexing that I've spent so much of my life in the American Midwest, particularly the sleepy little town of Wheaton, Illinois. Had things worked out as I originally hoped, I would have settled in an area like Santa Fe, Boulder, or San Francisco, and on several occasions I've spent considerable time in those areas.

Yet to paraphrase Al Pacino in one of those big *Godfather* films, circumstances just kept *pulling me back in*. Sometimes that was out of necessity, sometimes it was due to family responsibilities or relationship matters. Either way, the result is that I've either lived or worked in the town of Wheaton since late 1989.

Don't get me wrong. This is a perfectly nice little town in some ways, with beautiful natural areas scattered throughout its boundaries, all of which I've explored thoroughly on the nearby bike paths.

But it's also a very conservative and religious town, with lots of churches and right-wing voters. Aside from the Theosophical Society— a decidedly paradoxical presence here, rest assured—it's not somewhere I would have expected to wind up. I simply feel more myself around mountains, deserts, or the oceans, none of which are here.

So, I naturally turned to astrology to try and help me make some sense of all this.

So, What Am I Doing Here, Anyway?

I first looked to techniques such as Astro*Carto*Graphy, devised by Jim Lewis, as well as the locality-based astrology practiced by Stephen Arroyo and my late friend Steve Cozzi. But nothing really seemed to click for me as far as explaining that connection to this particular region of the Midwest.

Then I came across something that seemed to hold a key to this mystery. An old friend from my college days, Victoria Martin, sent me a copy of the horoscope drawn up for the city of Wheaton, with a "birthday" of February 24, 1859 (calculated for when for it was likely incorporated as a village, using noon as a probable time). What immediately jumped out at me was the fact that it showed Jupiter at 12° Gemini — *one degree away from my 9th house Sun at 13° Gemini.*

That suddenly made a great deal of sense to me. Consider the fact I owe the lion's share of my writing and publishing career to Wheaton, due not only to my work on the editorial staffs of the Theosophical Society throughout the 1990s but the fact that all my subsequent books and articles were either written here or submitted to publishers from here. It hardly seems accidental that I'd find myself drawn to an area that amplifies my Geminian publishing energies as powerfully as this.

I look at this in a similar way to how I'd study any synastry reading between two people. As in any relationship, how one's own chart meshes with that of the city one lives in makes a considerable difference in how one's energies are either enhanced or diminished. It's hardly an accident that so much of my writing and publishing has happened for me while living under the umbrella of Wheaton's Jupiter in Gemini.

In many cases, of course, there can be more than one horoscope involved for a given locale. The horoscope I constructed for Wheaton was the date of its incorporation as a *village*, but it was later incorporated as a *city* on April 24, 1890. As it turns out, though, the planets on that date *also* exert a profound impact on my own horoscope, especially in terms of publishing. Not only does the epic Neptune–Pluto conjunction in Gemini back then conjoin my Mercury and Venus in the 9th house (which aren't all that far from my Sun), but Jupiter at 10° Aquarius in that later horoscope forms a grand trine to my Gemini and Libra planets. So, which horoscope takes precedence when more than one is involved? Both do, but I personally chose to give a bit more priority to the earlier one, simply because of chronology.

So, what's my takeaway for readers here?

For one, simply consider the horoscope of the city or town in which you live, and compare it to your own. Even if you don't know the exact time of its incorporation or founding, just looking to the general positions of the planets alone can tell you a great deal. Is your city's Jupiter on your Sun? Or is Saturn on your Ascendant? Is Mars squaring your Venus? Or Uranus on your Mercury? There can be dramatic differences.

So, What Am I Doing Here, Anyway?

Likewise, when making a decision about any city you're thinking of moving to, take a moment to consider what your priorities are. If your chief desire is to get married, you might look to see how that city's horoscope affects your Venus, your 7th house, or your Moon. If your priority is more professional in nature, look to see how that city's chart complements your Sun, your 10th house, or your 6th house—and on it goes.

Taking this one step further, you might even consider the horoscope of the *nation* you're living in, or one that you're thinking of moving to or traveling through. I had a client in France who decided to move to the United States but encountered innumerable problems once she settled here, especially with her marriage. As it turned out, the United States' Saturn in Libra was precisely on her Venus!

A somewhat different example is that of filmmaker George Lucas, born on May 14, 1944. His Uranus sits at 8° Gemini—precisely on the Uranus of the U.S. (cast for the July 4, 1776 birth date, whichever time of day you use). As I mentioned in my book *Signs of the Times*, it's interesting how tuned-in to the technological side of the American psyche Lucas has been, not only in terms of filmmaking, special effects, and media, but also in the actual subject matter of his movies. His early film *American Graffiti* paid homage to American media and technology—cars, radio, TV, films, etc.—while the first *Star Wars* film from 1977 essentially replicates the symbolism of the original Revolutionary War, interestingly, featuring a group of rebels going up against an oppressive empire. I think it's safe to say that Lucas incarnated into just the right country to actualize the potentials of his horoscope. (Incidentally, Lucas's Uranus at 8 degrees of Gemini is closely conjunct my Venus and Mercury in Gemini, at 7 and 6 degrees, respectively. It's little wonder I felt so drawn to connect with him in such a technological way, as I described in the previous chapter.)

So, without discarding the value of other locality-based astrological methods, it's worth experimenting with the birth charts of your city, state, or nation to see what they tell you about your own compatibility with your area. Likewise, if you happen to be considering a move or a trip to a different area, take some time to look at the horoscopes associated with that area; it could possibly make a difference in how your fortunes do—or don't— unfold there.

This essay first appeared in The Mountain Astrologer, 2023 Yearbook.

CHAPTER 18

Are We "Pattern-Seeking" Creatures? (Yes—And It's A Good Thing, Too)

Every now and then I come across an article which dismisses those of a more symbolic or "synchronistic" mindset—i.e., individuals who seek to find hidden meanings in the events around them—with the critique that humans are simply "pattern-seeking" creatures.

"It's a way of finding comfort in an otherwise chaotic world," one scientist said. That's the real reason people find solace in such things as astrology, synchronicity, omens, and other such imaginary things. Or so we are told.

What critiques like this invariably fail to mention is that, while much nonsense has indeed resulted from this sort of pattern-seeking function, it's also what drove figures like Isaac Newton, Albert Einstein, Tycho Brahe, Galileo, and Johannes Kepler. These, and many other world-class geniuses, were also compelled by that urge to uncover the patterns which underlie our existence.

In other words, the fact that we "seek out patterns" does not in itself mean there are no patterns to be found! It's really just a matter of ferreting out which of those that are "real" versus those which are pure illusion or fantastical, such as the child who swears they see a unicorn in the shapes of clouds.

So how are we to ferret out the "real" patterns?

Are We "Pattern-Seeking" Creatures?

According to science, one of the key ways for judging this is the element of *predictability*. Can a particular pattern be replicated or foreseen in advance? That is, *can it be tested*?

Consider the origins of astronomy and the efforts by civilization's early sky-watchers. These ancient observers carefully looked for recurring patterns in the stars and planets, and the cyclical patterns of days, months, and years. For example, it eventually became clear that the Sun and Moon came together in certain 19-year cycles that led to eclipses, which could then be reliably predicted in advance. The eclipse model was thus more than just fantasy, it was real and predictable.

Astrology is based on this close observation of cycles as well, but it added another layer of significance—and difficulty—to those patterns. How? By adding the dimension of *meaning*.

By analogy, it's one thing to speak about a copy of Melville's *Moby Dick* as being nothing more than a collection of ink molecules inscribed on paper. But it's quite another to say those ink patterns contain a *story*, and that those markings harbor complex *meanings* above and beyond those chemical marks.

Likewise, it's one thing to say that the patterns of the stars and planets over time are simply material realities that operate in mechanical ways and can be carefully analyzed and predicted in visible ways. But it's another thing to say those patterns contain *symbolic importance* above and beyond those physical properties, and are entwined with a complex network of symbolic correspondences that extend beyond the purely obvious range of connections recognized by science. This is a considerably more complex matter!

Yet those layers of symbolic importance *can* be tested and predicted, though not in the normal way a strict materialist might think about it. That's because it requires, as we touched on earlier, a "hermeneutic" or symbolic mindset with an eye for analogies, correspondences, and symbols.

For instance, one might study the cycles of Jupiter in a person's horoscope over decades of time and find that each time it crosses over someone's Midheaven that person experiences a boost to their reputation or career; or every time an eclipse lands in their 6th house they experience a major shift in their health; or every time Saturn squares their Sun they experience some sort of career setback or a frustration involving an authority figure or goal. To someone with an eye for analogies, these would be readily noticeable, yet they're not easily quantified or measured strictly using the tools of science. Not impossible, mind you, just difficult. It's a metaphoric sort of thing.

My point is simply this: astrology evolved from much the same pattern-seeking function that drove many of the great geniuses of science and astronomy—and in the case of figures like Kepler, it evolved *side-by-side* with that eye for symbolic meanings and associations. After all, Kepler was also an astrologer who didn't just erect horoscopes for money, as some critics have claimed; he erected horoscopes for family members, who certainly didn't pay him for his services! If science is to ever recognize the worth of astrology, it will need to do what Kepler and others like him did, which is to open their minds to the possibility of a world filled with meaning and symbolism, rather than a cosmos entirely bereft of it.

CHAPTER 19

Whatever Saturn Touches....

As anyone familiar with my earlier books and articles knows, I've long had a particular fascination with the ringed planet Saturn. For various reasons I feel there are nuances to its impact and meaning in horoscopes that are often overlooked and which can provide an especially critical key toward understanding not just an individual's personality but the unfoldment (and pace) of their destiny over time.

In this chapter I'd like to offer a few more ways of approaching those nuances, by means of some very simple phrases that can serve as jumping-off points for broader reflections. Simple guidelines like this can sometimes provide an especially effective way of acquiring quick insights into planetary or zodiacal influences—that strikes me as especially true in the case of the ringed planet. With that said, here is a brief list of some Saturnian influences to hold in mind.

1. *Whatever Saturn touches in your chart can show what you have to work especially hard for.* By contrast, Jupiter aspects in the horoscope—especially trines, conjunctions, and sextiles—show where things tend to come relatively easy for you, where doors are opened up with much less effort. On the other hand, Saturn makes you work hard for whatever you get, to where it almost feels like having to use a crowbar to pry open those same doors Jupiter flung wide open.

In close aspect to Venus, for instance, one may feel one has to work hard for satisfaction in love, social relationships, or possibly even money. In connection with Mars, Saturn may make you feel you have to work hard to develop courage, assertiveness, physical strength, or sometimes sexuality. Individuals with strong Saturn/Mercury contacts can be quite profound and brilliant, intellectually (Einstein had the conjunction, Isaac Newton had the square), but realizing that potential can feel like a long, hard journey, involving a great deal of thought or research over time.

2. Whatever Saturn touches in your chart tends to have a "late bloomer" quality about it. I touched on this briefly in an earlier chapter, as well as previous books, but it's worth saying a bit more. Simply put, one of the silver linings to Saturn aspects is that whatever areas they touch tend to unfold their fuller potentials either later in life or after considerable struggle and hard work. Precisely because of that element of struggle, however, those areas can sometimes become areas of personal mastery, where you reap the rewards of that hard work.

An example of this was my client who was born with Saturn closely conjunct her MC. Throughout her 20s, 30s and early 40s she struggled to get several businesses off the ground. But all of them ended in disappointment. She kept at it, though, and finally achieved great success in her 50s! A far more negative example of the late-bloomer dynamic was Adolf Hitler, who was born with Saturn in the 10th house squaring his Mars and Venus in the 7th, and went from being a failed artist and jailed dissident to a powerful military leader—and a psychopathic one at that. Clearly, the fact that one's horoscope reveals late-bloomer potentials doesn't in itself guarantee how well one is going to express those energies!

Saturn/Moon contacts can indicate emotional blockages or frustrations early in life, especially in the ability to give or receive nurturing, but at its best this can over time transform into a far healthier sense of emotional openness. Consider my client born with a tight Saturn/Moon conjunction who went from feeling emotionally starved in childhood to working hard to become a model parent in adulthood. It was a factor of "compensation"; she consciously chose to turn things around and not to see her own child subjected to the same privations she experienced. We'll be returning to this "late bloomer" dynamic yet again in our next chapter.

3. *Whatever Saturn touches in your chart shows where you can have a capacity for discipline and tenacity.* Along similar lines, Saturn aspects often give a considerable "work ethic" in whatever areas it targets, where one generally exhibits greater tenacity and endurance than in other areas. Fred Astaire had Saturn/Neptune opposition and worked countless long hours to master the art of dancing (Neptune ruling both the feet and dancing). A friend of mine with an exact Saturn/Mars trine has long displayed a degree of physical endurance when it comes to exercise and yoga that practically leaves me speechless. Similarly, I've seen individuals with Saturn/Sun aspects who display an enormous capacity for discipline and work when it comes to professional ambition and leadership, like famed football quarterback Tom Brady, born with the conjunction. Individuals born with Saturn/Mercury aspects (like myself) tend to have greater persistence and focus when it comes to activities like writing, research, and deep thought.

4. *Whatever Saturn touches in the chart shows what you are driven to crystallize.* As the symbol of physicality *par excellence*, close aspects Saturn can reveal where you're compelled to *bring something into tangible reality*. I've come across many sculptors and architects born with prominent Saturn/Venus aspects who had a talent for materializing subtle ideas into tangible form. As mentioned previously, architect Frank Lloyd Wright had the opposition, while sculptor, architect and artist Michelangelo had the square. Normally, Neptune governs subtle or even ethereal impulses and feelings, so when touched by Saturn there can be an ability for bringing these into physical manifestation. Mozart was born with Saturn opposite Neptune and had a nearly supernatural talent for "drawing down" angelic musical creations into our world. In a very different vein, Thomas Edison was born with the conjunction between these planets and crystallized dreams of a more technological sort. Writers with strong Saturn/Mercury aspects can be driven to crystallize ideas, such as J.R.R. Tolkien or Isaac Newton.

Along related lines, I'm fascinated by how many leading figures in the arts had Saturn/Moon conjunctions: Miles Davis, David Bowie, Bob Dylan, Elvis Presley, and William Burroughs, as some examples. Why would that be? Here as well, a possible explanation is that the Moon—not unlike Neptune—symbolizes relatively non-tangible phenomena like emotions, so what better tool for an artistic figure to help bring those into form than a Saturn/Moon alignment?

This principle may also help explain why so many ultra-rich figures have been born with strong *Saturn/Venus* contacts. For example, Jeff Bezos and Bill Gates have the conjunction, Mark Zuckerberg has the opposition, while Oprah Winfrey was born with the square. It makes perfect sense, really, when you consider that Saturn not only confers great tenacity and discipline in areas of moneymaking but a strong impulse to crystallize wealth (along with the pleasures it brings). Which brings me to our next point…

5. *Whatever Saturn touches in your chart may be where you attain—or even seek—a degree of authority or status in the world.* I remember a conversation with one of the first astrologers I consulted in my youth, when I asked where he thought I could be most successful in life. To my great surprise, he immediately checked to see what my closest Saturn aspects were. It's not hard to unpack the reasoning there, actually. Precisely because it *is* the planet of materiality, whatever Saturn touches can indicate where you may be most driven to achieve worldly recognition or status. Is it Neptune? Then maybe the arts, imagination, or spirituality. Or is it Jupiter? Then perhaps religion, spirituality, politics, travel. Mercury? Intellectual work, teaching, writing, even business. Pluto? Psychology, the occult, power dynamics. Mars? Courage, athletics, the military, sometime even sexuality.

Perhaps that latter one may help shed light on why so many icons of beauty or sexuality in our culture were born with strong Saturn-Mars contacts. Consider this list: Marilyn Monroe, Claudia Schiffer, Nicki Minaj, Julia Roberts, Margot Robbie, Ariana Grande, Brooke Shields, Penelope Cruz, Jessica Biel, Khloe Kardashian, Zoe Kravitz, Rihanna, and Emily Ratajkowski, among others.

Whereas Venus tends to be more concerned with pure beauty or ordinary allurement, Mars tends to be about intense animal attraction or overt sexuality. As a result, Saturn in contact with Mars could indicate a potential for being a role model or "authority" in areas of sexual areas, or even tantra.

On the other hand, a more prosaic (and unsettling) explanation for this astro-signature could be the fact that many attractive women experience great difficulties or frustrations confronting male aggression *in response* to their attractiveness, which compels them to develop aggression or even anger as a result. In a case of Marilyn Monroe, her Saturn-Mars square likely helped explain her early instances of sexual exploitation and abuse (no doubt amplified by her Scorpio Saturn at the focal point of a t-square in her 4th house).

6. *Whatever Saturn touches—especially by hard aspect—indicates where you may experience loss or even rejection.* Where is Saturn in your chart, by aspect, sign, or house? This can be where you have to deal with a dramatic amount of loss. In the case of Saturn-Venus, this may involve romance, social acceptance, or money. In the case of the Moon, that may involve women, the mother, or the home and family. With the Sun, it may involve your reputation and public personae, or even the early loss of a parent; with Mercury, it can involve criticism or setbacks over one's intelligence or academic efforts.

However, due to the "later bloomer" effect mentioned earlier, this can sometimes boomerang in surprising ways. After all, Saturn may indeed taketh but it can turn around and giveth quite generously as well, with previous losses setting the stage for later advancements, a "build back better" sort of dynamic. In the case of someone with Saturn in the 2nd house, for instance, that could manifest as losing a fortune but winding up coming back and making an even greater fortune later. In the case of a Saturn-Venus person, they may feel wounded in love early on but wind up finding a deeper, more durable love later in life. (Our earlier example of Tina Turner exemplifies that.)

7. *Whatever Saturn touches in your chart shows where your key karmic challenge in life is.* The whole chart is likely "karmic," in a sense, but Saturn seems to indicate a *particularly concentrated symbol* of karmic lessons in this lifetime. For instance, someone with Saturn-square-Mars is certainly forced to learn important lessons about the proper measure of anger, assertiveness or sexuality in this lifetime, whereas someone born with a prominent Saturn-Venus connection is learning lessons about love and the proper balance between selfishness and unselfishness. Saturn-Mercury invariably has to do with the lessons about right thought, communication skills, and choosing words carefully, whereas someone with a strong Saturn-Moon conjunction may be dealing with issues and nurturing—though that may also involve a key area for potential for grounding and emotional growth. After all, "karmic" doesn't necessarily mean bad! It may simply show where a soul has set up challenges in connection with longer-range goals one has set for oneself in this life.

8. *Whatever Saturn touches in your chart may indicate where you lack confidence—at least initially.* Whereas Jupiter aspects tend to instill a degree of confidence in whatever areas it touches—sometimes to the point of hubris—areas closely affected by Saturn tend to have an element of insecurity about them, even to the point of fearing failure.

Yet it's for that very reason that the native will often compensate by trying even harder to succeed in those areas. Consider my client with an almost exact Saturn-square-Mercury who claimed to feel "stupid" early in life then wound up obtaining eight different college degrees! Similarly, someone with Saturn in Capricorn may well struggle with concerns over their reputation and status early in life, then wind up working their way up through the ranks into positions of respectability or leadership.

9. *Whatever Saturn touches in your chart can become an area of obsessive concern for you.* Normally, Pluto is the planet associated by astrologers with "obsession," but Saturn confers its own form of obsessiveness—with a subtle difference. Precisely because it does set up major challenges or problems in life, whatever it touches can show where you're *forced* to focus your attention that much more intensely. Were you born with Saturn closely aspecting your Sun? Then you may well be extremely focused on obtaining respect or worldly recognition and respect. Does Saturn closely aspect your Mercury? You may find yourself obsessed with acquiring knowledge or recognition for your intellect. Do you have a close Saturn-Uranus aspect? Then you may well be deeply concerned with finding freedom during your life, as was the case for Bob Dylan, born with a close Saturn-Moon-Uranus conjunction.

10. *Whatever Saturn touches in your chart says much about your connection to older people.* Finally, what sort of relationships do you enjoy with individuals older than yourself? The quality of your Saturn can provide important clues to that. Saturn-Sun tells you a great deal about your relation with authority figures or parents, with the quality of that connection being shown by the specific aspect. A close square between Saturn and the Sun will lead to quite a different experience than a trine or a sextile! (Curiously enough, conjunctions in such cases can go either way, positively or negatively, depending on supporting aspects from the rest of the chart, or the maturity of the native.) Saturn-Neptune or Saturn/Venus aspects can point to the quality of your connections to those in the film, music, or fashion industries, among others. Ernest Hemingway had a Saturn-Mercury trine, and throughout his life enjoyed an exceptional relationship with older writers and editors like James Joyce and Ezra Pound.

CHAPTER 20

My Astrological Guessing Game and the "Late Bloomer" Dynamic

Occasionally, I like to play a guessing game with myself where I'll see a story in the media about a certain celebrity, artist, or politician, and try to guess what might explain their experiences or personality from their horoscope. Sometimes I get it wrong, but more often than not I get it right. Mind you, I only attempt this when I'm fairly positive of what I'm picking up. It's usually those times when I'm on the fence about things that my predictions turn out to be wrong.

Does an exercise like this by itself "prove" the validity of astrology? Of course not, but that isn't the point. Aside from being an interesting learning experience (and I should add I've learned almost as much from my misfires and wrong guesses as from my successes!), the examples I've chosen to use here help illustrate something I've mentioned in earlier chapters—namely, the "late bloomer" dynamic. It's a particularly important feature of some horoscopes, as I hope these examples make very clear.

The Author

Consider the case of writer Maya Angelou, noted author of *I Know Why the Caged Bird Sings* and 30 other books. While watching an interview with her on TV one day, I learned that following a traumatic event in her childhood, she essentially became mute for six years. Her mother would put her arm around her and say, "I know you're not stupid or a moron like all the kids say you are, I

My Astrological Guessing Game and the "Late Bloomer" Dynamic

know that one day you'll be a great teacher and you'll travel the world imparting wisdom."

That immediately struck a chord with me, because it resonated closely with the "late bloomer" quality of Saturn I've seen when it comes into contact with Mercury (the planet most associated with communication, thinking, and writing). Here is what I wrote about that combo in my essay "Saturn, the Late Bloomer" in *Under a Sacred Sky*:

"This one might be called the *struggle to communicate.* I know of no better story to illustrate this combination than the life of legendary Greek orator Demosthenes. According to Plutarch, Demosthenes experienced great difficulty speaking publicly while young, because of both a speech impediment and breathing difficulties, which caused him to talk in staggered, clipped sentences. But in classic late-bloomer style, he tackled this problem by working on his diction and projection, using such unorthodox means as speaking with stones in his mouth and shouting into the surf. The end result was that he became what some regarded as history's greatest orator."

I've often found this planetary combination in charts of people who were considered stupid or slow early in life, or who have may even felt that way about themselves early on. That's especially true in cases where this planetary combo involves the conjunction, square, or opposition. These individuals struggle hard to communicate their thoughts while growing up, but can eventually blossom and become quite brilliant at times. Isaac Newton had the square between Saturn and Mercury, and Einstein had the conjunction, to cite two famed examples. Maya Angelou's case seemed like a likely instance, too, I thought, considering the way she eventually broke out of her shell to write scores of books and become a sought-after speaker.

Her chart? Unsurprisingly, she was born with a very tight square between Mercury and Saturn. (Her birthday: April 4, 1928, 2:10

So, What Am I Doing Here, Anyway?

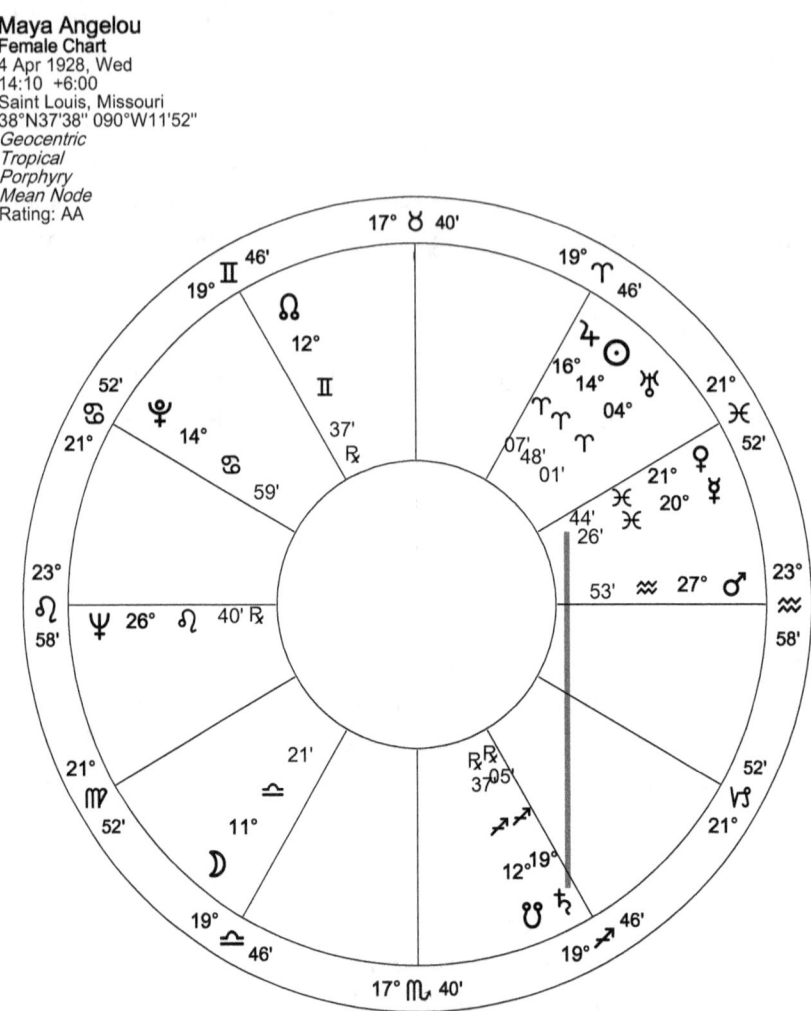

PM, St. Louis, Missouri.) As difficult a pattern as this can be, it often indicates a deep thinker—and in exceptional cases, a great writer or orator.

The Actor

Or consider the example of celebrated actor, Marlon Brando. Early in his career, especially in films like *On the Waterfront* and *The Wild One*, Brando was frequently criticized for a perceived tendency to mumble. The sense I also gathered from his body language during interviews was almost that of an inferiority complex. He certainly didn't have an academic background, yet he turned out to be an impressive thinker, and was impressively multilingual (he taught himself five languages—English, Japanese, French, Spanish, and Italian). Along with several other factors, this also strongly suggested an intellectual "late bloomer" dynamic, most likely involving either a square or opposition between Saturn and Mercury. Looking up his chart (April 3, 1924, 11 PM, Omaha, Nebraska), I saw he indeed had the opposition.

Actor #2

I found a similar dynamic in the life of actor Matthew McConaughey, known for films like *Contact, Dazed and Confused,* and *Interstellar,* among others. I turned on the TV one morning to hear him promoting a new book he'd just written, a memoir titled *Greenlights*. During that interview, he addressed the great difficulties he experienced when younger with reading comprehension. He mentioned how it took him many months just to get through a fairly short book of essays by Ralph Waldo Emerson.

Despite those struggles—or perhaps specifically as a result of them?—he eventually developed his communication skills to the point where he not only became an effective public speaker but wrote that very well-received (and best-selling) memoir relatively late in life.

Here as well, it sounded for all the world like a classic Saturn-Mercury dynamic, especially due to the slow-developing process he described. As a result, I looked up his horoscope to see if he had a square, opposition or conjunction to Mercury. Lo and behold, he had a tight opposition between Saturn and Mercury. (November 4, 1969, 7:34 PM, Uvalde, Texas.)

So, What Am I Doing Here, Anyway?

The Architect

Frank Lloyd Wright is celebrated now for his genius at architecture, but his road to fame and fortune was a decidedly staggered one. Besides going through difficult times in his professional career, his personal life was marked by scandals and sometimes even tragedies.

Probably the most fascinating aspect of his life, from a "late bloomer" perspective, is the fact that he peaked so late in life. His most productive and successful years were between the ages of 69 and 90! Unlike Angelou, Brando and McConaughey, this wasn't so much an intellectual late blooming as an artistic one, so I wondered if he had a prominent Saturn-Venus aspect in his chart, since Venus has more to do with the arts. It turned out he not only had an opposition between those two bodies, but that opposition was aligned with one of his chart's major angles—the Ascendant/Descendant axis. Few lives exemplify the "late bloomer" dynamic in creative ways more than Wright's. (June 8, 1857, 5 PM, Richland Center, WI.)

The Martial Artist and Podcaster

Perhaps my favorite example of my "guessing game" involved watching a video clip of podcaster and martial artist Joe Rogan talking about how he originally got into martial arts while still in his teens.

He was 14 when he found himself on a school bus getting beaten up by a girl, no less, followed minutes later by yet another pummeling from a classmate who saw a wonderful window of opportunity to join in on the fun. The double beat-down was so humiliating than he decided from that point on to learn self-defense, in the process becoming a well-known practitioner and proponent of the martial arts.

My Astrological Guessing Game and the "Late Bloomer" Dynamic

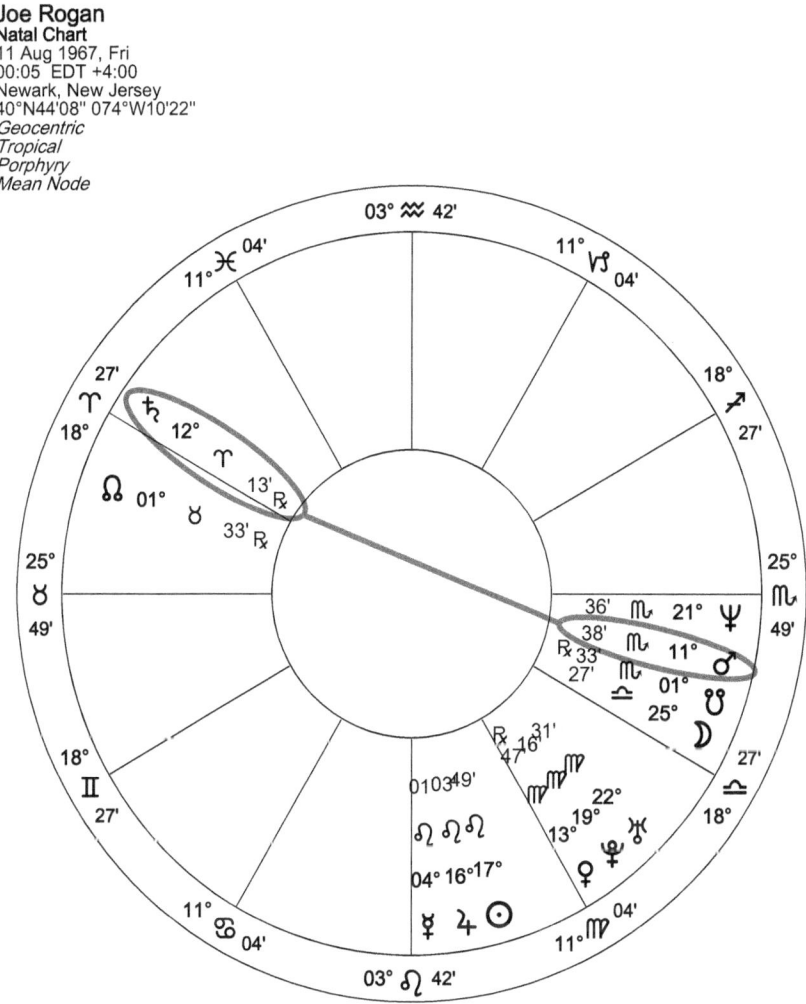

On hearing that story, it immediately reminded me of a particular "late bloomer" dynamic I'd written about involving two different yet extremely similar astrological signatures: 1) close aspects between Saturn and Mars, and 2) Saturn in Aries. As I've been saying, whatever Saturn touches usually assumes a "late bloomer" dynamic, and in *Under a Sacred Sky*, I had this to say about that first combination:

So, What Am I Doing Here, Anyway?

"(I describe the Mars-Saturn dynamic as) *the struggle for courage.* Some of us remember ads from our childhood comic books about the 97-pound weakling who gets sand kicked in his face by the bully at the beach, then goes on to become a body-building marvel who can stand up to anybody. That's a pretty good depiction of the Saturn–Mars dynamic. As a result of feeling insecure about their assertiveness or physical strength, these individuals often wind up working that much harder to develop their muscles, figuratively or literally, and can become surprisingly powerful in the process.... Bruce Lee, who was born with an opposition between Mars and Saturn, worked his way back from a crippling injury to become arguably the most famous martial artist of the 20th century."

In my book *StarGates* I wrote about the horoscopic dynamic that's extremely similar to the Saturn-Mars one, and that's when Saturn is positioned in Aries. About that placement I wrote:

"In its more evolved form, Saturn in Aries can bring a serious degree of mastery when it comes to expressing qualities of courage and accessing one's 'inner warrior.' Those early struggles with fear or confidence can eventually transform into a capacity for leadership and considerable fearlessness when venturing onto life's battlefields....The discipline that Saturn potentially brings to one's 'warrior' nature is especially obvious in the case of martial artists like Chuck Norris and Jason Stratham, as well as actress Lucy Lawless, who played the fictional warrior princess, Xena, on TV."

As a result, when I heard Joe Rogan describe his own involvement with martial arts, I immediately thought back to those two patterns I'd written about, and naturally wondered if he might have either one in his birth chart.

As it turned out, Rogan had *both*—and prominently so. Saturn was not only in Aries when he was born, but it was also forming an extremely tight aspect to Mars, a less-than-one-degree inconjunct. (I pay great attention to inconjuncts, or 150-degree aspects, when

My Astrological Guessing Game and the "Late Bloomer" Dynamic

they involve tight orbs like this.) In addition, Saturn is also the highest planet in his chart, bringing that Saturn/Aries energy even more prominently out before the public, while making it a factor of aspiration for him through his life. Significant, too, is the fact he had that life-changing humiliation at age 14—which was his first Saturn half-return, and thus a major activation of that natal dynamic.

These, then, are a few examples of my "game." If you haven't ever tried this yourself, I'd suggest giving it a shot sometime. Besides being a good way to put your own astrological knowledge to the test, it's potentially a way of gathering some new astro-insights in the process.

CHAPTER 21

What is "Mother"?

During the short time I spent at Zen Mountain Monastery in upstate New York, five months in all, the head teacher in residence was an imposing American by the name of John Loori, though most students knew him by his Buddhist name, "Daido." Of all the stories and teachings he shared with us throughout that time, one that stands out vividly in my memory centers around an incident involving his own teacher, Maezumi Roshi (1931-1995).

Maezumi was holding forth one evening to his students, Daido explained, and engaged in a teaching practice known in Buddhist circles as *dharma combat*. This is where a teacher poses a comment or question to the sangha (spiritual community), ostensibly meant to both challenge the students and test their grasp of deeper Buddhist principles, while allowing those students to in turn challenge and test their teacher. Each student taking part comes up and sits in front of the teacher to offer their own take on the question or comment at hand, with the teacher then responding to what the student said.

To anyone new to such interactions, these exchanges can seem cryptic to the point of being impenetrable, even nonsensical. I should know; they often did to me.

On this particular occasion, Maezumi posed the question, *"What is mother?"* to the group.

A number of students came up to offer their own responses, until Daido's fellow student and dharma brother, Bernie "Tetsugen"

Glassman, finally had his turn to parry with the teacher. Bernie proceeded to deliver a characteristically abstract, Zen-like answer to his teacher's query about the nature of "mother," one that probably only fellow practitioners would understand.

Upon hearing that, Maezumi firmly said, "No—*THIS* is mother!"—while pointing to a tear running down his cheek.

It was then that Bernie realized what Maezumi was getting at with his opening query. Bernie then began to tear up himself, with both of them now crying—as the rest of the students watching this exchange began tearing up as well.

So what does all this mean? In case the significance isn't readily apparent to those reading this, I'll offer a few words of explanation.

An integral aspect of Zen teaching emphasizes the need to balance the "Absolute and the Relative" in one's life and practice. What is the "Absolute"? Simply put, this refers to the highest, most sublimely spiritual perspective on life, as realized in the subtlest and most awakened meditative states. Seen from this perspective, one recognizes that all phenomena are "empty," surface appearances are fundamentally relative and transitory, to a certain extent even illusory.

On the other hand, the "Relative" refers to the ordinary experience of reality most of us perceive on a regular day-to-day basis. This is the world of conventional emotions and thoughts, with all the highs and lows of daily relationships, responsibilities, and concerns. It's called the "Relative" because it hinges on one's very personal and very subjective experience of life.

As I said, Zen stresses the need to *balance* one's sense of the Absolute and the Relative, since either extreme can lead to problems. For instance, one can become *so* spiritual—that is, so anchored in the Absolute by seeing everything in those highly rarefied terms—that one loses touch with the everyday world, like the obsessive meditator who forgets to pay his bills or tend to his loved ones. Conversely, one can become so engrossed in the Relative that one loses all sense of higher perspective, where life simply becomes a robotic pursuit of money, sex, and status, solely perceiving the world in terms of conventional values and emotions.

Neither of these viewpoints is complete in itself and needs to be balanced with the other, Buddhism suggests. Maezumi's gesture of acknowledging that tear flowing down his cheek demonstrated the need to value ordinary human emotions and experiences *on their own terms*—including the love felt for mother, and the grief felt upon her absence. Sure, one could put on one's "Zen glasses" and see mother in purely Absolute terms—as an embodiment of a deeply mystical or cosmic principle, say—but that would not be true to the full reality of who she was, or of one's deep emotional bond with her.

Here's another example to help drive the point home a bit further. Imagine you discover that a close friend has just endured the death of their child, who perished in a horrific accident. You attend the wake and see your friend standing there, clearly grief-stricken and barely able to talk. Now, do you walk up to them and say, "I'm deeply sorry for your loss"?—or do you instead say, "This sense of loss you're feeling is really an illusion, since all things are impermanent and insubstantial, so your grief itself is nothing to become engrossed in"?

It should be obvious which approach is the more appropriate one—presuming you're a normal, compassionate human being, that is. Yes, the latter response about impermanence and illusion may well be more accurate or "true" from an ultimate mystical perspective, but that is actually the false one, spiritually, since it doesn't recognize the truth of the moment—a truth that involves balancing the Absolute and the Relative, the mystical and the ordinary, the ultimate and the everyday.

What is "Mother"?

Nor is this simply a Zen Buddhist teaching, as one finds much the same idea in other spiritual traditions. For instance, I feel it's the esoteric meaning of Jesus telling his disciples to "render unto Caesar that which is Caesar's, and unto God that which is God's." Said a little differently, it's important to deal with the earth plane on its own terms, and the spiritual level on *its* own terms—and knowing how to keep those two in balance.

It's also what I believe Goswami Kriyananda was getting at in his comment I cited in an earlier chapter, when he said, "Everyone is trying to find God when they haven't even found their humanness yet." As important as mystical ideals and aspirations are, spirituality is not simply a denial of the everyday or of ordinary human emotions and perspectives.

Rather, at its most integral, the spiritual path is about learning to walk that delicate tightrope between the two, and reconciling each of those respective truths into a broader, more all-encompassing Truth.

That is "mother."

Postscript: Shortly before publication I shared this chapter with my old friend Ray Bonini, who was a young man (19) when I first met him at the monastery during my time there. He also was present when Daido related this story, and like me, had been deeply impacted by it. Though he liked what I wrote about it above, he suggested another layer of meaning to be considered, and shared what I thought were some extremely insightful comments about it. Rather than try to paraphrase what he said, I thought I'd simply include what he wrote, leaving his comments largely as he intended (edited slightly for clarity). Here they are:

"Daido's story is a really good example not just of balancing the Absolute and the Relative, or of respecting the truth of each one on its own terms, so to speak, but also as a demonstration of how the Absolute IS the Relative. The tears running down his face, or saying 'I'm sorry for your loss,' is itself the coming together of Absolute and Relative. Each is a complete

So, What Am I Doing Here, Anyway?

presentation of the whole, as Mumon says in his comments on the Koan 'Mu' in the **Mumonkan.** *It shows how ordinary emotions that* **seem** *to be the opposite of the Absolute can also be seen as the* **manifestation of** *the Absolute in the here and now. A big point in Mahayana Buddhism is that samsara is nirvana—they're not really two things. Absolute and Relative are not two things. If the ocean is the Absolute and the wave is the Relative, then the wave manifests the ocean—the entire ocean is manifested in one wave."*

CHAPTER 22

Thinking Outside The Box: A Closer Look at Uranus-Mercury Aspects

"Talent hits targets no one else can hit. Genius hits targets no one else can even see."

—Arthur Schopenhauer

My old friend, the dearly departed Carl Fitzpatrick, shared a helpful way of explaining something important about the meaning and influence of the planet Uranus, and he did it by comparing its effects with those of the planet Jupiter.

"Both planets have a quality of 'expansion,'" he pointed out, "but in uniquely different ways."

To explain that difference, he used the example of the 13th century explorer Marco Polo. The daring Venetian traveled great distances and visited exotic cultures, which for a person of that time surely was extraordinary. With all that travel came an incredible expansion of knowledge and a tremendous broadening of horizons, quite possibly unprecedented for his time.

Yet for all of that, his allegiance to his own Euro-Christian viewpoint was so fixed that he still regarded those other cultures and their religions as fundamentally inferior to his own. For all of those expanded horizons, he was unable to step outside of his own ideological, ethno-centric perspective and see the intrinsic worth of those other non-Christian cultures.

Compare that now to Uranus, Carl suggested. It expands one's horizons too, but with the added ability to step *outside* one's shoes and see other viewpoints as if from *their* shoes. Unlike Jupiter, Uranus has what I've often called a more *decentralizing* effect—much in the same way that the discovery of Uranus forced astronomers to stand outside of the old Saturn-bound view of our solar system.

Said a little differently, Jupiter gives the ability to think *big*, whereas Uranus gives the ability to think *differently*—to see, and do, things in a way outside of the norm, outside of the conventional.

At its most harmonious, that ability allows one to give birth to unique or unusual ideas and structures, and come up with unorthodox solutions for problems that others simply can't see. It's unconventional and deeply independent, thus it is the planet most associated not just with outsiders or progressives but sometimes even with that thing we call "genius."

On the negative side, though, it can think so *far* out of the box that it can come off as crazy to others sometimes, and shake things up to such a degree that it becomes a veritable wrecking ball to existing structures. On the personality level, Uranus thus veers sometimes to the eccentric, weird, or downright anarchic. We've even witnessed a few political leaders in recent years with dominant Uranus's who left a trail of wreckage behind, some of which could well take years or decades to repair, if ever. At this level, Uranus isn't merely "independent" but more like an outlaw—e.g., Charles Manson, John Wayne Gacy, and Diamond Jim Brady all had strong Uranus-Mercury aspects. That alone doesn't account for all their behaviors, to be sure, but it certainly contributed.

These Uranian qualities, both positive and negative, can act out when it comes into contact with *any* of the horoscope's bodies or angles. For instance, when Uranus links to the Sun, it affects one's professional status, general creativity, and ego-drives, causing one to work and create more independently; when in contact with Venus, it affects one's love nature or economic attutides; in relation

A Closer Look at Uranus-Mercury Aspects

to the Moon, it affects one's emotions, close relationships, and domestic instincts—and so on.

What I'd like to focus on here is how this planetary energy specifically affects the planet Mercury—the symbol of mind, communication and thinking. As I think the following examples make clear, this combination makes for a fascinating case study in its influence through different fields and perspectives. [1]

(A technical note: in terms of aspects I've generally allowed for an orb of up to six degrees, though in most of these examples it's considerably less, and in a handful of cases, somewhat more. In those few instances involving inconjuncts [150-degree aspects] or semi-sextiles [30-degree aspects], I've allowed for a much tighter orb of two degrees or less.)

Science, Mathematics, and Technology

In relationship with the planet Mercury, that Uranian ability to "think outside of the box" can be an especially productive tool for uncovering or understanding important truths about the cosmos. Following are just some of the thinkers who advanced the development of science and math through the centuries:

Johannes Kepler (conjunct), Neils Bohr (conjunct), Louis Pasteur (conjunct), Allesandro Volta (conjunct), Demitri Mendeleev (conjunct), Max Planck (conjunct), Thomas Young (wide conjunction), Margaret Mead (conjunct), Richard Feynman (sextile), Srinavasa Ramanujan (sextile), Edward Witten (sextile), Joseph Priestly (square), Benoit Mandelbrot (square), Claude Shannon (square), Luigi Galvani (square), Kurt Godel (square), Alfred North Whitehead (square), Stephen Hawking (trine), Paul Dirac (trine), Charles Darwin (trine), Francis Crick (trine), Albert Einstein (inconjunct), John Archibald Wheeler (opposition), and Carl Sagan (opposition).

So, What Am I Doing Here, Anyway?

Johannes Kepler, born with a Mercury-Uranus conjunction

Uranus is also the planet most associated with technology and machinery, so we naturally find Uranus-Mercury connections in the charts of important innovators here as well, such as aviation pioneer Orville Wright (sextile), Elon Musk (square), Wilber Wright (square), rocket scientist and occultist Jack Parsons (square), actress/inventor Hedy Lamarr (square), Dutch inventor Boyan Slat (opposition), and Ben Franklin (opposition).

Politics

Uranus doesn't simply involve an impulse towards innovation, although that's true enough, but often includes an awareness of broader social concerns. For example, on the more progressive and activist side of the spectrum—including ordinary citizens promoting "reform" agendas—we could cite such figures as Rosa Parks (conjunct), Alexandria Ocasio Cortez (square), John F. Kennedy (square), Robert F. Kennedy Sr. (square), Andrei Sakharov (square), filmmaker Michael Moore (square), filmmaker Oliver Stone (square), Bernie Sanders (trine), singer Joan Baez (trine), Lyndon B. Johnson (trine), and Abraham Lincoln (trine).

It would be wrong to think Uranus always leans towards the liberal side of things, however. On the other end of the spectrum we find more right-wing figures like William F. Buckley (square), Ted Cruz (square), Dick Cheney (square), Bibi Netanyahu (square), Vladimir Putin (square), and Rush Limbaugh (opposition). In these cases, we're not seeing the liberal qualities of Uranus so much as its more independent or sometimes extremist side, which can manifest through political ideologies of *any* sort, be they liberal *or* conservative.

When it comes to true, die-hard revolutionaries, though, it's no surprise that Mercury-Uranus contacts are common in these charts as well. For instance, consider such figures as Emiliano Zapata (conjunct), Che Guevera (sextile), Napoleon Bonaparte (square), Leon Trotsky (square), "Chicago 7" radical Jerry Rubin (square), and Mexican revolutionary Pancho Villa (square).

Speaking of revolutionaries, I was curious to see if there were any prominent Mercury-Uranus contacts in the charts of America's "Founding Fathers" and their associates, since they were among modern history's most famous exemplars. Though I expected to find some, I was frankly surprised by just how many there were, such as James Madison (conjunct), Samuel Adams (wide conjunct), Paul Revere (conjunct), Thomas Jefferson (sextile), George Washington (sextile), Alexander Hamilton (sextile), Martha Washington (inconjunct), and Benjamin Franklin (opposition). I have no doubt a deeper dive into the horoscopes of Declaration of Independence signers would reveal quite a few more.

So, What Am I Doing Here, Anyway?

The Arts

Though it's probably more natural to expect Uranus-Venus, Uranus-Moon, or Uranus-Neptune aspects in the charts of artistic innovators and "stars," we find a surprising number of cases with Uranus-Mercury aspects, too. Why would that be? I'd suggest it's because creativity in *any* field—not just writing but music, painting, dance, and cinema—involves an ability to think differently, not just in the conception of one's work but in matters of self-promotion, marketing or sometimes even personal fashion!

Some examples from the art and entertainment worlds are actor, activist, and filmmaker Sean Penn (conjunction), pioneering surrealist Giorgio di Chirico (square), photographer Richard Avedon (square), Stanley Kubrick (square), Alfred Hitchcock (square), Orson Welles (square), Rodin (square), Monet (square), Francis Bacon (square), Andy Warhol (trine), Jean-Michel Basquiat (trine), Lenny Bruce (inconjunct), Woody Allen (inconjunct), David Lynch (inconjunct), actress and producer Margot Robbie (opposition), and Edvard "The Scream" Munch (opposition).

From the music world, we find figures like Taylor Swift (conjunct), Brian Eno (wide conjunct), Prince (sextile), Mick Jagger (sextile), Igor Stravinsky (sextile), Miles Davis (sextile), Lady Gaga (square), Frédéric Chopin (square), Justin Timberlake (square), Weird Al Yankovic (square), Chet Baker (square), Charles Ives (square), Bjork (square), Jack White (trine), Roger Waters (trine), Eddie Van Halen (inconjunct), Buddy Holly (inconjunct), Jimi Hendrix (opposition), and Johnny Rotten (opposition).

Since it's an inherently Mercurial profession, it's natural to expect notable Uranus connections in the charts of writers and poets. That ability to think outside the box isn't simply an invaluable key for writers in coming up with unconventional ideas and perspectives, but in helping to enhance their awareness of social issues and circumstances.

Some prime examples of this planetary combo, on either of those fronts, are Whitley Strieber (conjunct), investigative journalist Ronan Farrow (conjunct), Paul Verlaine (conjunct), Gabriel Garcia Márquez (conjunct), Henry Miller (sextile), Charles Dickens (sextile), Herman Hesse (sextile), "gonzo journalist" Hunter S. Thompson (square), Charles Baudelaire (square), Franz Kafka (square), Ursula K. Le Guin (square), Philip K. Dick (square), "anomalist" writer Brad Steiger (square), Norwegian novelist Knut Hamsun (square), poet and independent Egyptologist Normandi Ellis (square), Sylvia Plath (inconjunct), Virginia Woolf (inconjunct), Charles Bukowski (inconjunct), Arthur Rimbaud (opposition), John Steinbeck (opposition), and Oscar Wilde (opposition).

Philosophy and Religion

Here as well, that Uranian talent—sometimes even genius—for perceiving things from unconventional perspectives shows itself in the lives of many key figures in philosophy, religion, history, mysticism, and mythology.

Kriya Yoga Swami Yukteswar Giri, born with a close conjunction of Mercury and Uranus.

So, What Am I Doing Here, Anyway?

This ranges from more popular or mainstream figures like Joseph Campbell (square) to those on the more openly spiritual or mystical end of the spectrum like Kriya Yoga teacher Sri Yukteswar (conjunct), famed yogi Ramakrishna (conjunct), Theosophical figures like William Quan Judge (conjunct), Alice Bailey (sextile), and Annie Besant (oppose); religious and esoteric scholar Richard Smoley (square), Franz Hartmann (square), Buddhist writer and explorer Alexandra David-Néel (trine), and even such controversial "outsider" figures as Aleister Crowley (square), David Icke (square), and Mormon founder Joseph Smith (square).

Especially noteworthy is how many historical figures now regarded as transformative or even revolutionary in the history of philosophy were born with notable Mercury-Uranus aspects. This includes Friedrich Engels (conjunct), John Locke (conjunct), the figure John David Ebert calls "the Picasso of philosophy," Martin Heidegger (conjunct), Alfred North Whitehead (square), Oswald Spengler (square), Georg Friederich Hegel (trine), Friederich Nietszche (opposition), and the French philosopher Voltaire (opposition).

Sigmund Freud, born with a Mercury-Uranus conjunction

A Closer Look at Uranus-Mercury Aspects

When it comes to psychology and our understanding of the human psyche, we have to add the towering figure of Sigmund Freud (conjunct), since his impact since the publication of *The Interpretation of Dreams* in 1899 has been as much on philosophy and global culture as on psychology. In turn, his foremost colleague and successor, Carl Jung, was born with a tight semi-sextile, while arguably *his* foremost successor, James Hillman, was born with a tight conjunct. Radical thinkers, all!

Media Celebrities

During my research I was surprised by the sheer number of ultra-famous figures from contemporary pop culture who weren't necessarily notable for outstanding intellectual, spiritual, or artistic achievements, but whose charts featured prominent Uranus-Mercury aspects. Why might that be?

A possible explanation is that in our media-saturated age, one necessary key to fame and fortune is an ability to work with the Uranian media. Unless someone knows how to promote themself through the media—whether through talk show appearances, social media posts, or interviews on the proverbial "red carpet"—it's difficult if not impossible to become particularly famous or successful these days.

Prominent Mercury-Uranus aspects are thus among those factors suggesting a connection to (and talent for) the media. Consider the following personalities, all just in the category of Mercury-Uranus conjunctions alone: Kim Kardashian, Jimmy Fallon, Adam Driver, Tiffany Haddish, Timothée Chalamet, Gwyneth Paltrow, Trisha Yearwood, Matt Damon, Adam Sandler, Gwen Stefani, Megan Thee Stallion, Keanu Reeves, Leonardo DiCaprio, Jack Black, Sophie Turner, Kit Harrington, John Krasinski, Florence Pugh, and Kevin Bacon.

Casting our gaze back a bit further, we might also include a few of those figures from past decades who have been influential in

TV or radio, whose charts displayed notable Mercury-Uranus connections. These include pioneering broadcaster Edward R. Murrow (square), radio, film and TV genius Orson Welles (square), liberal media personality Jon Stewart (square), talk show host Jack Paar (square), his "Tonight Show" successor Johnny Carson (wide trine), Dan Rather (inconjunct), Larry King (inconjunct), Oprah Winfrey (inconjunct), Ted Turner (inconjunct), conservative radio host Rush Limbaugh (opposition), and "shock jock" Howard Stern (opposition).

Astrologers

Last but certainly not least, this survey wouldn't be complete without a look at the role this planetary combo has played in the horoscopes of astrological practitioners or theorists through the years. While I was limited in obtaining the birth data of many contemporary astrologers (since the info wasn't available online), the ones I *did* find made for an interesting group, especially when coupled with those well-known figures from earlier eras.

These include such individuals as Johannes Kepler (conjunct), Ebenezer Sibly (conjunct), William Lilly (conjunct), Glenn Perry (conjunct), Sri Yukteswar (conjunct), Joan Quigley (conjunct), Mountain Astrologer magazine founder Tem Tarriktar (semi-sextile), Alice Bailey (sextile), Demetra George (sextile), Noel Tyl (square), financial astrologer W.D. Gann (square), Manly Palmer Hall (square), Aleister Crowley (square), Stephen Arroyo (trine), Andre Barbault (trine), Evangeline Adams (trine), Steven Forrest (inconjunct), Marc Penfield, Michel Gauquelin (inconjunct), and Cyril Fagan (inconjunct). And while U.S. President Theodore Roosevelt wasn't a professional astrologer himself, he was a vocal proponent of the discipline during his life, and born with an exact inconjunct between the two planets.

Final Thoughts

Looking over all the examples cited above, you may have noticed the seemingly disproportionate number of square (90-degree) aspects in many of these cases. Why would that be?

The answer is fairly simple. While squares are normally considered difficult or even "malefic," they can be extremely constructive in several ways. One of those is that they involve and generate a huge amount of energy, far more than trines or sextiles—energy that can be necessary for manifesting ideas or projects in the real world.

In turn, precisely because the square aspect *is* innately more challenging or even frustrating, especially in youth, it essentially *forces* one's attention onto a given area, skill, or challenge—which can ideally lead to mastery of that area. There is an element of drive involved with the square that isn't experienced to quite the same degree with any other aspect, except perhaps the conjunction. As I heard an astrologer say many years ago, if you hope to be successful at anything in this world, it's probably best to incarnate with some strong squares in your chart![1]

But while it's true the "hard" aspects have more energy behind them, it's important to stress that even the "softer" aspects (sextiles, trines, sexi-sextiles, and inconjuncts) can play a critical role in helping *anyone* think "outside of the box," whether they be a scientist, writer, revolutionary—or simply the average man and woman on the street.

Notes

1. While researching this chapter, I came across quite a few instances of important innovators where I expected to see prominent Uranus-Mercury aspects—but didn't. So what might explain that? In many of those cases, I found a strong Uranus-Sun aspect instead. Some examples of that: Walt Disney (conjunct), test pilot Chuck Yeager (conjunct), Werner von Braun (tight sextile), Nikola Tesla (sextile), scientist Richard Feynman (square), futurist Buckminster Fuller (trine), J. Robert Oppenheimer (tight trine)—

and many, many others. My own take on this? Simply, while there are subtle differences between the influence of those two planets, the Sun being somewhat more ego-involved in its desire to express that creativity more publicly, I think this speaks to the allied role they *both* play in creative innovation.

2. When I showed a draft of this essay to a long-time colleague, he pointed out that at least 30-40% of all charts picked at random would likely have *some* aspect between Uranus and Mercury, so a selection of this sort isn't terribly impressive from a statistical standpoint. I said I understand, but that I'm not trying to sway skeptics and disbelievers about astrology here so much as to simply illustrate the role these aspects play in the charts of notable historical figures. Had I wanted to solely address skeptics, I would have focused more on charts just with conjunctions and squares. Using that metric, I'm sure the correlation of Mercury-Uranus contacts would be considerably more impressive. For instance, consider a few of the noted "revolutionaries" or rabblerousers from our survey focusing only on the square aspect alone: Pancho Villa, Leon Trotsky, Vladimir Putin, Jerry Rubin, Benoit Mandelbrot, Kurt Godel, Joseph Priestley, Charles Baudelaire, Aleister Crowley, Stanley Kubrick, Orson Welles, Alfred Hitchcock, Napoleon, Franz Kafka, Manly Palmer Hall, Alfred North Whitehead, Philip K. Dick, and Oswald Spengler. Quite an incendiary crew!

CHAPTER 23

What the Movie *Barbie* Has to Teach Us About Planetary Retrogrades

Following its premiere in July of 2023, there were numerous discussions in the astrological community about the Greta Gerwig film *Barbie*, and the fact that its release coincided so closely with Venus turning retrograde. Some of those commentaries were particularly interesting, including one that looked at how the movie's storyline echoes elements of the ancient tale of Inanna.[1]

But there's one aspect of this Venusian connection that hasn't been emphasized as much—that being the lesson it holds for us about the nature and meaning of retrogradation generally. Rather than delve into the movie in all its intricacies, I'll break this down very simply.

In the movie, Barbie is shown at the outset to be an essentially extraverted, "sunny" embodiment of Venus— pure beauty, charm, pleasantness. Hers is a perfectly nice existence, but for the most part, a largely shallow one as well.

As the story progresses, the movie shows her becoming increasingly aware of deeper issues like death, social inequality, relationships, and femininity generally, while simultaneously becoming more conscious of her own mortal flaws (cellulite, bad breath, etc.).

In other words, she's becoming more reflective, thoughtful, and introspective. Having started to turn more inward, she assumes greater depth and complexity as a person. Having been relatively two-dimensional before, she becomes a more three-dimensional being.

This says a great deal about retrogradation generally—not just when it comes to Venus but any of the planets. While the stigma around retrogradation has lessened considerably in recent years, one still encounters astrologers who see it as an essentially negative factor, as though a planet that's reversed direction has somehow shifted into a more dysfunctional or inferior mode—whether that be Venus, Mercury, or any other body. (When I interviewed a famous, now-deceased astrologer for the Mountain Astrologer magazine years ago, I was surprised to hear him speak about Venus retrograde in exclusively negative terms! For him, there apparently was no upside to Venus retrogradation.)

While I don't deny this "turning backwards" can pose certain complications—just as it did for the movie's Barbie—sometimes those complications can result in productive, ultimately positive outcomes. Staying with our Barbie analogy, imagine if she had stayed in that superficial, two-dimensional mode forever. She would have remained all so pleasant and "sunny," to be sure, with far fewer complications to contend with—but also living a more shallow, boring, and less adventuresome life.

Ditto retrogradation of any planet. When it appears from Earth's perspective to go backwards, a planet turns more inward, more reflective. That planet pauses to take a breath, as it were. Or you might think of an archer drawing back a bow before releasing an arrow; the quivering of that string may feel difficult to manage at times, especially the further back it's drawn. For a purely superficial person, that may indeed seem "bad" in some ways, and certainly uncomfortable. Yet for any creative or spiritually-minded individual it can actually amplify that planet's potentials—especially once that arrow is released.

Take our opening example of Venus retrograde: consider some of the celebrities born with that placement: Amy Winehouse, Robert

What the Movie Barbie Has to Teach Us About Planetary Retrogrades

DeNiro, Christian Bale, Dead Can Dance vocalist Lisa Gerrard, and—surprise, surprise—Greta Gerwig, director of the film *Barbie*. Do you think Greta would have even been drawn to helm a film like that had she not been born with Venus retrograde?

A film which, by the way, has made her very, *very* rich. So much for Venus retrograde hindering a person's earning capacity, as I heard one not-so-brilliant astrologer suggest many years ago.

It's a good thing that that astrologer never informed Greta early on in her career just how little potential she really had on that front.

Notes

1. https://wildhunt.org/2023/07/barbie-is-the-new-inanna.html

CHAPTER 24

When the Planets Change Their Clothing: Ten Examples of Planetary Ingresses

Over the years that I've been following planetary movements through the signs, it's been fascinating to see what sorts of historical changes happen around those times when the slow-moving planets first move into new zodiacal signs—a process astrologers call "ingresses."

As most astrologers know, this sort of socio-cultural change generally unfolds fairly slowly rather than immediately. Yet I've sometimes been surprised to see major shifts of emphasis happen within those first few weeks, months, or even *days* after the ingress occurs.

With that in mind, I've compiled a short list of some of the more intriguing correlations I've noticed from recent times, which expands on a short list I mentioned briefly in an earlier book.[1] To be clear, these select events hardly represent the full impact of such ingresses, as there are *many* manifestations which emerge whenever a planet moves through a sign, on various levels—culturally, politically, religiously, scientifically, even geologically. These are just some of the more interesting correlations I've seen happen around these starts, but which may sometimes serve as clues or "omens" to the broader ramifications of those placements that unfold in their wake.

Before diving in here, I need to explain that slow-moving planets customarily dip in and out of a new sign before finally settling in "for the long haul," as it were. Some of the events compiled here are those which took place shortly after that initial entry, some of which happened shortly after its final ingress into the sign. Either way, the expressions of the zodiacal/planetary influence involved are ones that invite close examination and reflection.

1. Due to its irregular orbit, Pluto can reside in a given sign for anywhere from 12 to 30 years (!). During the 20th century, Pluto first ingressed into Cancer on September 11, 1912, but moved back into that sign "for the long haul" on May 28th of 1914. It was exactly four weeks after that latter date that Archduke Ferdinand was assassinated, which in turn triggered WWI. As for the possible Astro-significance there, consider that Cancer is domestic in nature, and relates to such matters as family, property, and emotional boundaries. With turbulent Pluto moving through this sign, WWI devastated virtually all of those for large segments of the population, while enacting a massive "transformation" of property and national boundaries throughout much of Europe.

2. Uranus characteristically resides in a given sign for six or seven years. On April 1, 1927, the planet of technology first moved into the pioneering sign Aries—the sign of "new beginnings." Several days after that ingress, on April 7, an event sometimes considered the birth of modern television occurred when Bell Telephone Company transmitted an image of Herbert Hoover from Washington, D.C. to New York City—the first successful long-distance demonstration of televised technology. Several weeks later, Philo Farnsworth achieved another televised milestone when he transmitted the first electronic television motion pictures (as opposed to the electromechanical TV systems tested previously).

The next month, on May 20-21 of 1927, another iconic breakthrough took place when Charles Lindbergh made the first solo nonstop transatlantic airplane flight from New York City to Paris, France, in his single-engine aircraft, the Spirit of St. Louis. Still another benchmark of modern times came several months later when, on October 6th, the film *The Jazz Singer* premiered in New York City—

the film widely regarded as a key turning point in the history of cinema. Though it wasn't the first "talkie," it became the highest grossing movie up to that point and popularized sound motion pictures from that point forward.

3. Though it had dipped in and out of Leo temporarily the previous year, Pluto entered Leo "for the long haul" on August 4, 1938. Several months later, on December 17, scientist Otto Hahn discovered the nuclear fission of Uranium, which caused some to call it the "birth of the Atomic Age." Considering that Leo is associated by astrologers with the Sun, the movement of transformational Pluto into this sign seems a fitting symbol for an unlocking of true "solar power." As we'll also see later, the ascendancy of Hitler during this time reflected the darker side of the powerful forces being tapped into during that period, but in more psycho-political ways. In that vein, I want to include here a comment posted on social media by my astrological colleague, Sheri Robin Hartstein, which I think makes a valuable point regarding the importance of this particular ingress:

"The most notorious example (of planetary ingresses) from the last century is one that involved a double-whammy ingress of Saturn into Taurus while squaring Pluto in Leo during July-September 1939 leading up to the start of World War Two. Pluto had first ingressed into Leo in late 1937 for two months, then again the following year at critical junctures (i.e., on September 30, 1938 coinciding with the infamous 'Peace for our Time' Munich Agreement between England and Germany.) But it wasn't until Saturn ingressed into Taurus and squared Pluto in the first degrees of Leo that Germany invaded Poland on September 1, 1939 and the world war began. (A third important factor at that juncture was transiting Pluto exactly square the Nodes in Scorpio/Taurus, with Saturn conjunct the Taurus South Node.)

4. Neptune spends roughly 14 years in a given sign, and is the planet most often associated with music, film, and mysticism.

Ten Examples of Planetary Ingresses

Elvis Presley (publicity still from *Jailhouse Rock*).

Neptune first moved into Scorpio on December 25, 1955. Less than two months later, on February 22, 1956, Elvis Presley exploded onto the charts with "Heartbreak Hotel." Shortly after, on March 13, he released his first gold album, simply titled "Elvis Presley," then on April 3 appeared on the Milton Berle Show, prior to his more famous appearance on the Ed Sullivan Show. In light of the Scorpio influence, it's worth noting the controversy surrounding Elvis during that period over the overtly "sexual" nature of his performances, with conservative viewers objecting strongly to his onstage hip-thrusts in particular—causing producers of the Ed Sullivan Show several months later to film him only from the waist up!

Interestingly enough, this was also a seminal period for the evolution of The Beatles. To begin with, the musical venue most associated with their early career, the Cavern Club, opened on January 16, 1957, in Liverpool England. On July 6th of that year, John Lennon and Paul McCartney met for the first time, and one month later, John Lennon's first group, the Quarrymen, played at the Cavern Club, literally setting the stage for the yet-to-be-formed Beatles.

On a very different note, on October 4, 1957, eight weeks after Neptune moved into Scorpio for the final time, the very first artificial satellite, Sputnik, was launched into space by the Russians. How might this tie in to Neptune's entrance into Scorpio? One possibility is this: as I mentioned in an earlier chapter, I remember watching that pinpoint of light streaming far overhead as a child, and it was an unspeakably mysterious—and Neptunian—experience for me. It certainly felt like a new world of the imagination had opened up—and with it came the true birth of the "Space Age" and our collective entry into the dark realms far beyond *terra firma*.

5. In the years leading up to 2008, a growing number of astrologers predicted that the imminent entry of Pluto into Capricorn could trigger a major shake-up on Wall Street and the global economy, due to the turbulent impact of this planet on the sign associated with business and government. For me, this seemed a prime opportunity to test out the viability not just of ingresses, but of the tropical zodiac itself (since its boundaries are different from those of the "sidereal," more heavily star-based zodiac). I say that because the financial forecasts being proposed were so dramatic and severe that this seemed to offer a relatively clear-cut "before and after" case study in astrological prediction.

As it turned out, within just weeks of Pluto's move into Capricorn in 2008, Wall Street went into a historic melt-down precipitated over a disastrous mortgage crisis, leaving the global economy teetering on a financial precipice.

6. On March 11, 2011, the planet Uranus was scheduled to move into the tropical sign of Aries, signaling a major transition that could seriously impact culture and society. What made this ingress especially important to me was the fact that Uranus was also starting to enter into a long-term stressful relationship (a square) with Pluto in Capricorn, suggesting this impending change could be turbulent or even revolutionary. On the day before this ingress occurred, on March 10th, I spoke with an old friend, Tim Boyd (about to become president of the Theosophical Society in America, where I had previously worked as an editor), and mentioned this planetary shift to him. I specifically suggested that he watch the news carefully for any major "shake-ups" on the global front those next few days.

As it so happened, the *very next day*, exactly as Uranus moved into fiery Aries, the Fukushima disaster occurred. A massive earthquake shook Japan and triggered a tsunami that took the life of thousands and caused a disastrous melt-down at the Haichi power plant. The destruction of the nuclear generator spread radiation across a wide region and continues to pose a serious risk for both humans and marine wildlife to this day.

7. On May 15, 2018, Uranus then entered the tropical sign Taurus. Because of the widely accepted association of Taurus with the Earth, many astrologers wondered whether we might start seeing major geological changes taking place at the point of its entry into this sign.

As it turned out, the week leading up to this ingress saw major volcanic activity starting up in Hawaii, and on May 16th, the day after its entry into Taurus, there was a significant eruption of Mount Kilauea, sending an ash plume 30,000 feet into the air. Nor was this the only Earth-related development occurring during that general period. Indonesia's Mount Merapi volcano began erupting in mid-May as well, sending plumes of smoke almost 4 miles into the air, while on May 29 Guatemala's Fuego volcano violently erupted, killing at least 62 people. On that exact same day, an earthquake of magnitude 5.5 shook the Big Island of Hawaii, sending plumes of ash thousands of feet upward from Mount Kilauea (again). Indeed, this general surge of volcanic activity led to the journal *New Scientist* publishing an article on June 6, 2018, titled "Why Are So Many Volcanoes Erupting Around the World?"

8. The planetoid Chiron is associated by many astrologers with issues of wounding and healing. This celestial body shifted into Pisces—the sign most associated with the ocean—on April 22, 2010. The Deepwater Horizon rig sank in 5000 ft. of water in the

Gulf of Mexico that same day, causing incalculable damage to the Gulf and many of its creatures.

9. On March 21, 2020, Saturn moved into Aquarius, precisely at a point when the theme of "social distancing" became prevalent around the world, as a result of the Covid-19 pandemic; this was coupled with a worldwide governmental crackdown on citizens who congregated in groups. One could hardly imagine a more fitting manifestation of Saturn (the planet of constriction and authority) moving into Aquarius (the sign of groups and social interactions) than this!

But while concerns over the pandemic lingered for some time, things became even more complicated in a different way when Saturn backed out of Aquarius, then re-entered it *alongside Jupiter* in late 2020—making for a simultaneous double-ingress of those two planets in zero degrees of Aquarius on December 21. Writing that previous summer, prior to the Biden/Trump presidential election, I made this comment in my book *StarGates*:

"As of this writing, one of the more interesting (celestial triggers ahead) is set to happen around December 21st of this year. Besides this being the date of the Winter solstice, it will also be when Saturn and Jupiter precisely conjunct for the first time in 20 years, in zero degrees of Aquarius...In addition to that, this is precisely when Mars in Aries will be forming a tight square to that epic Saturn/Pluto conjunction from January of 2020 at 22 degrees of Capricorn, serving as a trigger to that pattern as well. *The fact that three major triggers will occur so shortly after the U.S. Presidential election naturally leads one to wonder whether the impact of those celestial markers will somehow involve fallout from that political event—a 'perfect storm' of political proportions, maybe?"*[2] (Emphasis added.)

As it turned out, that "perfect storm" did happen, when just a few days later, on January 6, 2021, an angry mob attempted to overthrow the U.S. government. Numbering in the thousands, rioters stormed the D.C. Capitol in hope of halting the next president's certification.

Having failed at that, the formal inauguration of Joe Biden as president then took place two weeks later, on January 20.

It was a dramatic event like none other in America's history, and represented a dramatic "changing of the guard"—but a complex and very double-edged one at that. Coming on the heels of the arch-conservative Saturn-Pluto conjunction in Capricorn shortly before, some astrologers had been predicting the Jupiter-Saturn conjunction in Aquarius might point to a progressive or liberal "wave" ahead.

On the surface of things, that did seem to be the case, not only with the election of the Biden/Harris ticket (a moderately liberal President alongside the first female and first woman-of-color Vice President), but with the installation of a far more diverse U.S. Congress as well. Yet as the attempted insurrection in reaction to Biden's election made clear, any potential sea-change ahead wasn't simply going to settle into place without a fight. In addition, the storming of the Capitol by a determined group also revealed that the influence of collectively-minded Aquarius isn't necessarily always a constructive (or liberal) one. If indeed the events around an ingress are omens of a sort, then these developments strongly hinted at a complicated state of affairs ahead, not just the U.S. but likely for many other countries, as we collectively struggle to reconcile the opposing forces of constriction and expansion, of "conservative" and "liberal."

10. On March 23, 2023, Pluto moved into Aquarius for the first time in over two centuries. It was exactly during this period that we saw a massive upsurge of discussion about both the perils and promise of A.I., or artificial intelligence, especially with the introduction of graphic programs like Midjourney and writing programs like ChatGPT. That was certainly "Aquarian," as was the fact that this same period witnessed a virtual explosion of discussion in the media about UFOs/UAPs, and the possibility of humanity's contact with extraterrestrial or non-human intelligences. This climaxed in a highly publicized U.S. Senate hearing in late July (involving live testimonies from figures like David Grusch about possible crash retrieval programs), as well as the controversial work of physicist Avi Loeb and his claim of obtaining possible evidence of materials from beyond our solar system.

On a more political level, Pluto in Aquarius symbolizes the "power of the masses" (versus Pluto's meaning in its opposite sign, Leo, symbolizing the power of the reigning monarchal individual, or "star"). The last time Pluto moved through Aquarius was the late 1700s, which was a period that witnessed both the American and French revolutions. When Pluto moved into Aquarius this time, we quickly saw massive street protests in countries like France and Israel railing against the policies of their leaders, while in the U.S., the Department of Justice was launching unprecedented legal actions against former president Donald Trump, which some might well interpret as an effort by Aquarian "We the People" forces to take down a would-be autocrat.

The movement of Pluto in Aquarius also seems behind the extended writers' and actors' strike in Hollywood—which began on May 2, 2023, within just twenty-four hours of Pluto's station point at zero degrees of Aquarius, then ended five months later on the eve of Pluto's next station point. The strike involved creative artists of various stripes banding together against the corporate "kings" and "queens" of the entertainment industry, protesting unfair contractual terms around residual payments from streaming media as well as the possible replacement of writers and actors by artificial intelligence. The year 2023 witnessed other acts of popular resistance, including members of the United Auto Workers union (UAW) going on strike against America's three largest automakers—Ford, General Motors, and Stellantis.

Some Implications

To my mind, examples like these here don't simply offer an intriguing illustration of astrology-in-action but may also provide compelling circumstantial evidence for the influence and reality of the zodiac itself (in this case, the "tropical" one). Surprisingly enough, this is something debated even by some within the astrological community, with a number of astrologers I've communicated with over the years suggesting we should dispense with zodiacal factors entirely in favor of focusing solely on planetary angles and "aspects." (Though my colleague and friend Richard Tarnas doesn't align himself dogmatically with that viewpoint, he did adopt it for his book, *Cosmos and Psyche*, mainly for reasons of simplicity and clarity, choosing instead to focus primarily on planetary cycles through history without reference to zodiacal placements.) Do lists of ingresses like we've seen here provide ironclad *proof* for the reality and influence of the zodiac? Of course not. But are they compelling? Without a doubt.

Final Thoughts

Turning our gaze to the road ahead, it's worth calling out a few of the upcoming planetary ingresses that readers should watch for in the years immediately ahead. Here are the ones I'll be watching closely:

* Neptune moves into Aries on March 31, 2025.

* Saturn moves into Aries on May 24, 2025.

* Uranus moves into Gemini on July 7, 2025.

* Chiron moves into Taurus on June 19, 2026.

* Saturn moves into Taurus on April 13, 2028.

In particular, note the three ingresses taking place close to each other between the months of March and July 2025. Earlier we saw the unusual double ingress of Saturn and Jupiter in Aquarius within days of each other in late 2020; it's even more unusual to see three major ingresses happening so close to one another like this.

So what could that possibly mean? We'll be finding out soon enough!

Notes

1. Grasse, Ray. (2020). *StarGates: Essays on Astrology, Symbolism, and the Synchronistic Universe.* Inner Eye Publications, Chicago. See footnotes to chapter 22.

2. *StarGates,* see chapter 20.

CHAPTER 25

The Great Pyramid as a Cipher to Existence

I'll begin this chapter with a riddle:

In what way do the Great Pyramid of Giza and our conventional twelve-fold zodiac express the same essential symbolism?

We'll come back to this question shortly, but to get there I first need to explain a few essential points.

A veritable cottage industry of books, videos and essays has sprung up over the years exploring the implications and meanings of the Great Pyramid of Giza, and the ways it possibly encodes such mathematical principles as Pi and Phi, the dimensions of the Earth, or even predictions about humanity's future, among still other things.

So, What Am I Doing Here, Anyway?

What I'd like to briefly explore here is one aspect of the pyramid's form that builds on certain other relatively familiar theories but which hopefully adds another dimension to that discussion.

It's actually quite simple—so simple, in fact, that we may well say it's been hiding in plain sight all this time. Now, whether the Egyptian architects themselves consciously intended what I'll be saying here, specifically in the way I'm saying it, I don't know—maybe, maybe not. Either way, it doesn't really matter, since what we'll be looking at are fundamentally universal and archetypal principles, I believe, ones that exist innately within the essential meaning of forms and shapes.

To begin with, let's look at one simple feature of the pyramid that *has* been touched on many times before—that being its basic triangular shape, as seen in profile:

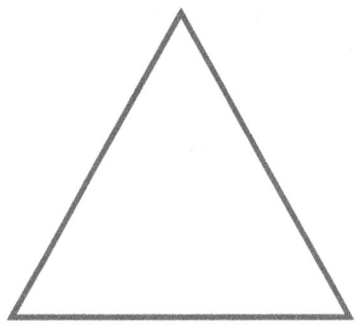

When you look at any one side of the pyramid, you find a simple triangle. Within that basic triangle, which consists of a pointed tip at the peak widening down to a much broader base, we find an expression of what some have seen as a symbol for the unfoldment of creation. That is, creation begins as a point within the unmanifest above and precipitates down into visible manifestation below. We even find this imagery stamped on any ordinary one-dollar American bill, with its Masonic symbolism of the all-seeing eye above and the multi-leveled pyramidal structure fanning out below it.

The Great Pyramid as a Cipher to Existence

On a numerological level, this triangular form implies a relationship between the concepts of the One and the Two, which together comprise a Three.

In Kabbalistic terms, for instance, this can be equated with the so-called Tree of Life, which depicts the various creative energies of existence in relation to one another. At the top of that Tree of Life (shown here), we see the neutral sephiroth Keter giving birth to the dual sephiroths beneath—Chokhma and Bina, symbolizing the relationship of divine unity to the archetypal masculine and feminine principles, respectively.

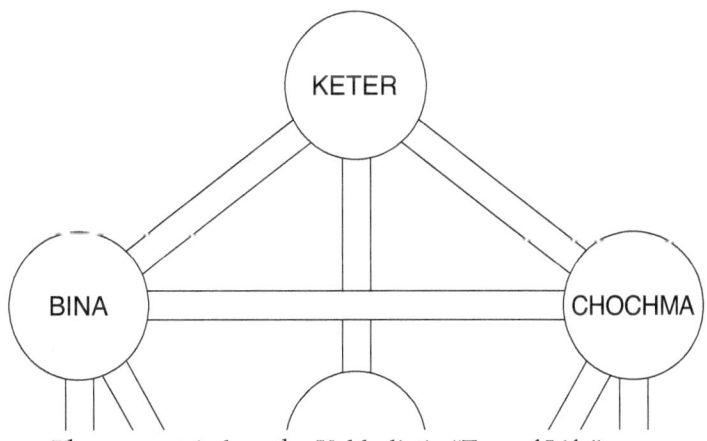

The upper triad on the Kabbalistic "Tree of Life"

From Three to Four to Seven to Twelve

But there is considerably more going on with the pyramid's shape than just these three principles found in a simple triangle.

That's because within the conventional pyramidal form there is not only a single triangle but *four* triangles, with each of the pyramid's faces likewise displaying those same three points. Through the mathematical process of addition, of course, that naturally leads to the mystic "7." But through multiplication, it also gives us this formula:

$$4 \times 3 = 12$$

What's so significant about that?

If you're an astrologer, you'll immediately recognize how this relates not just to the fact there are also twelve factors involved with the signs of the zodiac, but specifically to the zodiac's breakdown of twelve signs *into groups of four and three*.

In astrology, in other words, there are four "elements"—Earth, Water, Air, and Fire—relating to the fact there are four basic states of consciousness (simply put, *practicality, emotionality, intellectuality,* and *energetic awareness*); in turn, each of those four states express itself in one of three distinct modes—Cardinal, Fixed and Mutable (simply, *initiating, stabilizing,* and *flexible*).

In turn, at the peak of that pyramid those four sides converge in a fifth point, the proverbial "quint-essence"—that is, *fifth essence*—where the four elements find both their perfection and union in the subtle element of *Ether,* associated with the planet Mercury. The peak therefore represents the principle of pure mind, from which all creation ensues.

Let's stop and reflect on all this for a moment.

Within the pyramidal form there is not just the symbolism of a simple triangle signifying something precipitating down into manifestation, or even just of a twelve-fold manifestation emerging from the pyramid's peak. Rather, it's the fact that this twelve-fold manifestation has *four distinct faces, each of which has three distinct points*.

Encoded within the deceptively simple form of a four-sided pyramid, in other words, lies a profound truth about the nature of existence—one that is symbolically resonant with that of the twelve-fold zodiac. As different as these two might appear on their surface, these forms are actually profoundly similar, with both pointing to the nature of what Shelly Trimmer described as the "Maze of Self."[1]

But we can take all this one important step further.

In my book *The Waking Dream*, I spoke about how one can associate the matrix of symbolism I've been laying out here with that of the Sphinx—or more precisely, what is generally referred to as the *tetramorph*, or four-fold (*tetra*) form (*morph*).

In some ancient sources, most famously the Bible, we find references to a mythological creature sporting the features of four distinct creatures—in some depictions, the body of a lion, the hooves of a bull, the wings of an eagle, and the head of a human. These four beings are associated with the four fixed signs of the zodiac, of course—Leo the lion; Taurus the bull; Scorpio the eagle (in that sign's higher potentials); and finally, Aquarius, the human.

While there are certain similarities here with the Great Sphinx of Egypt, specifically in the joining of a human head with the body of a lion, there are differences, too—namely, the Sphinx of Egypt lacks the wings of an angel and the hooves of a bull.

The origin of the tetramorph is commonly traced back to Babylonian times, with the Jews likely having acquired it during their time in captivity. To my mind, though, it strikes a deeply archetypal and universal chord that resonates far beyond any one cultural tradition. I say that because of how it embodies the union of those four basic elements—Earth, Water, Fire, and Air—which together symbolize the four fundamental parts of consciousness.

Let me explain just a bit further.

As Shelly Trimmer explained it, the simplest that one's consciousness can possibly be reduced to is *four factors*. These are: *the observer, the observed, the act of observing, and finally the "all of the parts," or the memory track*. This relates not just to the four elements of astrology but to the four-lettered name of God described in Kabbalism, or IHVH. These four factors comprise the essential factors of your own consciousness at this very moment.[2]

The tetramorph thus symbolizes the coming together of all these factors of consciousness into one. As I expressed it in *The Waking Dream*, we live as though we are "dismembered gods"—divided beings—but in the state of enlightenment,

"...the dismembered god is *re-membered*: observer and observed collapse into one, and all dualistic qualities, contrasts, proportions, and meanings are subsumed into pure awareness, having been reduced to ashes by the radiant light of the enthroned Self."

The state of unity symbolized by the tetramorph is therefore related in astrology to the center of the horoscope, the balance point, as well as to the peak of the pyramid, where all twelve parts coalesce. In visual terms, I've depicted that concept with the following illustration, with the tetramorph at the pyramid's peak symbolizing fully balanced awareness, and the four creatures associated with the four fixed signs, representing the four essential elements of self-conscious awareness, shown at the four corners of the pyramid's base.

The Great Pyramid as a Cipher to Existence

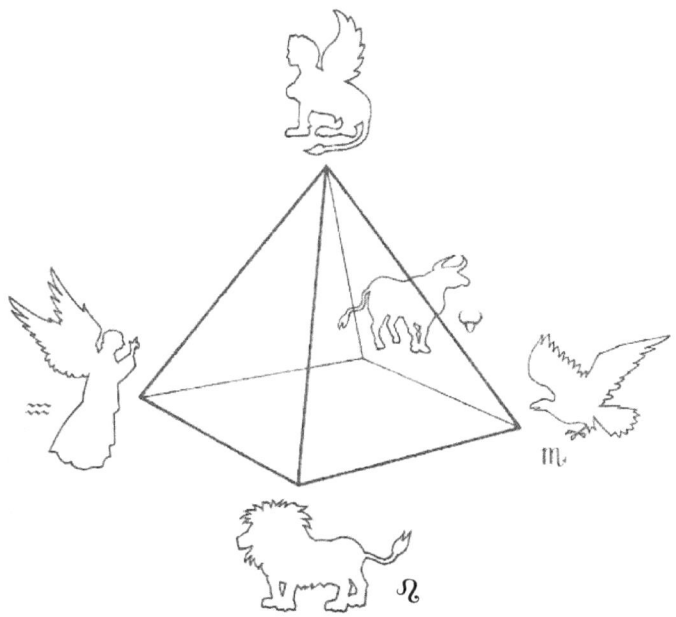

The four creatures associated with the four fixed signs of the zodiac, with the tetramorph at the pyramid's peak, representing the integration of those parts into one.

So returning to our original riddle: *In what way does the Great Pyramid and the twelvefold zodiac express the same essential symbolism?*

Simply, while their forms may seem completely different on the surface, both the four-sided pyramidal shape and the zodiac embody the same essential combination of 3, 4 and 12. In turn, this conveys something profound not only about creation, but the "structure" of own consciousness, with these properties extending as well to the symbol of the tetramorph.

In that way, it's possible to say that the Great Pyramid—or any four-sided pyramid, for that matter—can be viewed as a cipher to something truly profound about existence, and to the timeless truths encoded within the great "Maze of Self."

So, What Am I Doing Here, Anyway?

Notes

1. See my book *When the Stars Align,* chapter 41, "Esoteric Astrology: A Discourse by Shelly Trimmer."

2. You may notice how two of those letters in the holy name IHVH are the same—the two "H's." What could that mean? As Shelly Trimmer put it, it refers to the fact that *the observer and the observer are really the same thing.* Consciousness is eternally standing off and viewing itself, in an act of perpetual self-regeneration, esoterically symbolized by the image of a snake eating its own tail, known as the *ouroboros.* Think of it like this: right now you think that you're seeing a world outside of you, but it's actually *you* that you're seeing. In fact, you can't possibly see anything *outside* of your awareness; which is to say, *it's all you.* The problem is, because all these various parts of consciousness haven't been brought into balance, into unity, confusion arises as to what is really what, and who is really who—the result being you believe you are separate from the world. The Self "in here" appears to be something different from the not-Self "out there"—yet the truth is, *it's all you.*

CHAPTER 26

Fritz Lang's *Metropolis* and the Challenge Of A.I.

It may have been something of a commercial and critical flop on its release in 1927, but Fritz Lang's film *Metropolis* has since gone on to earn a place on the "best of" film lists from many critics around the world. While its highly theatrical acting may seem over-the-top to most contemporary audiences, its vision of a dystopian future continues to surprise even today for its pioneering special effects and imaginative depiction of a futuristic society. It was, in its own way, far ahead of its time.[1]

The film's story combines a number of interrelated themes, including morality, brotherhood, social justice, and still others. Yet Lang's film is perhaps most often analyzed these days for its critique of modern (and still-to-be) society, which depicts a world of extreme class divisions.

On the one hand, the film portrays a class of ultra-wealthy industrialists and their top employees living in luxurious settings aboveground, pursuing lives of hedonistic pleasures and trivial pursuits, while on the other hand we see the impoverished workers toiling away in their subterranean realm below. It was an obvious commentary on the growing inequality taking place in Lang's own time, but which he imagined becoming even more extreme and unjust in the years ahead.

In that respect, the movie follows in the footsteps of H.G. Wells famous story, *The Time Machine*, from nearly 30 years earlier. Wells' story likewise depicts a future of extreme social division where the childlike elite, or "Eloi," live in the world above while a disfigured class of sub-humans, the "Morlocks," exist below ground. Though it's remembered today mainly as an imaginative science fiction tale, for Wells it was actually a socialist critique of Victorian capitalist society projected far into the future, predicting an increasing division of society into upper and lower tiers of wealth and labor.[1]

But there is another, largely overlooked aspect of Lang's film that I want to focus on here, which makes Lang's futuristic depiction seem even more prophetic now. I'm referring to the fact that the film not only deals with the growing problems of class divisions, scientific progress, and big technology, but more specifically the increasing threat posed by artificial intelligence—or A.I.

In Lang's movie, that threat finds its embodiment in the form of a robot created by the mad scientist, Rotwang, who is sought out by the elite class and their "Masters." While the scientist originally created the robot to be a replacement for a lost love from his past, things take a very different turn when that robot—or *artificial intelligence*—is instead used to maintain control and manipulate the masses, in order to prevent a revolution.

As a way to make this robot more acceptable to those toiling masses, though, it is bestowed with the features of a beautiful and somewhat saintly commoner named Maria. In a scene that remains visually mind-blowing even today, the robot is transformed by the mad scientist from a purely metallic creation to a deceptively human-like "woman."

As I said, the purpose of the robotic "false Maria" becomes that of manipulating the masses. Her deceptive allures are considerable, and she manages to sew chaos and bring the workers and their children to the brink of catastrophe, resulting in the workers' city being largely destroyed by flooding.

Yet in the end, the faux-Maria is exposed for what "she" really is. In a scene reminiscent of the witch-persecutions of old, she's burned

Fritz Lang's Metropolis and the Challenge Of A.I.

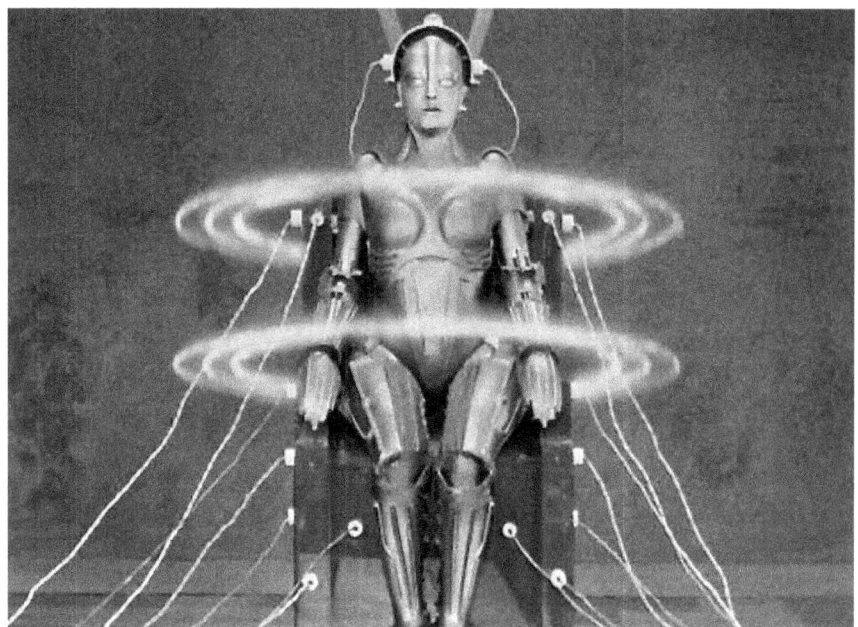

The robotic "faux-Maria" in the process of transforming into a (seeming) woman.

at the stake by the furious workers. The real Maria, meanwhile, becomes a savior to the workers by rescuing their children from the flood, and the movie concludes with a sequence depicting a reconciliation between the elites and the workers—a balancing of the "head" and the "hands" by means of *the heart*.

The symbolism and message of the robotic Maria seems an especially poignant one in light of current events in our own time. Consider that the film shows the masses being manipulated by this human-like form of artificial intelligence, which is all made possible by the fact that the robot is made to look alluring, even *sexy*—so much so, in fact, that even intelligent, full-blooded humans are taken in by her charms.

In an analogous way, the role of artificial intelligence in our own time is made appealing not just because of its functionality and usefulness—after all, A.I. makes modern life possible in virtually all aspects of life, from telephones and refrigeration all the way to our cars, credit cards and electrical grids, all depending on computers, either directly or indirectly.

No, it's also made appealing because of its tangible *beauty*—yes, beauty. I'm not just referring to how A.I. has given us art-generating programs like Midjourney and DALL-E 2, or to the sleek design of our smart phones, but to the mass appeal of CGI-laden blockbuster films, animated features, TV shows, commercials, Youtube videos, Tik Tok clips, and Instagram accounts—all of which are appealing and seductive in their own way, and which come to us by virtue of computers.

The end result of all this is a kind of modern-day "bread and circuses," a society of citizens hooked on and manipulated by A.I. in various forms, whether for recreational or practical purposes. Like the proverbial teenager staring into their phone for hours on end, we've surrendered our autonomy quite willingly, in a way that recalls Mark Crispin Miller's clever twist on George Orwell's famed catch phrase from his novel *1984*: "Big Brother is *you, watching!*" In the meantime, all of this activity leaves digital footprints that can be tracked and sold to the highest bidder, as more of our jobs become replaced by automated machines and sometimes even literal robots—and on it goes.

Not unlike the working masses in *Metropolis*, we have essentially been taken over by "robots," just as that artificial intelligence is simultaneously being used by the wealthy to control and manipulate us. In its own way, Fritz Lang's *Metropolis* pointed to all this way back in 1927.[2]

But there is a "punchline" here which I've saved until last, and that's this: although Lang's *Metropolis* was released in the 1920s, the movie's storyline was set a full century into the future from when it was created—specifically the year 2026.

In other words, the film's message is essentially directed towards those of us alive *in this decade right now*.

Fritz Lang's Metropolis and the Challenge Of A.I.

If you're like me, you'll find it fascinating that the film's narrative about extreme class division and the dangers of A.I. would have specifically pinpointed our own period as its focus, considering how pressing these concerns have actually become in recent years.

In light of the film's powerful resonance with future developments, it's worth noting the remarkable planetary energies at work around the time of its release. The year 1927 was significant not just because it was when Uranus moved into Aries; nor was it just because Uranus also happened to be conjuncting Jupiter at the time—a once-every-14-year aspect associated with cultural or "futuristic" breakthroughs of one sort or another. No, what's rarely mentioned—even in astrological circles—is that this important conjunction also happened to be aligned with the ultra-distant, super-slow-moving "minor planet" Eris. (We call it "minor," yet that planetoid is actually larger than Pluto!) That transformed an already potent conjunction into a *triple* conjunction of three slow-movers in the early degrees of Aries. To my mind, this simply amplifies the fact of 1927 being a "breakthrough" year in different areas—not just film but aviation, media, science, and others still unmentioned. (In cinema, incidentally, this year not only saw Fritz Lang's *Metropolis* but such other pivotal works as *The Jazz Singer*, F.W. Murnau's masterpiece *Sunrise*, Abel Ganz's *Napoleon*, and William A. Wellman's *Wings*. Cinematically, the so-called "Roaring 20s" were roaring quite loudly in 1927!)

So should we read Fritz Lang's remarkable prescience with *Metropolis* as nothing more than an interesting coincidence, or instead as a "prophetic synchronicity" of a sort, an omen, in which a cultural artifact somehow foreshadowed later developments? (Interesting, too, is the fact the disaster befalling the workers' city in Lang's film is one of *flooding*—just as our world is itself facing the threat of growing floods and rising sea levels due to global warming and melting icecaps.)

Either way, it's a bit of cinematic history I'd suggest is worth pondering very, very closely.[3]

So, What Am I Doing Here, Anyway?

Notes

1. Interestingly, H.G. Wells hated Lang's *Metropolis*. In a review penned for the *New York Times* shortly after the movie release, Wells wrote: "I have recently seen the silliest film. I do not believe it would be possible to make one sillier. It is called *Metropolis*, it comes from the great Ufa studios in Germany, and the public is given to understand that it has been produced at enormous cost. It gives in one eddying concentration almost every possible foolishness, cliché, platitude, and muddlement about mechanical progress and progress in general, served up with a sauce of sentimentality that is all its own." Considering that Wells was already considered something of a futurist and near-prophet during his time, it's hard not to wonder if some of that animosity might have been due to professional or artistic jealousy.

2. Some might point to Mary Shelley's *Frankenstein* as preceding Lang's film in warning of the dangers of A.I., yet the symbolism of the two narratives is distinctly different. Shelley's *Frankenstein* wasn't about robots or artificial intelligence so much as about resurrected life and a reconstructed "person." In Shelley's book, the monster's brain was still a human brain, not a cybernetic one.

3. In an earlier chapter, I discussed the curious way horoscopes seem to continue working even after their owners' deaths. The same principle seems to operate with *events* as well—Lang's *Metropolis* being one such example. Shortly after its release, the film's running time was severely cut by the studio and distributors, the result being that what audiences saw was just a pale shadow of Lang's original work. But to the delight of film lovers around the world, much of the film's original missing footage turned up in South America and a restored version of the film was finally re-released in 2009—on the film's Uranus return! As with the posthumous examples of individuals I looked at previously, we're forced to ask—if astrology indeed involves some sort of causal "force," what could it possibly be acting on here, when the subject in question isn't even a person but an event? (The same question could be posed in regard to the practice of horary astrology, where horoscopes are cast for the even more intangible phenomena of *questions*. One casts a horoscope for the time a question is asked—but what is being acted on *there*?) It does seem as though such events enjoy a tangible reality all their own, but more as "memes" in the cosmic mind than as biological entities.

CHAPTER 27

Stage Fright: Confronting Fears and Transmuting the Horoscope

I remember all too clearly the first time I gave a public talk. I was about 30 at the time. Only three people showed up, yet despite that small number I felt like my heart was going to explode. I'd been nervously anticipating the occasion for weeks, and almost cancelled the class the morning of the talk due to my mounting nervousness. I managed to get through it, fortunately, concealing my fear as best I could, but when I went home that day I collapsed from exhaustion, feeling like I'd just finished climbing Everest without the aid of oxygen.

Whenever I'd come across formal polls showing how so many people rated the fear of public speaking as being equal to or even greater than the fear of dying, I understood that. It was my greatest phobia for years, and something I harbored enormous shame about, since it seemed like such an obvious weakness. It looked like such a natural and easy thing for various friends and associates to do, that I simply couldn't understand why it would be so difficult for me.

That case of social anxiety held me back in many areas besides just lecturing or teaching. Going to parties back then was practically a fate worse than death. In my 20s I'd become a fairly good guitarist, to the point where I was asked on a number of occasions to join one band or another, yet each time I'd simply wind up making excuses for declining, agreeing to play only on recordings done in studios on occasion for some local group or performer.

So when a close friend suggested I struck them as being on the (autistic) "spectrum," I couldn't help but think he was on to something.

Because this was such a monkey on my back, it haunted me for years. I felt like I had to at least *try* to overcome it, even if the prospect of facing up to the challenge struck terror in my heart. Even more terrifying, though, was the prospect of going to my grave with this problem hanging over my head, still unresolved.

I finally took the plunge of attending a public speaking class in downtown Chicago, which proved difficult but it moved the needle a little. I also used self-hypnosis and affirmations for several years, which also made a dent. After that first small talk to those three people I mentioned, I continued to give talks to a few other small groups.

But strangely enough, the real turning point for me came from a most unexpected source: watching an actress being interviewed on a TV talk show.

Actress Barbara Hershey was a guest on the "The Tonight Show" plugging a movie she was appearing in at the time, and was speaking with Johnny Carson about the paradox of performers like themselves often being so outgoing in public yet so shy in private.

At one point, Barbara interjected, "You know, Johnny, I think that shyness is really just a form of self-centeredness."

Obviously taken aback by that comment, Johnny asked her to explain what she meant. She went on to suggest that shy people tend to focus too much on themselves, and it's that fixation on themselves which often causes them to be so fearful and timid.

Whoa… That was an eye-opener, since I knew she was largely right. Sure, there was more to stage fright than *just* that for some people, such as hyper-sensitivity to stimuli, the after-effects of early trauma, or other factors.

But for many of us, it really does come down to that concern of, "What are these people going to think about *me*? How are they going to judge *me*?"

To a large extent, in other words, it's a matter of ego—not ego in the sense of "I'm so great!" but more in terms of that narcissistic focus on oneself. As the teacher in that early public speaking class said to us one day, when talking about that fear, "What makes you think those people out there in the audience are really that concerned about *you*?"

Many decades later I heard something that struck a very similar chord for me—this one also from a most unlikely source: professional boxer Mike Tyson. Someone asked him about being on the receiving end of harsh criticism many times, and whether that was hard for him to deal with. His response was very wise—and surprisingly Zen:

"You know, when I think I'm somebody, I'm really offended by it. But when I remember I'm nobody, it's okay."

That says it all, really. Here as well, it comes down to that principle of self-importance. When I think I'm really special or important, the smallest criticism or judgment hurts; but if I remember that I'm really no one special, then it's not such a big deal if those people sitting out there don't like me or what I'm saying.

That early fear of being exposed as some sort of failure or imperfect creature started lessening when I began letting go of that attachment to "self." When I'd get up to present a talk, I made a concerted effort to focus more on the audience, or on the subject at hand, but far less on "ME!"

So, What Am I Doing Here, Anyway?

Simply getting more experience under my belt doing talks made a big difference, too, of course. I became certified as a yoga teacher at one point and taught that to small groups for years (which was especially helpful back in early days since it allowed me to talk with my back to the students much of the time, while demonstrating poses). I also taught an evening class at a local community college for two years (the College of DuPage), which was an experimental course I called "New Directions in Modern Thought." Things took an unexpected turn when I moved to Arizona for a while and wound up teaching classes for celebrities and wealthy guests at a resort called Canyon Ranch. While there was still some residual nervousness involved during much of this, the experience became easier over time. Most important of all, I was learning how to *relax*.

As a result of all this, I became reasonably good at public speaking, at least judging from the feedback I received. While there's much room for improvement, it's generally something I feel comfortable doing now, something I couldn't have even imagined happening back in my twenties. I'd be remiss not to mention that another key step in this process for me was always making sure I fully understood the material at hand—inside and out, almost to the point of over-preparing for talks. That allowed me to talk more casually and extemporaneously about the subject I was dealing with. That way I wouldn't be nearly as worried about stumbling over facts or losing my way. To this day I still often use a rough outline to help guide my way, but I *never* deliver lectures in a word-for-word manner from precisely written notes. To my mind, that is the kiss of death for any good presentation.

So it naturally raises the question: what is it in my horoscope that accounts for this?

While there are a number of horoscopic patterns that can relate to stage fright like I've described here, here, in my case I chalk it up to one in particular: a Saturn-Moon-Neptune conjunction in Libra, positioned largely in my 1st house at the focal point of a t-square. (I

Stage Fright: Confronting Fears and Transmuting the Horoscope

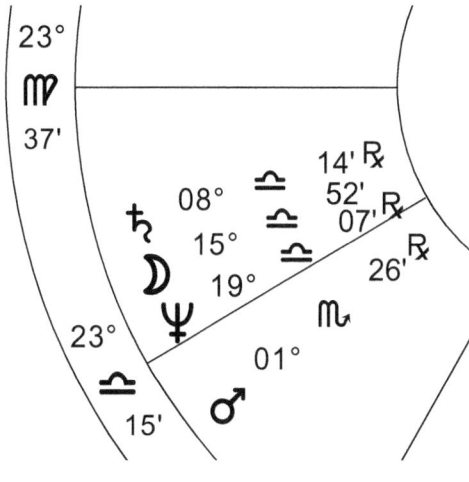

say "largely because the Neptune end of that Libra trifecta bleeds over into my 2nd house, by Placidus house standards.)

For the uninitiated, a configuration like that can be an especially challenging one in terms of social interactions and general self-presentation. That's particularly true during one's youth, due to the fact that the Moon and the 1st house are involved (both of which tend to be especially influential during one's early years). The net result is that it can make one's early years an emotional hellscape as far as dealing with public gatherings of any sort.

Yet that configuration also has certain potential silver linings, and they're important to understand.

One of those is the "late bloomer" dynamic I've touched on earlier, related to the heavy influence of Saturn in that configuration; while another involves the creative gifts that a configuration like that can bring due to the artistic potentials of Neptune and the Moon in Libra. But the key "silver lining" I want to call attention to here is a subtler one, not nearly as obvious to the casual eye.

I mentioned earlier in this book is how the most difficult pattern in someone's chart—for example, the closest square or opposition—can sometimes point to one's greatest potentials as well. The reason is that the sheer energy and attention required to contend with that problem can eventually lead to mastery of that area, presuming one responds to it constructively, of course.

So, What Am I Doing Here, Anyway?

I'm reminded of a Jungian psychologist I once heard who suggested that our greatest fears in childhood sometimes hold clues to our greatest potentials as adults. As he put it, it may simply be that the latent potential inside of us is simply too great for our youthful personality to contain; so instead of feeling comfortable with those potentials, he explained, we respond with terror, we're overwhelmed by the enormity of those energies. (Using his logic, in other words, for someone to whom being successful on stage didn't matter in the slightest, fear of failure might not be nearly as big a problem.)

One's biggest fears, in other words, sometimes are the doorways to our biggest achievements. Fascinating way to look at it, I thought—and it tied in closely with how I began looking at my own horoscope.

It also reminded me of a story I once read concerning the ancient figure Demosthenes, someone I've often referred to in lectures and writings. According to the Greek historian Plutarch, Demosthenes was criticized early on by his peers for his problems speaking in public, among them being an "inarticulate and stammering pronunciation." This prompted him to work especially hard at overcoming those shortcomings, which included going off to the seashore to shout into the surf as a way to develop projection, and trying to speak with pebbles in his mouth as a way to develop better diction. As a result of those efforts, along with others, Plutarch says, he eventually became acclaimed as one of ancient Greek's greatest orators. It's a classic late bloomer story, and offers a good illustration for how one's greatest challenge can sometimes become one's greatest talent.

While I may not go down as one of "history's greatest orators," that isn't the point. I was able to finally deal with those fears, and in so doing, "transcend (actually, *transmute*) my chart"—and that's good enough for me.

CHAPTER 28

The "Jazz Band" Principle and the Aquarian Age

In various books and articles over the years I've written about the significance of jazz as one of the key symbols for the historical period we're entering. When my colleague Michael O'Reilly asked if I'd sum that up for a short article to be posted on his astrological website Neptune Café, I drew together and distilled material from all my earlier sources to produce this short piece. —R.G.

If I were asked to sum up the difference between the Piscean and Aquarian Ages as simply as possible, I'd point to the difference between an old-time Gregorian choir and a modern-day jazz band.

In a Gregorian choir, all the members surrender their personal creativity and individuality in service of a greater ideal, while in a jazz band each member is actually *encouraged* to express their individual creativity, in a way that not only maintains but enhances the vitality of the larger group.

Under the influence of Christianity and Islam over the last two thousand years, the role of the individual was seen as largely subservient to God or to religious authorities. During the emerging Aquarian Age, we're seeing a greater emphasis on personal worth and autonomy, yet with each person's voice in the cosmic choir seen as having an importance all its own—all within a decidedly more secular rather than religious context.

So, What Am I Doing Here, Anyway?

Here as well, we're seeing the influence of the Leo/Aquarius polarity at work, with the spark of Leonine creativity filtering through the social collective. Both Pisces and Aquarius are "group" signs, relating to larger masses of people; but in the case of Aquarius, as with the jazz band, each individual is potentially able to contribute something of worth to the collective, whether that be in terms of creativity, science, politics or social activism.

This shift has already been expressing itself across a broad range of areas, as in the growing influence of democracy around the world—democracy expressing jazz principle *par excellence*. This has had its most visible proponent in the United States, which emerged as a political force in the late 1700s—almost exactly coinciding with the discovery of Uranus, the modern ruler of Aquarius.

I've often suggested that the United States can be seen as the spearhead of the emerging Aquarian Age—for both better and worse. Jazz has often been called the one truly American art form, and not surprisingly, the U.S.A. is itself based upon the jazz model, viewed symbolically.

Think about it: the United States is a conglomeration of fifty states, all of them following the same basic "sheet music" of the Constitution, yet with all those states being allowed a certain creative latitude in improvising their own creative visions for its citizens. In turn, the President is to those fifty states and their governors what Louis Armstrong or Duke Ellington were to their jazz ensembles, spearheading the collectives while allowing each member to make its contribution to the mix.

That delicate tension between the federal government and individual states reflects precisely the same tension that exists within any jazz ensemble, as well as in the sign of Aquarius itself, with its precarious dance between strict individualism and "We the People" group consciousness. I've sometimes been asked, "Does Aquarius rule groups, or the individual?" In fact, it's both.

The "Jazz Band" Principle and the Aquarian Age

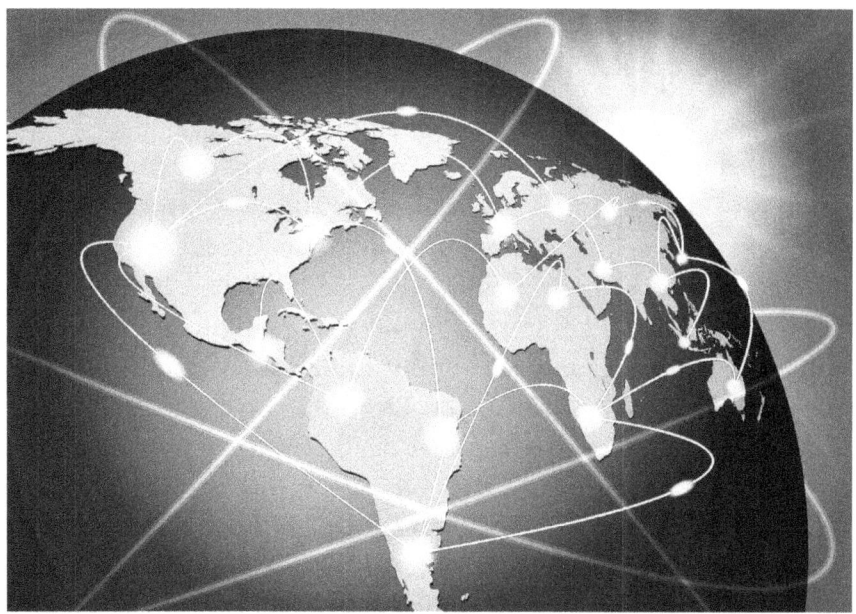

Image: Shutterstock

Aquarius is best understood as the creative tension *between* those two extremes.

Nor is it just in music or politics where we find this archetypal dynamic in play. This is the same essential dynamic underlying modern phenomena like the Internet, where separate individuals interact with one another similar to members of a jazz ensemble, with each person offering their own personalized input and no one person tightly dictating those interactions. (Who owns or "runs" the Internet, for example?)

And it's also apparent in the model of employee-owned businesses, where each worker has a say in the running of a company. It's also the underlying principle of corporate think tanks, where individuals pool their ideas rather than everything being decided by a single innovator or leader. Thomas Edison's workshop was a perfect expression of the "jazz" dynamic; he essentially played the role of a band leader to a selected group of unique innovators, each of whom contributed their own ideas to the group's output.

In a way I find particularly fascinating, the jazz model is even embedded in some of the popular mythologies of our times—most notably L. Frank Baum's *The Wizard of Oz*. This tale features a classic "heroic" quest, with Dorothy and her companions setting out to find the answers to their pressing life-queries. Whereas the mythic tales of old generally centered around a single figure on their own heroic quest, or a group setting out to find a common goal such as the Holy Grail or the Golden Fleece, Baum's story features a group of *totally different beings, each one seeking something completely different*. One wants a heart; another a brain; another hopes to find courage; while Dorothy just wants to get home. Despite those differences, they're somehow able to harmonize and coordinate their respective quests—not unlike how diverse figures in a jazz ensemble coordinate their respective creative voices towards creating something above and beyond any one of their goals.

In yet another "Aquarian" touch, there's also this: the story shows them all traveling together to the fabled city of Oz in hope that the great and powerful Wizard might grant them these boons. But rather than discovering that the answer to their quests lies in some external wizard, they discover what they had sought all along actually resided much closer to home. As the Good Witch says, "The answer to your journey has always been *within* you!"

Symbolically, that's telling us that in our own spiritual journey, the external "wizard" (i.e., God, guru, religious authorities) must ultimately be set aside in order to awaken the God *within*, to realize our role not just as God's children but as divine co-creators. In his late book *Answer to Job*, Psychologist Carl Jung referred to this process as the "Christification of many." In *Masks of God, Volume 4: Creative Mythology*, Joseph Campbell described it this way:

"Just as in the past each civilization was the vehicle of its own mythology…so in this modern world––where the application of science to the fields of practical life has now dissolved all cultural horizons, so that no separate civilization can ever develop again—each individual is the center of a mythology of his own, of which his own intelligible character is the Incarnate God, so to say, whom his empirically questing consciousness is to find. The aphorism of Delphi, 'Know thyself,' is the motto. And not Rome, not Mecca, not Jerusalem, Sinai, or Benares, but *each and every 'thou' on earth is the center of this world....*" [1] (emphasis mine)

What could be more Aquarian, really?

Notes

1. Campbell, Joseph. *The Masks of God, Vol. 4: Creative Mythology* (New York: Viking Press), 1968, p.36.

CHAPTER 29

Planting Seeds: Seeing the Long-Term Impact of Transiting Conjunctions

It's probably a sign of my own arrogance that I find myself shaking my head at the mistakes I sometimes see experienced colleagues making about interpretations I'd assume we'd all know better about by now.

One of the biggest of those involves failing to understand the long-range effects of transiting conjunctions, whether those occur in personal charts or mundane (socio-political) horoscopes. Let me explain what I mean.

Transiting planetary conjunctions are what might be called "seed-planting" times that inaugurate much large arcs of unfoldment. As I've mentioned on a number of occasions, they have a "New Moon" quality about them, recalling the old axiom of "What the New Moon promises, the Full Moon delivers." (In fact, a New Moon is itself a conjunction, involving just the Sun and the Moon.) The key here is that the *full impact* of any transiting conjunction won't be felt for quite some time after the actual conjunction itself.

For example, suppose you see a transiting Uranus coming along and conjuncting someone's Sun. Sure, you will see some important things happening around the time of that conjunction; but that transiting conjunction is just the start of a much larger phase. True, those initial events will provide important clues as to what lies ahead— omens, sneak previews, call them whatever you like—but

Planting Seeds: Seeing the Long-Term Impact of Transiting Conjunctions

it's decidedly not when the *entire impact* of that conjunction will take place. Indeed, in the case of a slow-moving planet like Uranus, the implications of that conjunction for that person could unfold over many months or even years.

Despite that, on countless occasions I've seen astrologers express confusion or even disappointment when they don't see something major happening right at the time of the transiting conjunction itself. Or, they'll see something significant happening but with little if any thought given to the longer-term implications involved. Here are a few examples of what I'm talking about, on both the personal and collective levels.

1. Saturn Return in the Personal Chart

The first return of transiting Saturn to its place in the natal chart happens to all of us in our late 20s, and typically ushers in a time of deepening reflection, a reexamination of priorities, and often a restructuring of life-goals.

Many times, though, clients or colleagues have expressed surprise at how *un*-dramatic the developments around that return seemed to be, beyond that general mood of reflection and heightened seriousness. There can be changes, yes but they're generally not of the magnitude many expected based on the popular reputation of the dreaded *"Saturn return!"*

The reason for that is simple: the return of Saturn to its "birthplace" is really a time when one is *laying the foundations for the future*—or, as some put it, a time when one is setting the things of childhood aside to start becoming an adult. It's probably the most iconic "seed-planting" time of life when the first signs of a broader life-change are taking place, but which may actually take months or years to manifest.

Take my own case. My first Saturn return (in Libra) was a time of enormous uncertainty, when I was straddling between life-chapters. I was shifting from a life devoted almost entirely to the arts to one devoted mainly to writing. But whereas my first attempts at writing began around age 28, smack dab in the midst of that return, it would be a full decade before I had my first article published. Looking back now, it's all perfectly clear how the events of that period fit together, but at the time I couldn't really grasp that, which made it a painfully confusing period for me.

Similarly, I've spoken to many others through the years who felt they could only recognize the meaning of their first return long after—sometimes not even until their *second* Saturn return! As I said, there will undoubtedly be important clues surfacing around that first return, when the proverbial first "shoots of change" start popping up, but it takes real discernment and foresight to recognize what those will eventually look like when fully grown.

2. The Uranus and Neptune Conjunction of 1993

The outer planets Uranus and Neptune only come together once every 170 years or so, so when those two bodies began inching towards an exact conjunction during the early 1990s, astrologers everywhere began looking forward to the event with anticipation. But when 1993 came and went with relatively little to show for it, there was some confusion as to the meaning of that epic conjunction.

In fact, it *was* a period of profound change, but many of those changes only became fully apparent in the years afterward. Some of those were more cultural in nature, such as advances in special effects and CGI with films like *Jurassic Park* in 1993 or computer gaming technology; or the rise of "World Music," which started gaining momentum in the late 1980s and peaked throughout the 1990s.

But arguably the two most important changes during that period were the full-blown rise of the Internet and the activation of the Hubble telescope, both of which profoundly impacted how we see

Planting Seeds: Seeing the Long-Term Impact of Transiting Conjunctions

The Hubble Telescope, activated in 1993. (Photo: NASA)

the world. Prior to 1993 and 1994, few people had heard of either the Internet or "e-mail," yet now they're both fixtures of everyone's life, with enormous consequences for the world's economy as well. On the other hand, the Hubble Telescope may not have had as big a practical impact on our lives, but philosophically it has permanently changed our view of the universe and our place in it.[1]

3. The Long-Range Impact of Stelliums (Multiple-Planet Conjunctions)

When only two planets come together, like Uranus and Neptune, it makes for a simple conjunction. But when a *number* of planets come together in close proximity, we call it a "stellium"—a *super-conjunction*, as it were.

I've written elsewhere about one such stellium that occurred in 1524 in the (tropical) sign of Pisces, when astrologers and mystics around Europe predicted an onslaught of floods and disasters that could possibly herald the end of the world.[2] Well, no such flood

205

took place—or at least not at that time, and certainly not a literal one. Yet a huge "flood" *did* take place, one that *did* change the face of our planet—but it was religious (and Piscean) in nature, and took place over a series of decades. I'm referring to the fact that in the years which followed that stellium, the Protestant Reformation occurred and brought about a profound change in the religious landscape of not just Europe but the entire world.

Likewise, early February of 1962 witnessed a hugely important line-up of planets in the tropical sign Aquarius. There was little at the time to indicate just how big a tectonic shift this really portended; yet when one broadens one's focus out a bit, one begins to glimpse just how important it was—while setting the stage for the revolutionary Uranus-Pluto conjunction climaxing several years later. On a purely cultural level, 1962 was a year when important seeds were planted for later years in the form of iconic figures like Bob Dylan, the Rolling Stones, the Beatles, and Andy Warhol—all of whom either started their careers then or experienced career-defining milestones that year. On a more political level, it was later that year when the world nearly ended in an atomic conflagration, as a result of the Cuban Missile Crisis.

Another highly significant planetary line-up occurred in the year 2000, when a series of planets congregated close to one another in the (tropical) sign of Taurus. As with both the 1524 stellium and the Uranus-Neptune conjunction of 1993, great anticipation had been building as to what this might bring. Earthquakes? New forms of energy? A spiritual revolution? Perhaps even contact with extraterrestrials?

In fact, the stellium didn't result in anything very earth-shaking, at least not to the passing observer. Some astrologers were even a little embarrassed by what had taken place—or *didn't* take place, as the case may be, since the build-up and anticipation had been so great. But those astrologers were simply fixating too closely on the actual days surrounding the conjunction, not their possible long-term effects. In my book *Signs of the Times* (finished in early 2000 but due to production delays not released until early 2002), I spoke about the stellium but with an eye to those events around the line-up as "omens" to the future. In addition to pointing to potential terrorist threats from figures like Osama bin Laden, I mentioned an overseas election that had taken place the very same week as the line-up:

> "To understand the 'revolutionary' effects of major planetary lineups like this, it's helpful to recall the astronomical connotations of this word. A celestial body is said to make a full 'revolution' each time it rotates completely on its axis or every time it comes back to its 'home' point during a larger orbit. In other words, it's about something coming full circle, an old order is dying off and a new one starting up. This certainly describes the events surrounding the period of the May line-up. For instance, *on May 7, Russia's leadership saw the beginning of a new political era with the inauguration of Vladimir Putin as president. Considering the proximity of this event to the lineup, it will be interesting to see what impact this former KGB spy eventually has on Russian and world politics.*" (Emphasis added.) [3]

Needless to say, it's fairly clear now just how consequential that election really had been, although its consequences were not clear much at all back in May 2000.

4. The Long-Term Effects of Solar Eclipses

Eclipses have long been considered one of the most important celestial triggers in virtually all astrological systems, be those East or West, modern or traditional. Where eclipses fall in horoscopes, whether personal or national, are seen as significant areas of change, where old chapters are closing off and new ones are opening up.

Yet as one student said to me, "If that's really true, then why do I see so few real-world effects happening when eclipses fire in my chart?" To some extent, that hinges on how close the eclipse lands to any personal planets (or horoscopic angles) in one's chart, which can impact their intensity enormously.

But it also ties in to what I said earlier—about the "New Moon effect" of all transiting conjunctions. Remember, New Moons are conjunctions, yet their effects don't manifest right away and often culminate around the time of the following Full Moons. Well, solar eclipses can be thought of as high-powered "New Moons," when those two luminaries don't simply align near one another but become *exactly* conjunct, causing the effects (and duration) of that Sun-Moon linkage to be amplified many times over. As a result, the effects of solar eclipses can linger for months, sometimes even years beyond the conjunction itself.

Is there some way to tell *when* those effects will actually manifest? Like any New Moon, the very earliest effects can sometimes be soon, within the first couple of weeks. But as for the *full* effects, those may be triggered over subsequent months by transiting Mars or Sun squares, oppositions, or conjunctions to that eclipse point. In fact, I've found that any energetic aspect by the heavier planets (Saturn, Uranus, Neptune, or Pluto) can serve as triggers to the latent potentials of the eclipse—sometimes even years later.

An especially dramatic example illustrating the long-term impact of not just solar eclipses but multi-planet stelliums involves no less than the JFK assassination, which occurred in the wake of a rare combination involving those two astro-triggers. That is, precisely when the Aquarius stellium of early 1962 took place, there was also a solar eclipse occurring right in its midst—a celestial combination the likes of which I've not encountered again in my lifetime.

As mentioned above, various pop cultural figures saw major developments in their careers in the weeks or months following that double-trigger; then came the anxieties of the Cuban Missile Crisis later that fall. But the real bombshell happened that next year, when President John F. Kennedy was shot in Texas, on

Planting Seeds: Seeing the Long-Term Impact of Transiting Conjunctions

November 22, 1963—which took place just as transiting planets were triggering the planetary placements of that earlier stellium.[4] Looking back, JFK's violent end now almost seems like the opening salvo in the cultural revolution which characterized that entire decade, all amplified by the Uranus-Pluto conjunction climaxing several years later. (Also note that solar eclipses literally represent a blotting out of the Sun's light—and JFK's assassination saw the blotting out of the light of a prominent "solar" figure in the world.)

5. The United States' Pluto Return

Finally, let's look at a planetary event that has been on the minds of many astrologers, especially here in America. I began here by talking about Saturn returns in the charts of individuals; but planetary returns occur in the horoscopes of nations and countries as well.

The most conspicuous one from recent times has been the much-ballyhooed "Pluto return" for the United States, when this distant planet circles back around to where it was at the time of this nation's founding in July 1776. According to one set of calculations (referred to by astrologers as "non-precessed corrected" measurements), this return first became exact in 2022; while according to another set of calculations (technically called "precessed-corrected"), its exact trigger point is in 2024. As I will make clear, though, the exact date may be less important since its effects actually extend well beyond either of those years.

As of this writing, I've already encountered astrologers who feel this planetary event has been relatively uneventful thus far. (I'd point out that that the attempted violent overthrow of the U.S. government is actually pretty eventful—but I digress.) But when you're talking about a planetary cycle that lasts over 240 years, its effects can't really be limited to a mere twelve or twenty-four-month period.

So, What Am I Doing Here, Anyway?

If there's any one lesson to be drawn from the Pluto returns of nations like England or ancient Rome, the effects of this return will be unfolding for decades after its first exact triggers. Just consider the example of England's second Pluto return, which coincided with the rise of Elizabeth I to the throne. Her reign inaugurated the entire "Golden Age" of Elizabethan England, a period which accompanied the emergence of figures like William Shakespeare, Christopher Marlowe, and occultist John Dee, among others—all of which unfolded years after the exact point of Pluto's return.

Applying such a forward-looking perspective to the U.S. Pluto return, I've suggested that we can safely forecast a period ahead of growing controversy over issues like abortion rights, social inequality, civil unrest bordering on Civil War, the growing threat of autocracy, among others. But in the 2019 article I wrote for *The Mountain Astrologer* about the U.S. Pluto return, I concluded by suggesting that one of the key manifestations of a nation's Pluto return involves facing up to that country's "shadow" energies, and having to confront unresolved issues from the past. So what Plutonian "darkness" from America's past will on the table for America throughout this entire period? I wrote:

> "It seems clear that, on one level anyway, it's similar to that of England during the early 1800s (during its third Pluto return)—namely, confronting the legacy of slavery. America was built upon it, the nation's economy thrived because of it, and while the institution itself was officially discontinued, we're still coming to terms with its legacy and all it implied—racism, bigotry, greed. Slavery and racism have long been a stain on the nation's soul, and though we've tried hard to deny that history, it's becoming increasingly hard to avoid.

Nor is this impending challenge solely about America's black population. The Pluto return also seems related to our national discussion around minorities in general, and our culture's uneasy relationship with Muslims, Native Americans, Asian Americans,

Latinos, and the LGBTQ community. Previously repressed elements of our population (including women) now seem poised to make their voices heard in ways like never before, something which became especially evident in the latest U.S. mid-term elections. The influence of Pluto is also apparent in our national debate over immigration and the ongoing crisis involving Mexican and Central American refugees at our southern border. [5]

Further complicating things is the fact that during this same decade, the U.S. will be experiencing *yet another* planetary return—this one involving Uranus. That is set to trigger exactly in 2027 and 2028 but with an orb of influence easily extending a number of years in either direction. Based on America's previous two Uranus returns (the first in the mid-1860s, the second during the 1940s), this one also promises to be powerful, especially piggybacking on the already revolutionary Pluto return. Could be a whole lotta shakin' going on, as a famous rock-and-roller once put it.

I'd suggest keeping all these points in mind in the years ahead, as the seeds planted by these two planetary returns continue to impact the lives of U.S. citizens, and possibly those across the planet.

Notes:

1. There has been a long-term dynamic surrounding the launching of the James Webb Telescope and its associated astrology similar to that of the Hubble Telescope during the 1990s. In my essay "Our Expanding Universe—Within and Without: The Jupiter–Neptune Conjunction and the James Webb Telescope," I discussed the Jupiter-Neptune conjunction that took place in April 2022 and how it might relate to the impact of the James Webb Space Telescope. Though launched on Christmas Day 2021, it wouldn't become fully active until several months later in the summer of 2022. As with the Hubble Telescope and the Uranus-Neptune conjunction back in 1993, I suggested there might be similar long-term effects with the JWST as far as expanding humanity's cosmological imagination over the ensuing years. Already, that seems to be taking place, as ultra-distant findings about distant galaxies from the telescope

So, What Am I Doing Here, Anyway?

are forcing astronomers to reconsider long-held notions about the age of the universe. (See "When the Stars Align," chapter 15, but originally posted on the Mountain Astrologer website, 4/6/2022, here:

https://mountainastrologer.com/our-expanding-universe-within-and-without-the-jupiter-neptune-conjunction-and-the-james-webb-telescope/)

2. "Wheels of Change: Stelliums, Mundane Astrology, and the Art of the Big Picture," from my book *Under a Sacred Sky: Essays on the Practice and Philosophy of Astrology* (chapter 12); The Wessex Astrologer Ltd., Swanage, England, 2015. (Posted online here: www.astro.com/astrology/tma_article141007_e.htm)

3. *Signs of the Times: Unlocking the Symbolic Language of World Events,* Hampton Roads, Virginia, 2002. See Appendix III.

4. Among those triggers at the time of JFK's death were these: transiting Saturn was closely conjuncting Venus, Mercury and the Moon in that earlier stellium; transiting Moon had returned to the sign it occupied back on February 5, 1962, thus signaling a "lunar return"; transiting Sun was closely squaring Uranus in the 1962 horoscope; transiting Uranus was conjuncting the 1962 Pluto; transiting Neptune was closely squaring the 1962 eclipse degree; and significantly, when JFK died the planets of the 1962 stellium were crossing over the Ascendant in Dallas, Texas.

5. First published in *The Mountain Astrologer* magazine, Nov/Dec 2019, also included in my book *StarGates: Essays on Astrology, Symbolism, and the Synchronistic Universe,* chapter 23. (Also posted online by Astrodienst, here: www.astro.com/astrology/tma_article210208_e.htm)

CHAPTER 30

One More Thing About the Sixties: Bigfoot and the Patterson-Gimlin Footage

As the story goes, the two men were traveling on horseback through an area of California called Bluff Creek, when they spotted a large dark figure in a nearby creek bed. While his partner Bob Gimlin remained atop his horse, Roger Patterson climbed down, grabbed the movie camera he had with him and proceeded to film the creature as it lumbered off into the woods—and into history.

To this day, the footage remains a source of heated debate, but despite repeated claims by skeptics of possible hoaxing, it's important to note that no one has ever successfully reproduced the appearance of that creature on film in a fully convincing way.

Whatever one's opinion about the footage—or even the reality of the creature itself—all parties agree it was a turning point in our modern fascination with this creature. For that reason, the iconic footage represents a synchro-Fortean event of the highest order.

Taking a more symbolic approach to that footage, we could begin by looking at it strictly in terms of its imagery, as if examining someone's dream symbols. In my book *The Waking Dream*, I suggested that the

213

events in our daily lives can be read as synchronistic reflections of our own unfolding consciousness, much in the way that our nightly dreams do. For some mystics, however, events on the world stage hold a similar significance but in a more collective way. "It is a vast dream, dreamed by a single being," Schopenhauer wrote, "but in such a way that all the dream characters dream too."[1] For our purposes, the "reality" or "unreality" of the creature filmed by Roger Patterson is of less importance, since we'll be looking at it in terms of what its appearance meant as an emerging symbol within the mass consciousness of the time, as a phenomenon within the *collective dream*.

The Phenomenology of Bigfoot

The creature in this footage is obviously wild and untamed, halfway between human and animal, straddling the threshold between organized civilization and raw nature. It's entirely naked and covered with fur, yet it stands upright and walks like a human. Its muscular figure conveys a sense of enormous power—yet it displays female breasts!

Viewed as a collective dream symbol, the appearance of this creature in 1967 signaled something primal surfacing from the "wilds" of the collective unconscious, an energy that's paradoxically both ancient and new. The figure embodies great power, yet its feminine gender hints at a consciousness that is more right-brain and intuitive than anything purely aggressive or animalistic. It personifies a consciousness midway between ordered civilization and untamed nature, betwixt pure rationality and raw emotional impulses.

With those points in mind, let's take a moment to adopt what Carl Jung called a Chinese "field thinking" approach and consider what other socio-cultural developments were taking place around that encounter, to see if anything stands out which might illuminate the symbolism I'm suggesting here. When I went back and carefully examined the historical record from that era, I came across a number of events that not only seemed relevant, but at times synchronistically uncanny:

* Two days before the Patterson-Gimlin encounter, on October 18, Disney Studios released the popular animated feature *The Jungle Book*. The film's scenario revolves around a boy raised by animals in the wild, and follows his escapades as he mingles on the threshold between nature and civilization, between life in the wild and domesticated village life.

* One day before that, on October 17, the enormously successful musical "Hair" premiered on Broadway. This long-running production was embraced by fans as a celebration of personal freedom and Dionysian self-expression, but was derided by some conservative critics as promoting amorality and regressive values. The musical's title itself hints at how the hippies at the show's core shunned the neatly groomed fashions of mainstream society in favor of wilder, more "natural" looks. The musical became especially controversial for a scene in which all the cast members appeared on stage fully naked.

* Less than a week earlier, on October 12, Desmond Morris's bestselling book *The Naked Ape* was released, a popularized attempt to frame human nature in the context of Darwinian evolution. It suggested that we need to view humans as just one animal species among many, and tried to explain our behaviors in light of those exhibited by our mammalian kin. The book's title came from the fact that out of 193 species of monkey and apes, humans are the only ones not fully covered in hair.

* Three weeks after the Patterson-Gimlin encounter, the conventional Bible of the rock-and roll counterculture, *Rolling Stone*, premiered. (November 9 was the cover date on the first issue, but as is common practice in the publishing industry, it appeared on newsstands earlier.) Contrasted with publications like the ultra-conservative Wall Street Journal with that paper's embrace of

short haircuts, business suits, and "square" values, Rolling Stone celebrated much the same ideals as the musical "Hair": alternate lifestyles, long hair, music, and Dionysian self-expression.

* The human/primate interface was a surprisingly popular meme in all the arts throughout this period. Several months after the P-G incident, on February 8, 1968, the first in the hugely successful *Planet of the Apes* film franchise premiered, centering around a society of unusually intelligent apes; while 1967 saw the peak popularity of the TV show *The Monkees*, showcasing a group of long-haired Beatle imitators (and whose records actually outsold both the Beatles and the Rolling Stones that year), with episodes frequently picturing the actors alongside images of actual or stuffed monkeys.

* Another way that the counter-cultural impulses of the period were making their presence felt was through the burgeoning protest movement, with ordinary citizens rallying to express their anger over governmental policies—a development some commentators at the time described as "the awakening of a sleeping giant." With that in mind, it's worth noting that one day after the Patterson-Gimlin encounter, a historic march in Washington, D.C. took place, with tens of thousands of citizens lining the streets of the nation's capital to protest America's involvement in the Vietnam War. As clearly as any other event from that period, that march embodied the grassroots energies of the 1960s rising to the surface in a dramatic way.

Putting all of these pieces together, the picture which starts to emerge is that of a powerful force welling up in the collective psyche—a force simultaneously rooted in the intuitive-emotional aspects of human nature as well as our more rational faculties. After all, developments like "Hair," *The Jungle Book*, *Rolling Stone*, and the march on Washington weren't simply expressions of Dionysian abandon and unbridled anarchy; in each case, their execution all involved considerable forethought and intelligence.

One More Thing About the Sixties: Bigfoot and the Patterson-Gimlin Footage

Just consider the 1960s, and all the countercultural forces coming to light at the time: people were shedding their conservative fashions and adopting wilder, more uninhibited appearances. The Back-To-Nature movement was on the rise, with 1967 ushering in the "Summer of Love" and "Flower Power." The Beatles released "Sgt. Pepper" that year. There was a general sense of heightened creativity in the air, as people from various walks of life woke up to the possibility of becoming forces for change in the world, whether as grass-roots activists or as celebrities and rock stars.

Yet alongside all this was a palpable sense of danger and potential violence, as all these pent-up energies were being unleashed, as reflected not just in protest movements, big city riots, or the Vietnam War, but even in the arts. One month before the Patterson-Gimlin encounter, on September 17, The Doors courted controversy by appearing on the Ed Sullivan show with frontman Jim Morrison singing a drug-related lyric in defiance of the host's wishes; that same night The Who destroyed their instruments while performing on The Smothers Brothers Comedy Hour, climaxing in an unexpectedly jarring explosion of Keith Moon's drum kit; while several months earlier, a relative unknown named Jimi Hendrix shocked audience members at the Monterey Pop Festival in California by dry-humping his amplifier and setting fire to his prized guitar. Wild thing, indeed.

In this context, the first major film appearance of an alleged Bigfoot now seems like an apt symbol for the entire period. Midway between human and animal, this creature mirrored a powerful instinctual energy surging forth through the collective, yet one coupled with a newly awakened sense of individuality and independent thought. Remember, this wasn't simply a beast, but an apparently intelligent creature who walked upright like ourselves. Similarly, people of that time were trying to juggle starkly polarized energies in themselves, born from that divide between our loftiest creative impulses and our most primal passions.

So, What Am I Doing Here, Anyway?

Astrologically, the Patterson-Gimlin encounter took place during a powerful astrological alignment between the planets Uranus and Pluto—a celestial duo typically associated with revolutionary change and volatile emotions, such as occurred in France during the 1790s, or in the U.S. during the mid-1800s.

When I first wrote the above essay (2013), the world found itself in the midst of the next major configuration involving those two planets to occur since the 1960s, as they reconnected in a stressful 90-degree angle. Not surprisingly, we not only saw signs of civil unrest in countries around the world but, curiously enough, the phenomenon of Bigfoot reached an all-time high, with TV series, books, and pop culture references to the creature popping up seemingly everywhere.

But if we turn the clock back to the *last* major Uranus-Pluto aspect occurring prior to the 60s, we arrive in the early 1930s, when Uranus squared Pluto the previous time. Curiously enough, that was when another famed "filmed cryptid" burst onto the scene—namely, *King Kong*. The famous oversized ape stormed into movie theaters the very same month the Uranus-Pluto square became exact. (The movie's release was on March 2, 1933, while the Uranus-Pluto square became exact on March 8.)

Powerful forces were stirring in the world then, too—with yet another "monster" storming onto the world stage just two weeks later, as Adolph Hitler formally ascended to power in Germany on March 23.

The message seems to be clear: whenever Uranus and Pluto join forces, the Earth doth shake!

This chapter has been adapted and revised from a longer essay, "Portals of Strangeness," which first appeared in Volume 8 of Greg Taylor's anthology series Darklore *(Daily Grail Publishing, 2014), and once again, in modified form, in my book* The Sky Stretched Out Before Me:

Encounters with Mystics, Anomalies, and Waking Dreams (Inner Eye Publishing, 2021).

Notes

1. Quoted by Joseph Campbell (from his translation of Arthur Schopenhauer's essay "On an Apparent Intentionality in the Fate of the Individual") in *Masks of God, Vol. IV: Creative Mythology*, p.344.

CHAPTER 31

A Mystical Look at War and Suffering

I once knew a woman who was fervently anti-war, a staunch pacifist who decried violence in our world every chance she had. Like many such pacifists, she fantasized about a possible future when peace and harmony ruled the planet, and society was finally freed from the horrors of war and injustice.

But one day, after watching a particularly gut-wrenching news segment on TV about war crimes being perpetrated by a distant country's leader, she said, "If karma is real, I sincerely hope that man gets payback in some future life, or better yet, many future lives, so he gets to experience the suffering he's caused to others."

A curious comment, I thought, since there seemed to be a split between those two viewpoints—on the one hand her professed pacifism and on the other her obvious desire for retribution.

You see, like me, my friend believed in reincarnation and karma. So far so good. However, if she really did hope to see the world rid of violence, injustice, and war then how exactly did she think a war criminal like that would come back in some future life to be on the receiving end of those same crimes and cruelties he committed himself *if it weren't for the continued presence of future horrific wars and conflicts?*

In other words, you either want to see that terrible person get his just desserts in a later life, or you want to see the world rid of horrific conflicts and wars—but I'm not sure you can have both.

To be sure, all sensitive souls are grieved by the existence of suffering and injustice on our planet. Who *wouldn't* like to see all that come to a stop?

Yet if karma and reincarnation are indeed real—and to my mind it's the only philosophy that really makes sense of my world—then how exactly is that supposed to happen?

It naturally raises the question of whether the Earth might not be serving precisely the purpose it's perfect for serving—namely, as a place where both pleasant and unpleasant karmas are acted out and fulfilled, a veritable playground of free will, as it were. But with all of that good also comes all of the bad—and that includes a lot of *very* bad (rather, unpleasant) things.

This doesn't mean we don't do everything in our power to improve things down here, to work hard to combat the injustices all around and try to lift others out of their miseries and sufferings (which, by the way, is supposedly a job best accomplished through teaching or spiritual education—*"teach a man how to fish..."* and all that—we'll come back to that in a bit). It simply means that at some point we need to face up to our limitations and accept what we can or can't really achieve. What's the old Alcoholics Anonymous saying?— *God, grant me the serenity to accept the things I cannot change, the courage to change the things I can, and the wisdom to know the difference.*

A Final Query

There's one last point I think is worth making here, and it takes the form of a question I've sometimes posed to myself when I'm not in a very good state of mind about the way things are going in the world. It crops up for me whenever I find myself getting riled up about the sheer volume of injustice, greed, and hurtful stupidity in the world around me, to where I almost feel like my blood will start to boil. It was on one such occasion that I heard a voice in my head verbalize a question which went something like this:

So, What Am I Doing Here, Anyway?

Of all the possible places in the cosmos where you could have incarnated, with all of the different kinds of civilizations that likely exist out there from the most peaceful and harmonious to the most corrupt and painful, why do you think you wound up in on this *one?*

If you're bothered by the same concerns I was in pondering that question, then I'd invite you to consider that query yourself. Of all the gin joints in this crazy cosmos (to paraphrase an old film), why do you suppose you wound up living in *this* world, with all of its perils and possibilities, if it didn't somehow relate to what you're learning at this particular stage?

Okay, but let's say you decide you *really* don't like it here, with all of this planet's harsh realities. Then by all means start looking for a planet or dimension other than this one, where there aren't such pesky problems as karma, reincarnation and free will to deal with.

Best of luck with that.

CHAPTER 32

Arnold, Madonna, and Tom: Three Exemplars of "Manifestation"?

I recently watched a three-part documentary on Netflix called *Arnold,* about the life of Arnold Schwarzenegger. It's a surprisingly interesting film but also a remarkable story of personal achievement, chronicling the life of someone who came from humble beginnings to become extraordinarily successful in not just one but *four* different careers: bodybuilding, moviemaking, real estate, and politics.

And if that weren't *quite* enough, he married into American "royalty"—the Kennedy family.

I recall when he first appeared on the scene and how he spoke about getting into movies in America, thinking to myself how completely improbable an ambition that was for him, due to all the things he had going against him.

Besides just being a foreigner, there was that barely pronounceable name of his that wouldn't fit easily on any theater marquee; add to that his almost comically thick accent; consider his less-than-Shakespearean acting skills; and last but not least, he didn't have what anyone regarded as "movie star" good looks.

Yet he succeeded beyond anyone's wildest dreams—other than his own, that is.

I'm intrigued by individuals like this, not because such achievements make them "saints," heaven forbid, but because how they exemplify the power to visualize a dream, go after it, and finally make it a tangible reality, often in the face of formidable odds.

I can think of at least two other instances from show business that readily fit this category: Madonna and Tom Cruise. These are all individuals who came from modest beginnings to achieve astonishing success in their respective fields, and were able to maintain—or even expand—that success over multiple decades.

My question is this. What is it in a horoscope that shows that ability to take an impossibly large dream or vision and make it a reality? Sure, hard work is a big part of it, but lots of people work hard but don't succeed like these individuals have.

The most obvious thing that jumps out at me when looking at their charts is the fact that two of those individuals are Sun-sign Leos (Arnold and Madonna) while Cruise is a Cancer but has his Moon, Venus and Uranus in Leo. How do I interpret that?

There's obviously an impulse with many Leos to seek the limelight and ascend to the heights, no doubt about it. The simplistic explanation for that is that it's all simply fueled by ego and the need to be seen in larger-than-life, "heroic" terms. On a more esoteric level, though, it's good to remember the zodiac-chakra correlation I've written amount in other books (drawn from esoteric traditions like Kriya Yoga), which has it that Leo is the zodiacal sign corresponding to the so-called "third eye" or *ajna* chakra. This chakra represents the visualizing, creative center of consciousness in the subtle body, and is thus ground zero for that very "manifestational" ability we're talking about here. (Among the planets and luminaries, that chakric center is in turn associated with the Sun itself, the celestial "ruler" of Leo, to the extent that many yogis even refer to that particular chakra as the "Sun center." Having the Sun in Leo therefore does seem to double up on the impact of that principle there.)

Arnold, Madonna, and Tom: Three Exemplars of "Manifestation"?

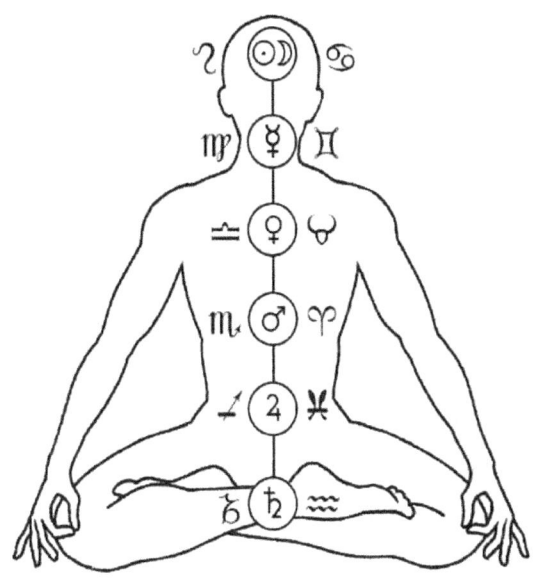

A depiction of the astrological correspondences between the zodiac and the various chakric levels. The "positive" polarity signs symbolizes the masculine (extraverted) expressions of the chakras and the "negative" polarity signs symbolize the feminine (introverted) expressions of those levels, whereas the planets governing the various signs represent the central "core" energy at each level.

What About Saturn?

The other factor I'd expect to see in this context would be a prominent Saturn in the chart (especially if placed in Leo or forming some angular relationship to the Sun). That's not only because Saturn relates to the quality of discipline and "hard work" so integral to success, but to the *crystallizing principle itself*—the capacity to brings ideas or dreams into material reality. (Notice too that Saturn relates to the lowest chakra of that system, and is thus the "grounding," materializing plane of consciousness.) So, do we see that planet pronounced in the charts of those four individuals?

I'd say, yes, pretty much.

To begin with, Arnold has his Sun approaching a conjunction to Saturn (as well as Pluto) in Leo. This is a pattern which shows considerable struggle but also considerable accomplishment, potentially, as well as considerable resilience. The fact that he became particularly well-known on the silver screen for James Cameron's *Terminator* films—a creature which *just keeps coming back* in the face of repeated setbacks—seems especially fitting to me.

Madonna's birthtime is up for debate, but based just on her birth day (August 16, 1958, Bay City, Michigan, with a *possible* 7:05 AM birthtime), we know that Saturn is forming a trine to both her Sun and Uranus, as well as a square to her Moon in Virgo. Among other things, that shows considerable opportunities with authority figures and success, as well as an impressive capacity for discipline. At its most positive, it also demonstrates an impulse toward manifesting her dreams into tangible reality.

There is also uncertainty about Cruise's exact birth time, but based on his birth day (July 3, 1962) Saturn is placed in Aquarius and forming a close inconjunct (within one degree) to his Sun, while opposing his Moon and Venus in Leo—all of which fits the bill of our crystallizing thesis. In general, his Saturn is exceptionally active, forming aspects to every other body in the chart except Mars. Among those aspects is a particularly close square to Neptune, which can likewise indicate a drive to crystallize otherwise diaphanous fantasies and ideas. (For example, Mozart had the opposition, with an obvious talent for putting extremely refined musical ideas into tangible form.)

How About Jupiter?

Is there anything else we might look for, in terms of this ability to materialize dreams or visions?

I'd expect there to be a prominent Jupiter in such charts, since that planet would surely play a big role in worldly "success," not just due to the confidence (or perhaps hubris?) it confers, but the element of "good luck" and windows of opportunity it opens for those born under its rays. Consider just a few of the successful figures from pop culture born with close Sun-Jupiter aspects: Paul McCartney, Brian Wilson, Bob Dylan, Sheryl Crow, Herbie Hancock, Woody Allen, Adele, Kanye West, and Mick Jagger were all born under the conjunction; Marlon Brando, Whitney Houston, Keith Richards, Justin Bieber, Martin Scorsese, and Justin Timberlake, all born under the trine; Jack Nicholson, Ariana Grande, Andy Warhol, Sylvester Stallone, George Lucas, Neil Diamond, Frank Sinatra, and Dolly Parton, all born under the square; while Sting, Kevin Costner, Doris Day, Duke Ellington, Herman Melville, and Robert Duvall were all born under the opposition.[1]

So, do we see prominent Jupiter aspects in the charts of our three individuals? Indeed, we do.

Arnold Schwarzenegger was born when Jupiter was forming a close trine to his Ascendant and Mercury, a fortunate influence often showing success, communication skills, or popularity.

Madonna was born with Jupiter *squaring* her Sun in Leo—no lack of confidence there!

And as for Tom Cruise, he was born with no less than a *grand trine* from Jupiter to both his Sun and Neptune, in addition to which Jupiter was stationing precisely at his birth, further amplifying the power of that grand trine.

So these are a few possibilities I'd propose on this fascinating subject. There could well be other factors at work that I've not touched on here—for example, I suspect Mars and Pluto play supporting roles of their own here, in providing both energy and assertiveness—but for now I'll leave it at these, and hope these cursory reflections might stimulate your own thoughts about the role and dynamics of manifestation in our lives.

Notes

1. It's worth noting the United States of America was itself born under a Jupiter-Sun conjunction, in early July of 1776, and in turn those two planets were squared by Saturn. That's quite a "manifestational" combination, I'd suggest, considering how the Sun-Jupiter conjunction shows a general confidence and openness to success, whereas the square

So, What Am I Doing Here, Anyway?

from Saturn suggests hard work, worldly ambition, and the ability to crystallize those potentials. Perhaps that trifecta may help explain why the U.S. has been viewed by many immigrants through the years as the proverbial "land of opportunity," where dreams can become reality.

CHAPTER 33

Teaching

One can't help but wonder about the karmic predicament of any soul who messes up badly on the reincarnational path and becomes a violent leader or warlord, responsible for the suffering and deaths of thousands or even millions of people. There are no shortages of examples from history to illustrate what I'm talking about.

What complicates things here is that, as some mystics have noted, there isn't just the karma incurred for harming any one individual to be dealt with but the ripple effects of all those lives who are in turn affected by the harm to that one person. You hurt one person and you affect all the friends, family members, and acquaintances in that person's orbit of influences.

Which naturally raises the question: how can such a soul possibly make all that up, karmically, when the debt has become so monumental?

According to some teachings, there are two primary ways such an unfortunate soul might go about that task.

The first is might be called the incremental or "long and winding road" approach—i.e., slogging through the karmic trenches, lifetime after lifetime, experiencing for oneself all the same abuses inflicted on others until that karmic ledger is finally balanced out. Not an easy path, to be sure, but it's certainly one way of going about it— presuming you have a few extra eons of time on your hands.

So, What Am I Doing Here, Anyway?

The other method is to come back as a great world teacher or healer, and in that capacity work hard to help and educate as many souls as you hurt or destroyed in past lives.

In fact, that's exactly what the famous yogi Paramahansa Yogananda claimed about himself (as told to Shelly Trimmer, as I recounted in my book *An Infinity of Gods*). In private, he claimed he had been William the Conqueror in a past life, during which time he hurt and killed a great many men and women while conquering England in 1066. As a result, he needed to balance out all the pain and suffering he caused others, which required teaching and healing as many souls as he harmed in that earlier lifetime. (Not the exact same souls, necessarily, as Shelly explained, but *as many*.) In fact, as Yogananda said to Shelly, so formidable was that debt of his that on departing Earth he would need to incarnate into another dimension or world entirely, one that housed many more souls than he could possibly reach and help here on Earth.

Whether all of that is really true, the irony here is that there conceivably may be some great spiritual teacher or leader you've admired in this life for their good deeds and unselfishness who is actually working off an ocean full of difficult karmas due to past selfishness, greed, and violence! Who knows; is it possible the Dalai Lama was some ruthless warlord in a past life? Or Mahatma Gandhi was previously Torquemada the Inquisitor? (On the other hand, it's equally interesting to contemplate that the horrid individual you're dealing with in this lifetime could—given another 10,000 years—become a respected spiritual teacher adored by millions!)

Well, maybe, maybe not—who knows? In the end it's best not to get too invested in one's imaginative projections on any teacher or person, and instead simply take them for who they are in this life, right here and right now. At any rate, I'd like to believe the karmic debt shouldered by most of us is not nearly so formidable as any of the extreme cases mentioned here.

Either way, there's something to be said about the value of teaching, whether that's done to make amends for anything karmic or not. Teaching can take many forms, of course, not just as someone standing before a room full of students. It can express itself as a parent educating a child about a more awakened and conscious life, or it could simply be teaching through the example of one's presence. As a friend said to me in passing nearly 40 years ago, "The most important thing you have to teach is your way of being."

Couldn't have said it better myself.

CHAPTER 34

Are the "Great" Ages Even Real? (And Does it Even Matter?)

A while back I came across a reader's review on Amazon of an early book of mine, *Signs of the Times*, in which I wrote about the shifting Great Ages and the transition from the Age of Pisces to the Age of Aquarius.

The reviewer's name was Abner Rosenweig, and what struck me about his review was he obviously didn't believe in astrology, and actually found my need for it "flawed" and "frequently contrived"—yet despite that found my insights into cultural trends "provocative," "impressively broad," and offering "fascinating critical insight into history, society and culture." Quite a blend of opinions, that was.

In other words, it didn't seem to really *matter* whether he believed in astrology or its interpretive value; the conclusions and theories I presented—primarily by means of an astrological paradigm—nonetheless still seemed valid or thought-provoking to him.

I bring this up because I think it makes a useful point about the potential value of the Great Ages doctrine as a way of thinking about historical matters. Over the decades that I've been involved with astrology, I've discovered that even some colleagues in the astrological community are skeptical about the validity or usefulness of the "Great Ages" concept. They may fully embrace the value of astrology when analyzing personal horoscopes, or the power of the role of planetary cycles in analyzing historical trends,

Are the "Great" Ages Even Real? (And Does it Even Matter?)

say, but for them the doctrine of the Great Ages poses another challenge altogether.

For the most part, that uneasiness seems to center, in part, on whether there truly are twelve clearly defined constellations through which the vernal point (i.e., the astronomical point signaling the first moment of spring) moves; while another concern has to do with *precision,* and exactly how one is to decide when a given Great Age starts or ends. Still others feel the doctrine is simply too broad to provide any useful, specific information. These are all perfectly understandable concerns.

But Rosenweig's review crystallized a point I've been mulling over for some years now, and that is the possibility it may not entirely *matter* whether the astrological Great Ages doctrine is "true"—at least not in the way we normally think about it. Let me explain what I mean.

If you look at the defining themes of the last three or four millennia, up to and including our present time, those themes match up quite well with what astrology says about the potential themes and symbols associated with the corresponding epochs of Aries, Pisces and Aquarius—the three zodiacal archetypes associated by astrologers with the Great Ages during that span of time.

To put it very simply, the sign Aries is governed by the planet Mars, a comparatively assertive and war-like energy. That matches up quite well with the two millennia prior to Christ, which culminated in the founding of great empires in Persia, Rome, China, Egypt and Greece (with conspicuous ram symbolism in several of those; besides Egypt, we find depictions of Alexander the Great having ram's horns in Greece as well as iconic Greek myths like Jason and Golden Fleece). Then, during the two millennia following Christ we saw the emergence of at least two worldwide religions (Islam and Christianity) characterized by an aggressive religious dogmatism, the latter of which even centered around conspicuous fish symbolism. In turn, Aquarius is a decidedly more mental sign,

233

and we've already begun to see a gradual replacement of religious values by scientific and secular ones.

Now, skeptics may well contend that Arian "war-like" impulses have existed through *all* of history, just as religious ones like those associated with the Piscean Age have in their own way, too. But there are subtle differences, especially in the way these eternal principles changed "clothing" from era to era.

For instance, whereas the Age of Aries largely witnessed wars of conquest, the Age of Pisces saw wars of religion, while the emerging Age of Aquarius has already begun to bring us wars of information, as well as battles fought in the air and wars between computers. In other words, there will always be wars, but they will change their form and motivations in line with the historical periods in which they occur.

Astrologers like myself tend to look at these intriguing correspondences as possible evidence for the workings of astrology in history. However, even if you choose *not* to read it that way and prefer instead to chalk these correspondences up to mere coincidence or scholarly cherry-picking, that's quite all right—because it may not really matter!

That's because there is another way to approach this subject, which I'd sum up like this: *the doctrine of the Great Ages provides us with an extremely rich language for discussing historical trends—whether or not that doctrine is technically "true" as astrologers normally think about it.*

Here's an analogy from the field of mythological studies that may help explain what I mean. As psychologists like Carl Jung, Freud, and James Hillman have shown, certain classical myths can be extremely useful for discussing important psychological truths and experiences. An example of that is the Greek tale of Persephone, which tells of an innocent young woman being dragged into the underworld where she becomes the bride of Pluto, and queen of the underworld.

Are the "Great" Ages Even Real? (And Does it Even Matter?)

In a beautifully *symbolic* way, this story illustrates what many of us have endured as a result of deep emotional or traumatic experiences in our lives, when we've felt like we were "abducted" into our own *psychological* underworld (an experience often associated with powerful Pluto or Saturn transits or progressions).

One might well ask, is the myth of Persephone really "true"? Of course, it isn't—not in any literal way. But it is *psychologically* true, in the sense of illustrating a profound and dramatic human experience most of us have experienced at one point or another in life.

In much the same way, I'd argue that the last two thousand years during which the vernal point has been moving through the constellation of Pisces, the historic changes we've seen taking place correspond in a striking degree with the symbolism and meaning of Pisces, while the characteristics of what's happening in our world now are corresponding closely with what astrologers have come to associate with Aquarius, especially this sign's highly mental and technological nature.

Now, do we chalk up these correspondences between astrology and real-world history to simple coincidence (as reviewer Abner Rosenweig seemed to do)? Or is it the result of some mysterious, synchronistic connection between celestial workings and earthly affairs? As I've suggested, it may not ultimately matter, since the correspondences appear to apply either way.

In short, whether the Great Ages doctrine is *literally* true, and represents a truly synchronistic phenomenon, I'd propose that it offers us a surprisingly useful language for discussing the profound changes taking place throughout our world. In the next chapter we'll be taking a closer (and rather unconventional) look at some of those changes taking place, and what they may really be saying as ciphers to our own changing understanding of the world.

CHAPTER 35

Science and Imagination: A Psychoanalysis of Scientific Discovery

The following essay was the first extended article of mine ever published, back in 1990 for a magazine called Magical Blend. *Reading it again now, I find myself still agreeing with its main premise, and hope that others may find it of interest as well.* —R.G.

"Few men have imagination enough for the truth of reality."
—Goethe

During the last few hundred years our understanding of the universe has been altered in profound ways by the advent of modern science. Largely displacing the religious and mythological notions that shaped our perceptions for millennia has been a new pantheon of material laws and principles dramatically different from the conceptions of earlier times. Relativity theory, quantum mechanics, entanglement, the quark, the laws of thermodynamics—these are just a few of the unusual new ideas that have come to populate the imaginal landscape of contemporary scientific thought.

But could there be a deeper significance to this process of scientific discovery than we've generally realized? Do the myriad findings of science describe for us the hard facts of an outside, physical world—or might they instead be ciphers to the exploration of an inner, more psychological universe that we've been engaged in?

In fact, as we're about to see, the truth may well involve a good deal of both.

Science as Symbol

We've largely been taught that science is a dispassionate search for truth, using experimentation, deduction, and rational analysis as its primary tools. In this way, scientists have sought to uncover the objective laws of nature as they exist in the world "out there," ideally unfiltered by personal bias or belief.

Yet there is good reason to believe that what we've been witnessing in the progress of science over the centuries has been as much the reflection of an inner process of psychological exploration, projected onto the outer world, as one of external discovery. This isn't to say science is *nothing more* than a psychological construct, with no objective relevance, but rather that the relationship between these two spheres may be far more intimate and symbiotic than we've generally realized.

Said a bit differently, it's entirely possible that the human imagination mirrors the world around it in ways that allows it to grasp those natural principles and laws commensurate with its own development and level of understanding. One only has to examine the history of scientific breakthroughs over time in relation to our shifting cultural values to notice the curious mirroring that's always existed between these two.

Consider the fact that just as "relativity" began emerging in the sciences we find much the same principle emerging in other fields, too, from the visual relativism of cubist art and the narrative relativism of James Joyce's novels, to the cultural relativism proposed by anthropologists. Or consider how just as our material universe was being decentralized by Copernicus, who dethroned the Sun as the center of our solar system, our *religious* universe was being "decentralized" by Luther and the Protestant Reformation, who were loosening the grip of Catholicism on the European imagination.

Understood this way, the ongoing history of scientific discovery begins to appear less like a succession of hard facts about the objective world than a series of shifting mirrors to changes in the human imagination. As the pioneer physicist Werner Heisenberg put it:

> "(We have seen) that the changes in the foundation of modern science may perhaps be viewed as symptoms of shifts in the fundamentals of our existence, which then *express themselves simultaneously in many places*, be it changes in our way of life or our usual thought forms, be it in external catastrophes, wars, or revolutions." (Emphasis mine) [1]

With this as our starting point, I'd like to briefly explore some other correspondences between scientific trends and corresponding changes in the collective imagination. In particular, I'd like to focus our attention on some of the major stages in our evolving views of the atom. Arguably more than any other, it's this basic concept that has defined and shaped the course of science in its development from the ancient Greeks up through modern times.

As the essential building block of nature, it's only natural to look toward this concept as an ideal screen on which to find the changing projections of our unfolding self-knowledge. As the basic unit of the world, the atom serves as a perfect analogy for that basic unit of human social experience—namely, the individual psyche. In this way, the *history of the atom reveals itself to be a mirror to the unfolding history of the modern Western ego.*

The Origins of Atomic Theory

The search for the origins of atomic theory takes us back to ancient Greece and the world of Democritus and Leucippus—the same general period as the origins of modern individualism and

Science and Imagination: A Psychoanalysis of Scientific Discovery

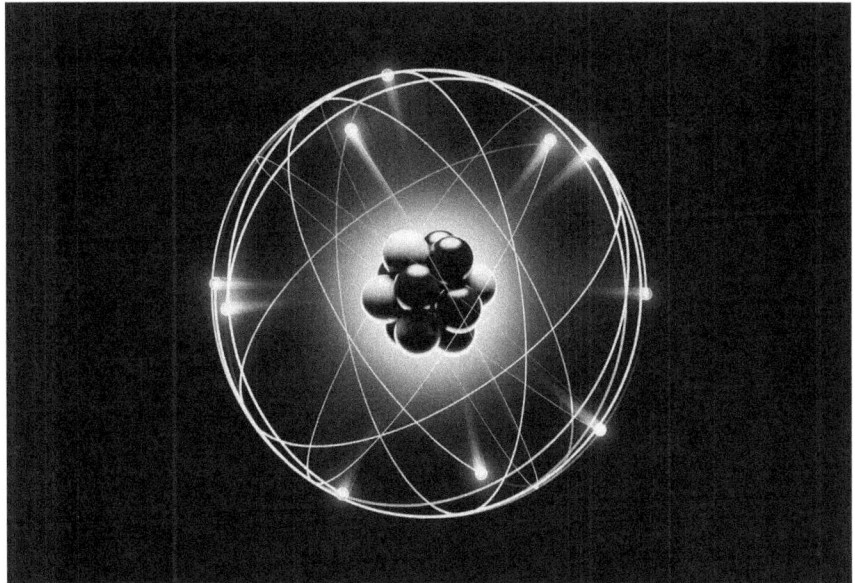

Image: Shutterstock

psychological thought. For just as Democritus was suggesting that the universe could be resolved into a world of indivisible particles, so Greek political philosophy was giving birth to the transformative idea that society could likewise be understood in terms of its primary component, the *individual* (from the Latin *individuus*, meaning "indivisible").

With the decline of Greek philosophy and culture, it would be another two millennia before the concept of the atom would become integrated into the corpus of scientific thought with the rise of the modern scientific method in the 17th century. It was then that atomic theory joined hands with the mechanistic worldview suggested by scientists like Newton and Descartes, both of whom likened the interaction between nature's discrete parts to the cause-and-effect interplay of billiard balls on a table.

Thus it was during that same period that we find the full-scale re-emergence of individualistic thought as well. As we view the world, so we view ourselves, and during an age when the archetypal building block of nature was increasingly defined in the discrete, analytic terms of the new science, so our view of human personality was becoming increasingly "atomistic" and independent as well, with the emerging belief that each individual's experience represents the fundamental reference point of social reality.

Indeed, the mechanistic model that helped scientists understand the interactions of atoms also served as a model for social theorists like Thomas Hobbes and John Locke (one of the founding figures of modern democracy), who used it to help explain the behavior of human society. Just as the actions of a gas cloud could be understood in terms of the interaction between its essential atomic and molecular components, Locke believed that the economic and political patterns of a society could likewise be understood through an analysis of its individual members.[2]

Opening the Atom

Perhaps the single most dramatic change in our understanding of the atom came during the late 19th century, when scientists obtained their first glimpse into its mysterious interior. Prior to this point, most scientists regarded the atom as something fundamental and concrete—nature's "ground floor" beyond which our conceptual tools would likely never penetrate. This appeared so certain and so final that some prominent scientists even suggested we'd finally solved most of nature's essential mysteries, with the only tasks remaining being those of tying up loose ends of existing theories.

Then, with the epic discovery of the electron by J.J. Thompson in 1897, that longstanding view underwent a seismic shift with the realization that beneath the atom's surface existed another, previously unknown dimension of reality: *the "sub-atomic" level of matter*. That is, it turned out that our visible world was just the proverbial tip of the iceberg beneath which there existed an even vaster realm of reality hidden from ordinary view.

At virtually the exact same time, an analogous development was taking place in our understanding of the individual psyche, with the advent of modern depth psychology and the discovery of the "subconscious mind." Earlier psychologists had largely regarded the conscious personality as being—not unlike the atom— indivisible and concrete, and that our waking thoughts, perceptions, and rational mind represented the essential boundaries of personality.

With the publication of Sigmund Freud's *Interpretation of Dreams* in November of 1899, that view was shaken to its core by an idea previously suspected mainly by poets and philosophers—namely, the *human subconscious*. In this groundbreaking volume, Freud argued that beneath the surface of everyday awareness lies a dimension of emotion and thought vastly greater than our conscious world of thoughts and feelings, but largely hidden from view like the submerged portion of an iceberg. While difficult to perceive, it was partially visible through such symbolic expressions as our nightly dreams and ordinary slips of the tongue. Whereas earlier psychologists sought to understand human nature in terms of our observable surface behaviors—not unlike how pre-20th century physicists studied the atom through its observable, quantifiable features—Freud believed the study of human psychology was properly understood only through a deeper understanding of this subconscious domain of experience.[3]

Continuing Revolutions in Atomic Theory

During the following decades, the discoveries unfolding in both of these spheres—the sub-atomic and the subconscious—continued to parallel each other in sometimes surprising ways.

At first, a simple "orbital" model was proposed to help explain the atom's structure and behavior. Suggested first by Niels Bohr and Ernst Rutherford, this model depicted the atom as a kind of miniature solar system, containing a central nucleus surrounded by orbiting electrons. In psychology, that model became a template for both Freud and his student Carl Jung as well, who employed the orbital image to illustrate the dynamics of human psychology. Interestingly, whereas Freud chose to place the ego in the central position corresponding to the atom's nucleus, Jung thought it more accurate to reserve that central position for his concept of the "self," in turn exiling the ego out to psyche's periphery.

It wasn't long before this simplistic model gave way to more complex understandings on both fronts, scientific and psychological. Having stepped into the vast interior of the atom, physicists found themselves encountering a world of unprecedented strangeness that resembled nothing so much as Lewis Carroll's tale of Alice through the looking glass. Here were particles that seemed capable of traveling both forwards and backwards in time, particles which could be in two places at once, or that might exist only as "probabilities." At this level of matter, scientists encountered laws and characteristics that seemed to defy the orderly logic of everyday, macroscopic reality.

In the realm of psychology, researchers were arriving at conclusions almost as unusual as those emerging in science. As a result of the work by not only Freud but Carl Jung, we were encountering a dimension of experience where the prevailing laws seemed more akin to those of dream logic and myth than the linear characteristics of ordinary rationality. An especially graphic expression of that shift became apparent in the works of artists and writers influenced by unfolding developments in psychology like Salvador Dali, Rene Magritte, and Max Ernst, as well as novelists like James Joyce. In their own way, all of these aimed to give expression to the subtleties of the unconscious mind. In books like Joyce's *Ulysses* and *Finnegans Wake*, for instance, we find a world of mythic resonances and dizzying correspondences that would seem perfectly at home in the newly emerging "zoo" of quantum physics. Indeed, there's something fitting about the fact that the name chosen by scientists to designate one of sub-atomic physics' most important particles—the quark—was drawn directly from the pages of Joyce's *Finnegans Wake!*

The Holistic Atom

Among these new discoveries about the atom was the surprising insight that it might be best understood not as an isolated "thing" so much as a complex web of relationships. According to quantum physics, the physical world itself must be seen

> "...not (as) a structure built out of independently existing unanalyzable entities, but rather a web of relationships between elements whose meanings arise wholly from their relationships to the whole." [4]

In psychology, theorists like Harry Stack Sullivan were proposing a similarly holistic view of human nature with the suggestion that personality is best understood not in isolation but as inseparably entwined within a web of social relationships. Likewise, Carl Jung increasingly came to perceive the human personality as playing host to a dynamically interacting array of "complexes" and archetypal patterns. He further believed, with his theory of the collective unconscious, that the psychic roots of each person were fundamentally entwined with those of *all* beings.

No less revolutionary in the realm of science was the unsettling element of "unpredictability" which characterized the behavior of particles at the smallest levels. In direct contrast to the secure determinism of macroscopic, everyday phenomena, physicists discovered that the more closely one examined the atom's interior, the less it lent itself to predictable analysis. At the level of sub-atomic matter, nature itself almost seemed to be ruled by chance. Yet as unpredictable as things appeared at the level of individual atoms, scientists learned that by examining atoms *in large numbers* they could establish a statistical curve which made accurate predictions possible. The larger the number of atoms, it turned out, the more accurate the predictions about them could be.

On a cultural level, that element of unpredictability was closely paralleled by the rise of a similar view in our understanding of human behavior. While the actions of any one individual may indeed be unpredictable, if analyzed in large enough numbers it was possible to predict behavioral patterns with great accuracy—an insight that held particular appeal for proponents of Marxism, with their emphasis on quantity over quality. As the philosopher Immanuel Kant said long before, whereas each lover may see their relationship as unique and all-encompassing, the man down at the registry office somehow knows there will be more marriages in Spring than in Winter!

Exploiting the Energies of the Atom

As important as these various developments were, they were superseded by an even more far-reaching development: unlocking the enormous energies within the atom. That began with Leo Szilárd's hypothesis about the possibility of atomic "chain reactions" in 1933, followed by the discovery of fission in 1938, and culminating in a fiery climax with the detonation of the first atomic bomb in 1945. As Carl Jung suggested, we might look to this historical development as a profound symbol for humankind's awakening to the enormous powers housed within the human psyche itself—energies that could be employed towards either constructive or destructive ends.

Importantly, 1933 was also the year Adolph Hitler began his ascent to power as Chancellor of Germany, and which likewise came to its apocalyptic climax in 1945 with Hitler's death. It's easy to see in the personality and life of Hitler an extraordinary—if horrifying—example of the human mind's ability to draw upon the latent energies of the psyche to effect change in the world. From the standpoint of the ego, Hitler's rise to power was indeed a "triumph of the will," to borrow Leni Reifenstahl's famed film title; yet it was a form of will that issued from the darkest instinctual layers of the psyche.

Some of those who witnessed Hitler's speeches remarked on the nearly hypnotic power he exerted on audiences, as though he was channeling a force larger than himself, one rooted in the depths of the European psyche. Hitler's political skills seem to have involved the realization that the secret of mass influence lay not in well-reasoned arguments, as most politicians believed, but in appealing to the primal impulses of the human psyche. Towards that end, Hitler and his associates often employed mythic and religious elements in Nazi ceremonies and iconography toward manipulating public opinion.

Carrying this analogy one important step further, we can see yet another correspondence in the scientific phenomenon known as the "chain reaction," whereby energies released from a single atom can ignite the energies contained within many adjoining atoms. That presents an apt metaphor for the way certain charismatic individuals like Hitler, Mussolini or Hirohito, or even Churchill and Roosevelt, were able to ignite the passions of fellow citizens towards effecting social change, for good or ill.

New Directions

Since the time of Hiroshima and Nagasaki, scientists have continued to deepen our knowledge of the atom, and in the process have expanded the list of sub-atomic particles from the roughly two-dozen known at the end of World War II to the hundreds of nuclear particles and anti-particles now officially recognized by physicists.

Among the more speculative developments resulting from this ongoing process of investigation has been the "Many Worlds" hypothesis, which suggests an endlessly proliferating number of worlds from out of the probabilities described by quantum mechanics. Then there is the hotly debated notion of "String Theory," with its proposed multiple dimensions of reality, as well as Alan Guth's theory of the "inflationary universe" and its notion of multiple universes emerging out of the Big Bang. If confirmed, any one of these theories would represent a revolutionary development in the history of science; but what could they possibly mean as mirrors to shifts in the human mind? One possibility may lie in the research of figures like Russell Targ, Hal Putoff, and Dean Radin into the realm of psychic and "paranormal" phenomena, and the hidden powers of the human mind. We may well be standing on the threshold of a dramatically new view of our world, both outwardly *and* inwardly.

And what of scientific discovery over the next 50, 100, or even 10,000 years? In a curious echo of the late 19th century, we've once again heard some scientists proclaim we might again be on the verge of unlocking nearly all of nature's essential secrets, and perhaps even creating an all-encompassing "theory of everything."

Yet if scientific discovery is as much an inner process of exploration as an outer one, one has to wonder whether there can *ever* be an "end" to our explorations. For if the limits of our science indeed mirror those of the human imagination, then our grasp of the external universe will end only when we've ceased plumbing the fathomless depths of the human psyche.

Notes

1. Werner Heisenberg, "The Representation of Nature in Contemporary Physics," *Daedalus,* Vol. 87, No. 3, Summer, 1958, p.101. There's something worth adding here. In recent years several distinguished scientists have come forward to support the controversial theory of "intelligent design"— the notion that the intricate patterns and design found in nature likely point to the existence of a creator or "God" underlying it. (See "Return of the God Hypothesis," by Stephen C. Meyer, as one prominent example.) Of course, few things trigger materialistically-minded scientists more vociferously than this theory, who dismiss its proponents as simply motivated by their pre-existing religious views. Yet if one chooses to invalidate Intelligent Design arguments solely on that basis, then one is essentially obliged to dismiss the work of figures like Isaac Newton, who

Science and Imagination: A Psychoanalysis of Scientific Discovery

also held strong religious beliefs fueling his search for the underlying laws of the universe.

2. For a more complete explanation of Locke's theory of the relationship between atomic and social behavior, see Fritjof Capra's *The Turning Point*, Simon and Shuster, New York, 1982, p.68, 69.

3. Freud's *Interpretation of Dreams* wasn't his first published statement about the subconscious (nor was he its only proponent; Josef Breuer suggested a similar idea in his book *Hypnotic Theory* back in 1882). However it's the work most often seen as introducing the concept of the unconscious to a worldwide audience. (Worth noting, incidentally, is the fact that Sigmund Freud and his scientific "doppelganger," J.J. Thompson, were almost exactly the same age, having been born just a few months apart in 1856.)

4. Henry Stapp, "S-Matrix Interpretation of Quantum Theory," quoted by Gary Zukav in *The Dancing Wu Li Masters*, William Morrow and Company, 1979, p.72.

This essay first appeared in Magical Blend *magazine, April 1990, and reprinted in Vol. 8 of the anthology* Darklore, *in 2007 (ed. Greg Taylor).*

CHAPTER 36

A Synchro-Historic Meditation on the Discovery of the Coelacanth

While flipping channels on my TV recently, I came across a segment on the coelacanth—the ancient creature found by fisherman off the coast of Africa in 1938 and which was thought to have been extinct for some 60 million years.

That's a whole lotta years.

The more I learned about this story, the more I realized what an extraordinary event this was, not just from a paleontological standpoint but as a seismic event in the collective imagination.

Think about it. An unimaginably ancient creature, having remained unseen in the ocean for eons and thought to no longer

Replica of Coelacanth, *Latimeria chalumnae*.
(Photo: Citron / CC-BY-SA-3.0)

A Synchro-Historic Meditation on the Discovery of the Coelacanth

exist, unexpectedly reappears in the present day after being hauled up from the depths into the bright light of day.

If this were a dream image described by someone in Jungian therapy, I'd say it likely pointed to something profound and archaic emerging from the depths of that person's psyche. In this case, though, it was emerging in the *collective* psyche. This event clearly exuded a sense of something deeply archetypal or even mythic to my mind—but what, exactly?

My first instinct was to wonder if there was anything astrologically significant happening at the time. I guessed that the most likely suspects would be something involving either Neptune or Pluto (since Neptune governs the ocean and Pluto relates to primal energies welling up from the distant past).

The fish was hauled up in the fishermen's nets on December 23, 1938 (no exact time recorded). The first thing I noticed from the ephemeris was that Neptune was stationing at the time (that is, standing still and about to change directions). That station climaxed on December 25-26 but exerted a powerful influence for several weeks on either side. Planetary stations are times when the energy of a planet is amplified considerably due to the "branding iron" effect they exert. Considering the connection of Neptune with the ocean, the fact that Neptune was so pronounced at the time of the coelacanth's surfacing seemed like a fitting correlation to me.

Then, similar to our earlier discussion of Bigfoot, I thought I'd try taking what I call a more "synchro-historic" approach by looking to see if any other developments of that period might be synchronistically connected to that discovery—this, in the spirit of seeing "what happens together." *Field thinking*, in other words. Isolated events are not strictly isolated, after all, but are actually part of a larger pattern, so we must look to the whole pattern to grasp the significance of any one part. Studying what happened during those adjoining months on either side of the coelacanth's discovery, I came across several things of interest.

So, What Am I Doing Here, Anyway?

A little less than six weeks before the coelacanth's discovery, on November 16, Swiss chemist Albert Hoffman discovered LSD—a development that eventually opened the floodgates of consciousness for millions during the ensuing decades. Besides the fact the drugs are commonly considered by astrologers to be a "Neptune" symbol, and involve activating very primal levels of the brain and consciousness, the historic discovery of an archaic creature from our deep waters seems like an apt symbol for what was starting to emerge as a result of work like Hoffman's.

Even closer to the time of the coelacanth's discovery, I saw that on December 17^t, scientist Otto Hahn discovered the nuclear fission of Uranium—a process that became the technological basis for nuclear power. While the *concept* of nuclear chain reactions had been proposed as early as 1933 by Leo Szilard, Hahn's discovery made it an actual reality, leading some to call it the true "birth of the Atomic Age."

Clearly, something seismic was occurring on several fronts, having to do with powerful energies being unleased into the world, both internally *and* externally. The fact of LSD's birth occurring so close to the origins of the Atom Bomb seemed like a thought-provoking synchronicity in itself—but what could *that* possibly mean?

A Different Possibility

All of this called another perspective to mind, one that takes us in a very different direction but which might provide yet another clue.

At the time of the coelacanth's discovery, *Time* magazine's "Man of the Year" issue featured no less a figure than Adolf Hitler on its cover, touting him as the "most influential" person of that year. Interesting, too, is the fact Hitler first rose to power in Germany in March of 1933—the year associated with the birth of the chain reaction theory I just mentioned. (Curiously enough, that was also a time when *another* "prehistoric" creature from the depths surfaced

A Synchro-Historic Meditation on the Discovery of the Coelacanth

into public awareness, that being when the first major news story about the Loch Ness Monster appeared, several weeks later.)

Yet Another Layer

But there was one more piece of the puzzle I'd been overlooking, which may help to bring some of these other elements together.

Taking one more look at the ephemeris (the catalog of planetary patterns), I discovered that the slow-moving planet Pluto had just moved into zero degrees of Leo several months before the coelacanth's discovery, on August 4. (It first entered Leo the previous year for a few months before temporarily backing up into Cancer, then moving more permanently into Leo in August 1938.)

As most seasoned astrologers know, the entry of an outer planet into a new sign can signal major shifts in the collective consciousness. Because these bodies move so slowly and have a reach that extends far into space, they symbolize broader and more generational effects, and the emergence of longer-term trends and themes into global culture.

I found it fascinating that the movement of Pluto into Leo took place so close to the "birth of the atomic age." Why? Because Leo is the sign governed by the Sun—and the discovery of nuclear fission essentially involved harnessing the power of the Sun.

In other words, *just as the planet most associated by astrologers with power and hidden energies coming into being (namely, Pluto) moved into the zodiacal sign most associated by astrologers with the Sun (namely, Leo), we saw the emergence of nuclear fission.*

In a closely allied way, Pluto's shift into Leo also relates to uncovering the powers of the individual human ego and personal consciousness—whether for better or worse. The discovery of LSD at that time obviously reflected one aspect of that development, having opened the proverbial doors of perception to new possibilities of consciousness. One obvious manifestation of Pluto's shift into Leo was the birth over subsequent years of various pop "stars" (a solar word, of course) like Mick Jagger, John Lennon, Jimi Hendrix and Robert Plant. Figures like these not only exemplified the power of the individual ego but of personal creativity—a kind of "nuclear fission" of personality.

But the flip side of that same development was the rise to power of older figures like Adolph Hitler, Mussolini, and Hirohito, who tapped into the hidden reserves of the ego and the unconscious in vastly more nefarious ways. As I touched on briefly in the last chapter, those of a more Jungian bent would perceive a close symbolic connection between the rise of the atom bomb and the emergence of powerful figures like these. *As without, so within.*

Concluding Thoughts

So what are we to make of all this?

It's clear to me from all of these developments that powerful energies were stirring in the collective psyche during the period when the coelacanth was discovered, and which "came to the surface" in their own way on several different fronts. To be clear, it would be a mistake to think of this trend as all good *or* all bad, since it's clearly a mixture of both constructive and destructive possibilities.

On the one hand, the discovery by Hoffman of LSD several weeks earlier signaled new possibilities of consciousness that were awakening in society, while the scientific discovery by Otto Hahn of nuclear fission represented a seismic shift of a more technological and intellectual sort—though with an even more ambiguous and complicated legacy than Hoffman's. On the other hand, the prominent emergence of a figure like Hitler during that same period—coupled with the appearance of an archaic creature from the depths both in 1933 *and* 1938—clearly represented much darker but equally powerful forces welling up from the collective unconscious.

As I've suggested in other places,[1] the appearance of anomalies, whether those take the form of rare but ultimately prosaic discoveries (like the discovery of the mountain gorilla in 1902) or as events of genuine "high strangeness" that defy conventional explanation (such as the so-called Phoenix Lights in 1997 or the appearance of "Mothman" in West Virginia between 1966 and 1967), typically seem to accompany seismic shifts in the collective consciousness, cropping up as they do in the midst of important socio-cultural shifts.

Did the appearance of the coelacanth that day late in 1938 serve just such a role? It's a possibility worth considering.

Postscript: While studying the planetary positions at the time the coelacanth was discovered, I saw that Pluto was at zero degrees of Leo. I discovered that on the very day I was finishing up this essay (February 26, 2023) Pluto was occupying zero degrees of Aquarius—exactly 180 degrees away from that earlier zodiacal degree. Interesting to think that my attention would be drawn to this historic event precisely on the half-return of Pluto to that degree, especially considering this planet is not only associated with "the depths" but with phenomena or memories resurrected from the past. It would be just one more curious footnote to this story for me.

Notes

1. See my essay "Portals of Strangeness, Or, What Does It Mean When Weird Things Happen?" in *The Sky Stretched Out Before Me*.

CHAPTER 37

The Divine Scale: Searching for a Skeleton Key to the Universal Mind

While I was still a student in college, I had the chance to talk with a visiting scientist from a nearby college. During our conversation, I asked what drew him to science in the first place, as opposed to, say, becoming a shoe salesman, actor, or race car driver. He was surprisingly open about his religious motivations.

"This may sound a bit grandiose," he said, "but I was attracted to the possibility of uncovering the secrets of the universe."

And just what did he mean by *that*?

"Well, I thought that if I could really understand the laws of nature," he continued, "I might be able to understand something deeper about existence itself. I've always felt as though scientific truths held a key to something more important. Spiritual truths, maybe."

Grandiose or not, his answer wasn't really all that unusual, at least not from the standpoint of the history of science. Fact is, figures like Kepler, Galileo and Isaac Newton all pursued their quests to unveil nature's laws not simply out of curiosity about mechanical workings but from a conviction that those laws offered clues to the spiritual dimensions of life itself—possibly even the mind of God. As Galileo famously wrote in *The Assayer* (1623):

The Divine Scale: Searching for a Skeleton Key to the Universal Mind

"Philosophy is written in that great book which ever lies before our eyes—I mean the universe—but we cannot understand it if we do not first learn the language and grasp the symbols in which it is written. The book is written in mathematical language, and the symbols are triangles, circles and other geometrical figures, without whose help it is impossible to comprehend a single word of it; without which one wanders in vain through a dark labyrinth."

Even more pointedly, Newton wrote in a letter to Richard Bently:

"When I wrote my treatise about our system, I had an eye upon such principles as might work with considering men for the belief of a Deity; and nothing can rejoice me more than to find it useful for that purpose."[1]

For scientific pioneers like these, nature was but the visible garment covering a deeper reality, and the key to unlocking its varied patterns was that of symbolism and analogy. In fact, this is a way of thinking about the world that has its roots in an intellectual tradition virtually as old as civilization itself, with hints at least as far back as Pythagoras, and likely much earlier. According to this perspective, for instance, light is not simply a physical phenomenon but a symbol for something divine; mathematical principles aren't just lifeless laws but mirrors of patterns in God's mind; water isn't merely a substance but the distillation of a higher state of being—and on it goes.

In reality, this philosophical perspective never completely disappeared. In a Twitter comment posted in 2021, physicist Michio Kaku wrote,

"The search for the God Equation is one of the greatest quests in all of science, the search for a single equation, perhaps no more than 1 inch long, that will unify all the laws of the universe, and allow us to 'read the Mind of God,' in the words of Einstein."[2]

So, What Am I Doing Here, Anyway?

Kaku has said on occasions he believes the key equation in that quest will be found in "string theory," a hotly debated model of physics that views the cosmos as consisting of exceedingly tiny "strings," roughly comparable to musical vibrations. String theory of not, I suspect that a central impulse of the emerging era will be unearthing the hidden patterns and laws of the manifest world towards the greater understanding of its dynamics and its hidden truths.

With that perspective in mind, there is one pattern I've long been fascinated by which I first mentioned in *The Waking Dream*, and that I believe may hold an important key toward unlocking a fundamental truth about the cosmos. It takes the form of certain recurring analogies that we find across various fields and domains of experience, including astronomy, music, esoteric psychology, geometry, and mathematics. On its surface, it's relatively simple, yet it strikes me as pointing towards something much, much deeper. For lack of a better term, I simply call it the *divine scale*, and we'll look at how this pattern appears in a number of different areas, beginning with the solar system.

The Solar System

The Sun is the center of our local group, surrounded by Mercury, Venus, Earth, Mars, Jupiter, Saturn, Uranus, Neptune, and Pluto, all of them circulating in their orbits around that central star. The essential point here is that the Sun is *dominant and primary amongst them all*.

Not only is the Sun the largest body in our system, not only does it represent the center of our system, but it's the primary source of light for all the other bodies in our system. Certain other bodies like Jupiter do radiate a certain amount of energy, even a little light, but it's relatively minor by comparison, and certainly not extensive enough to illuminate any neighboring bodies. When we look up and see Jupiter, it's actually the light of the Sun we're

The Divine Scale: Searching for a Skeleton Key to the Universal Mind

Image: Shutterstock

seeing reflected back to us. As such, the Sun represents the only truly "self-referential body" in our local group. Said another way, *all the planets shine by the reflected light of the Sun*. That is, all of the orbiting bodies of our system acquire their meaning in reference to that solar principle.[3]

Music

Next, let's look at music. In the various scales we use to play or compose music, there is a consistent pattern underlying all of them, which is that each contains a ladder of notes, a spectrum of tonal steps. In our familiar Western modality, these are known by the seven tones *Do, Re, Me, Fa, So, La, Ti,* culminating an octave higher at the next *Do*.

But notice how out of all those notes, *only one* is dominant or "primary," that being the *Do*.

So, What Am I Doing Here, Anyway?

In other words, pick any note on a keyboard and you can make it into a *Do*, a base note from which an entire scale can be constructed. But if you want to play any of the other notes of the scale, you can't do it until you've first established a baseline *Do*. Of all the notes of the scale, in other words, *Do* is therefore the most fundamental; it's the only one that's completely self-referential, with all the other notes deriving their meaning and existence by reference to it.

In a sense, you could therefore say that just as the Sun is to the solar system, so *Do* is to the notes of the scale. Analogically, *all the notes of the musical scale "shine by the reflected light" of Do*.[4]

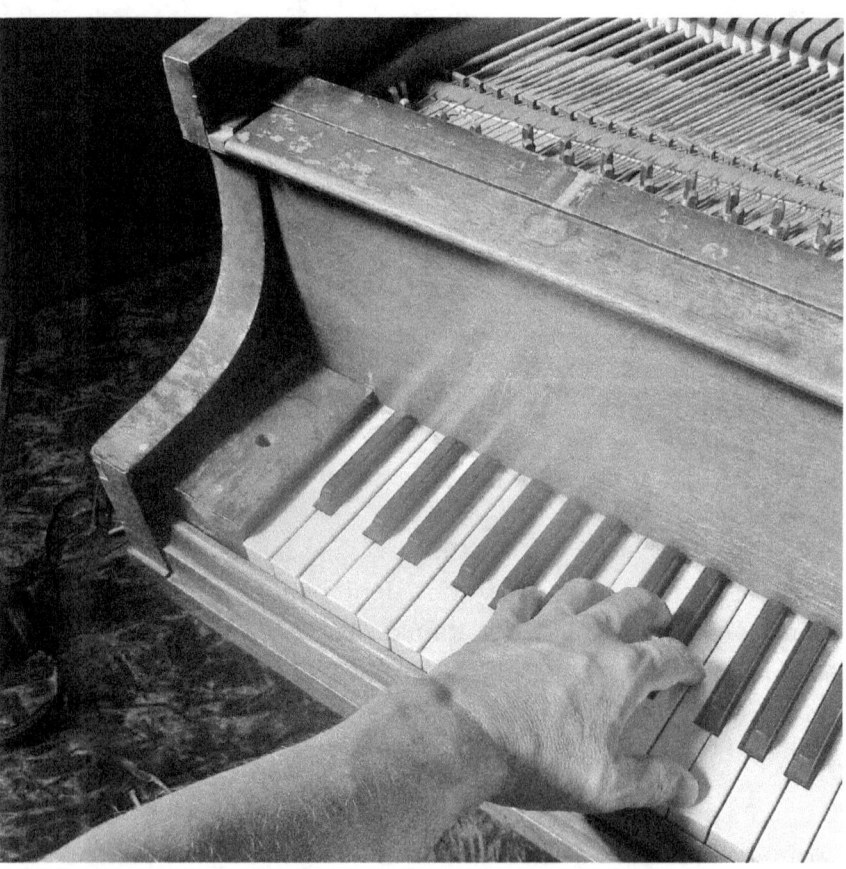

The Divine Scale: Searching for a Skeleton Key to the Universal Mind

Math

Our next correspondence is drawn from mathematics and the world of numbers. If you take the basic integers One, Two, Three, Four, and so on, you'll find something in common with these previous two systems we've just examined. That's because out of all the possible numbers in existence, *only one* of them is primary and fundamental—and that's the number One. All of the other integers are secondary in importance since they depend on One for their existence. You can't have the number Four without there being four Ones, just as you can't describe Seven without saying there are seven Ones, and so on.

As such, the number One is the only integer that is completely self-referential and self-existent. In a manner of speaking, we could say that all the numbers in existence *"shine by the reflected light" of One*. [5]

So, What Am I Doing Here, Anyway?

Esoteric Psychology

Now I'd like to introduce ideas from the system of spiritual psychology I've discussed in other books, that of the *chakras*. This doctrine holds there are thousands of energy centers throughout the subtle body, of which only a handful are primary.

Each of these primary chakras represents a particular state or level of consciousness, ranging from the more earthy and emotional concerns at the bottom end of the system

to the increasingly mental and finally spiritual concerns associated with the upper centers.

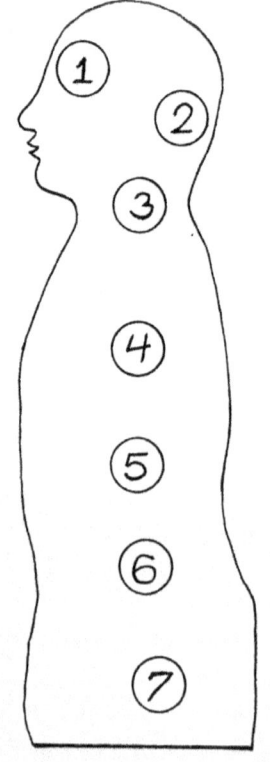

At the bottom of the spine (7) we have the root chakra, *muladhara*. Second from the bottom (6) is *svadisthana*. Third in line moving upward (5) is *manipura*. At the heart level (4) is *anahata* chakra. At the throat level (3) we find *vissudha*. At the back of the head (2) there is *chandra* chakra, while at the center of the forehead (1) there is *ajna* chakra, also known as the "third eye."

Of all these centers, it's believed that the chakra located in the forehead is primary. That's because it is the seat and source of personal consciousness itself, the pure witnessing consciousness of I AM AWARE THAT I AM. (By contrast, the so-called "1000-petaled lotus" at the top of the head, or *sahasrara*, is less a source of personal consciousness than a doorway to the Divine, or the transpersonal Self.)

To draw on an earlier analogy, the energy of this center can be likened to the light bulb in a movie projector, which illuminates all the images issuing out of it. Similarly, our essential nature is pure *spiritual* light, and informs all of the permutations of consciousness that arise within our field of consciousness. As we saw in previous chapters, some mystics believe that the analogy between the visible planets of our solar system and the chakras of the subtle body is actually quite precise, and goes as follows:

The ringed planet Saturn is equated with the lowest or "root" chakra; Jupiter with the second chakra; Mars with the third; Venus with the fourth, heart chakra; Mercury with the throat chakra; the Moon with the chakra in the back of the head (*chandra* means *Moon* in Sanskrit); and the Sun with the *ajna* chakra in the middle of the forehead. (There is no planetary correlate to the chakra at the top of the head, the "thousand-petaled lotus," although some have assigned the planet Neptune to it.)

Of those seven basic chakras, *ajna* is considered to be the predominant one. So, in much the same way that the planets of the solar system shine by the reflected light of the Sun, we could say that *all the lower chakras shine by the reflected light of the ajna chakra.*

The Pyramidal Form

We earlier looked at how the simple shape of a four-sided pyramid embodies a host of symbolic truths, centering around the numerical principles of 3, 4, 7, and 12. Yet all of those factors draw their meaning in relation to that singular point at the pyramid's peak. In a symbolic sense, we might therefore say that all those truths contained within the pyramid's form "shine by the reflected light" of that pyramidal apex.

So, What Am I Doing Here, Anyway?

Sacred Geometry

Finally, let's move on to geometry, where we find another level of correspondence with these other areas. Here I'll be taking a cue from Shelly Trimmer, who first made me aware of the geometrical implications of this system, and which starts with a simple circle.

Pick any spot on the rim of a circle, and place a dot on that spot, as shown above, and let that be your reference point. Geometrically speaking, this is the zero-degree angle, known to astrologers as a "conjunction." It represents something in perfect relationship with itself, and esoterically symbolizes *the observer*, the witnessing consciousness. We'll let this be our ground zero from which all other points and angles on the wheel are established.

Now take a point directly opposite from that one on the circle, which gives us a 180-degree angle.

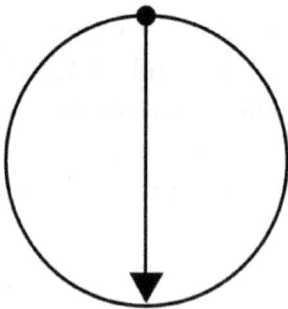

This angle represents the symbolic principle of *opposition*, of experiences and perspectives which exist at a polar remove from

The Divine Scale: Searching for a Skeleton Key to the Universal Mind

another perspective. When we say that someone "did a 180," for instance, it conveys the notion that they underwent a complete reversal in their opinion or approach. Astrologers refer to this relation, suitably, as an *"opposition."* And whereas the 0-degree angle is the symbol of self-consciousness, the observer, the 180-degree is symbolic of the *other*, the *not-self*—that which is *being observed*.

Or, we can choose to focus on point of the circle that exists at an exact 120-degree angle from that original starting point, what astrologers refer to as a "trine" relationship. As shown below, this extends out in dual ways to both sides of the circle, since there are two 120-degree angles. Symbolically, this represents a relatively easy or harmonious relationship, which can manifest in the real world as harmonious or even lucky situations or states of consciousness.

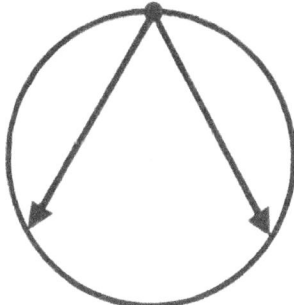

And there are of course many other angles possible besides these. Shelly Trimmer suggested focusing mainly on seven primary angles, which in turn give rise to twelve by polarity. Let me explain.

There is only one 0-degree conjunction and one 180-degree opposition, but two 90-degree angles (or squares) on either side, two 120-degree angles (or trines) on either sides, and two 150-degree angles (or inconjuncts) on either side. That makes twelve points along the rim of the wheel, of which five are dual and two are singular. But if we look at the what Shelly called the "balancing arcs" within the central spine of that circle, we find *seven points of balance along that spine.*

So, What Am I Doing Here, Anyway?

In short, twelve is the path of what some occultists call "the wheel"—that is, ordinary phenomenal existence—whereas seven is the path of balanced consciousness, the proverbial "straight and narrow" on which the mystic walks, and which requires self-discipline, meditation, and equanimity to attain.

But here's the crucial point needing to be made: *however* many angles along that rim you choose to create, only one stands completely alone and self-referential: the zero-degree point, our original dot upon the rim. All the others angles and degrees around the circle draw their meaning in relation to that starting point.

In other words, just as *Do* is the fundamental reference point in the musical scale, just as the Sun is the ultimate reference point in the solar system; just as the number One is the reference point for all integers; and just as the *ajna* chakra is the fundamental reference point of consciousness for all the chakras, so the zero-degree angle is the ultimate reference point for all the geometrical angles along the wheel. It is thus the only truly "self-existent" angle out of all possible angles.

Drawing upon our solar system analogy, you could well say that *all possible geometric angles within a circle "shine by the reflected light" of the zero-degree point.*

Conclusion

So what are we to make of all this? While all this may seem abstract to those unfamiliar with esoteric principles, I've come to believe there is something profound within this pattern, which I'll explain in the following way.

For one, the fact that this ladderlike pattern exists in so many systems, and in so similar a fashion—in each and every case involving a range of principles subservient to one dominant principle—strongly suggests that we're looking at a genuine archetype, a universal principle that exists everywhere, and everywhen. As such, it likely provides us with a skeleton key toward understanding something important about reality on both the cosmic or personal levels. Let's consider each of those levels, one at a time.

On the cosmic level, this ladderlike pattern seems to imply a hierarchical, multilevel structure to existence itself. If so, it suggests, among other things, *there are multiple planes of reality besides this physical one*. Whereas modern science conventionally regards the material world as the sum total of existence, it may be just one of many levels, an idea long suggested in connection with what some have called the "perennial philosophy."

But note that in every instance we've considered here, there is a series of principles subservient to *one primary principle*—be that a musical note, a celestial body, a number, a pyramidal or geometrical point, or chakra. This clearly suggests that one of the levels on that scale of principles is fundamental; there is an ontological primary "note" or "ground zero" of existence itself, whether we choose to call that Brahma, God, Jehovah, the Absolute or Plotinus's *the One*. There is a core truth underlying reality, which in turn gives meaning to all other myriad permutations and levels of reality.

Applying this concept now to a more personal level, this pattern seems to suggest that our own consciousness exists across multiple levels as well—and *that one of those levels is likewise primary*. Said another way, each of us possesses our own essential *Do* note, a fundamental ground of consciousness that lies at the core of our being, or what Shelly Trimmer referred to as the I AM AWARE THAT I AM from which all our other states, thoughts, and emotions draw their meaning and existence.

But where exactly is that essential *Do* note, that I AM AWARE THAT I AM?

To be clear, saying that it lies "at the core of our being" doesn't mean it lies somewhere *else*, like a vein of gold buried deep underground and out of sight. Rather, *it's the very awareness comprehending these words right now, the consciousness that's seeing through your eyes at this moment.*

In other words, *you* are none other than that essential *Do* note from which all the phenomena in your world draw meaning. The environment around you, the screen or page on which you are reading this now, all the sensations of your body and mind—all of these "shine" by the reflected light of your own observing consciousness.

So, while science may continue to uncover many more secrets concealed in nature's great menagerie of laws, from the mathematical patterns governing spiral galaxies to the tiniest atomic particles or "strings," it may well be that one of the most important of all is also the simplest, and is hiding in plain sight.

If so, then it's worth our while to consider what other implications this "divine scale" may hold in our understanding of both the world and ourselves.

Notes

1. Quoted from a letter found on the Newton Project website: http://www.newtonproject.sussex.ac.uk/view/texts/normalized/THEM00254 (spelling and punctuation modernized).

2. https://twitter.com/michiokaku/status/1382325614691160065

3. This naturally brings us back to the opening chapter of this book, with my discussion of the Sun sign. Yes, there are many other celestial bodies in the horoscope, but the Sun indeed occupies a central position of sorts, and that's because, in a manner of speaking, *all of the other bodies in the chart shine by the reflected light of the Sun.*

4. When I suggested to Shelly Trimmer the possibility that the musical note *Do* symbolized the spiritual "pinnacle" of consciousness, he gently disagreed, saying that since *Do* was the lowest note of the musical scale, it couldn't really be equated with the highest spiritual principle; that honor, he suggested, should rightly go to the highest note, *Ti*. Since then, I've come to think the problem could simply be resolved by flipping our

perspective around to see the scale as *precipitating downward* from Do, *rather than ascending up* from it. After all, the complete scale properly includes the eighth stage of the higher octave *Do*; as a result, our conventional bottom-up method of viewing the musical scale ascending from *Do* all the way up to *Ti* is really just a cultural preference, not a universal law. As a result, there's no intrinsic reason we shouldn't posit *Do* as the highest note, rather than the lowest, and that the other tones *precipitate down* from it—thus giving us the descending scale *Do, Ti, La, So, Fa, Me, Re,* and *Do*. This would not only allow the musical scale to intersect precisely with the model I've suggested here but would fit well with the classic esoteric notion that the manifest worlds precipitate downward from the Divine source.

5. It's worth noting that in ancient Egypt, mathematics consisted almost entirely of fractions, but specifically fractions of *one*—e.g. one-third, one-sixteenth, one-eighth, and so on. (The fractions two-thirds and three-quarters were also used, but far more rarely.) Viewed esoterically, that practice may well suggest a belief in the fact that all phenomena derive from a fundamental unity.

CHAPTER 38

At the Still Point of the Turning World

In the yogic traditions of the East, "samadhi" is a term used to describe a state of meditation variously defined as "transcendental consciousness," "one-pointed absorption," and "effortless concentration," among other terms.

Importantly, the yogic tradition states that samadhi isn't simply one singular level or stage of consciousness, but actually has *various stages,* ranging from the comparatively mundane (think of a sports player going "into the zone" in the midst of a game, or a musician in a moment of peak improvisation) all the way up to a completely formless and transcendental state, sometimes referred to by Buddhists as "mind and body dropped." To be clear, samadhi is not the same as full-blown "enlightenment," but is rather a useful stage in its attainment. As the Zen teacher John Daido Loori once said,

"Samadhi is the vehicle by which we arrive at enlightenment."

In my book *The Sky Stretched Out Before Me,* I wrote about a meditative experience I had at Zen Mountain Monastery in New York back in the mid-1980s, which was likely a state of samadhi, but a very rudimentary one. It was certainly nothing "cosmic" or anything an advanced meditator would find particularly extraordinary. Yet it was important for me in providing some useful insights into meditation, and heightened awareness generally. With that early experience under my belt, I would modestly venture my own very simple definition of samadhi:

At the Still Point of the Turning World

Samadhi is a state of being totally focused in the present moment, a deep dive into the Now, unencumbered by memories of the past or expectations of the future.

In that earlier book, I tried to explain that experience of mine as best I could, and to do that I drew on the metaphor of how a star arises out of a nebula, with matter floating around in deep space which condenses so tightly over time that the energy and light inherent in that matter breaks open—and a *star is born*, as it were.

But another metaphor has come into my mind since that time, which may help to explain samadhi in a slightly different way—in this case, not so much in terms of energy or light but in terms of *time*. Here is that metaphor.

Imagine you're at a carnival or amusement park, and at the center of the park there's a merry-go-round, the kind with horses on poles that bob up and down, all of them going around and around. Now, since this merry-go-round or carousel is moving quite fast, you'd have to run quite fast to catch up and hop onto it. So, imagine you're doing just that, running alongside it, faster and faster, exerting yourself in order to catch up—at which point you finally do catch up and hop on board.

It's at that point you realize something quite startling and unexpected—namely, that the merry-go-round has actually been standing still the entire time, and it's really the *whole amusement park that's moving round and around it*. So there you are, at the still point of existence, with everyone out on the fairgrounds thinking *they're* the ones standing still, and these passengers up here on the merry-go-round are the ones who are moving.

While all such metaphors are imperfect, I'd suggest this one says something useful about the nature of samadhi. When you hone in on the present moment, there's a sense of profound stillness—not stagnancy or boredom, because it's actually very vibrant and alive—just *stillness*. But once you start drifting off into thoughts

So, What Am I Doing Here, Anyway?

of the past or expectations of the future, you begin falling off the carousel and drifting back into the world, into the amusement park, with all of its movement and time. Said another way, *you fall out of the Now.*

That, I'd suggest, is a simple way to think about samadhi—if indeed you plan on thinking about it rather than attempt to experience it.

In which case you might as well enjoy the amusement park while you're there. After all, that has a truth of its own, too.

CHAPTER 39

LEGENDS OF THE FALL

"Why should a man's mind have been thrown into such close, sad, sensational, inexplicable relations with such a precarious object as his body?"

—Thomas Hardy

Towards the end of his life, Goswami Kriyananda made a series of deeply occult statements about the human condition, one of which in particular stood out for me:

"The Earth is the only planet in this solar system where the people have fallen from the astral world (of that planet) down onto the surface of the planet. On all the other planets, people are there, but they're not on the surface of those planets; they are in what is called the air realm, which we call the astral realm. So if you went to those planets you would not see people on the surfaces there."

Lots to unpack there, friends. It's an idea mentioned by other mystics and occultists through the years, including Rudolf Steiner and Edgar Cayce, among others. When I posted Kriyananda's comment on social media recently, it elicited a surprising number of responses, of which the key one was probably this:

> What would cause us to 'fall' from the astral down into bodies on a planet in the first place?

So, What Am I Doing Here, Anyway?

It's not a simple question, of course, but it's a critical one, since it touches on one of the most fundamental mysteries of all—namely, *why are we here?*

One possibility suggested by various mystics and spiritual traditions through history might be called the "allurement" theory. Simply stated, this suggests that we're gradually enticed by embodied life here on planet Earth by the various pleasures of this planet—particularly (though not exclusively) food and sex.

After all, look at the Earth compared to the other planetary bodies of our system. What is there to entice beings up on subtler levels to come down physically to the surface of a planet like Venus, say, with its scorching 867° F temperatures? Or Mercury, with its barren metallic features? Or Uranus with its icy cold atmospheres?

But Earth – ahhh! This most Taurean of all planets represents a veritable playground of sensual pleasures and "earthly delights." It's a supremely beautiful world with a seemingly boundless smorgasbord of sights, sounds, tastes, and textures to appeal to the

physical senses, ranging from the fragrance of flowers and flavors of exotic fruits to the luxurious settings of tropical islands and the sexual ecstasies offered by a loving partner.

One might well ask, wouldn't those experiences be just as enjoyable in their astral form as in the physical? Apparently not. As I heard Kriyananda once explain it, there is something about the sheer "tangibility" of experiences like sex and food that is more viscerally satisfying when experienced through bodies than with their more ethereal counterparts on the astral, or in dream states. A disembodied spirit may well draw close to appreciating such mortal experiences while hovering around our planet's surface, taking in the sights and sounds spread out before it—yet it just isn't the same.

As a result, we can imagine a scenario where a spirit plays with entering into the bodies of certain animals, plants, hominids, or even plants—all in order to "taste" those phenomena. (Imagine becoming a sequoia tree, even if just for a moment!) Though this may initially take the form of momentary experiments or earthly "vacations," the spirit may eventually find itself sucked in and stuck here, *addicted* to those worldly sensations, as it were—and in the process, forgetting its true home and original nature.

In one form or another, this is a theme that echoes throughout various ancient myths and legends—including, of course, the Biblical tale of Adam and Eve in the Garden. (Notice, incidentally, how it's specifically the taste of a fruit that leads to their fall!) But I'll be coming back to that story shortly.

I find it fascinating that we've seen a similar motif re-emerging in contemporary culture in recent decades, but framed in the clothing of science fiction. Though we find touches of this in the writings of authors like Stanislaw Lem, Philip K. Dick, and John Varley, one particularly high-profile expression was the 1982 film *Tron*. This Disney-produced movie features a central character (played by Jeff Bridges) who goes from being a game player and developer to becoming sucked into the virtual reality of his computer world, where he finds himself contending with the complexities of that digital reality. In stories like these, the computer becomes a metaphor for embodied existence itself; it's "the Fall," all right, but in a far more hi-tech setting. The message is clear: we may think we're just playing a "game," yet it's one we can easily get lost in—and in the end, forget who and where we are.

A Gnostic Reading of the Biblical "Fall"

I want to return now to the Old Testament tale of Eden, to offer up a more nuanced interpretation of "the Fall," since I think it can shed valuable light on another aspect of what that myth means. To be clear, I don't intend for any of what follows to be taken literally, as an actual account of real events that took place in ancient times. Rather, I see it as a way to mythologically convey certain truths about consciousness, particularly those involving spiritual awakening.

To begin with, imagine that you are God and you've given birth to this extraordinary creation. Yet you are not alone; there are other beings in existence, but of lesser awareness and power than yourself. (Whether you choose to see these other beings as created by God, or as fully independent beings or "mini-gods" distinct from the creator, as mystics like Shelly Trimmer and many Gnostics do, isn't as important for our purposes here. For the sake of our discussion, though, I'll be taking the latter view here—that of Adam and Eve as independent god-beings.)

Imagine that in your benevolence, as God, you allow those other beings in existence to enter into your creation, your "cosmic dream,' so they can benefit from the multifarious lessons and gifts your creation offers. At the astral level where these beings have settled in, it's a generally blissful existence. Let's suppose they are residing in the higher astral realms above a planet like Earth. In this scenario, God is akin to a protective mother who nurtures her children, who exist safe and sound within the cosmic womb of her sacred creation. [1]

There's just one downside, however. Having entered that protective Edenic state, those beings have yet to really *awaken* to their own inherent God-natures. Like proverbial infants in the womb, these beings are protected, nurtured, and quite comfortable in their seemingly "perfect" existence; there isn't yet any need to make decisions or think for themselves.

But as a result, they're also relatively unaware, relatively unawakened. There's nothing inherently wrong with that, any more than there's anything wrong with an infant remaining happy and blissfully unaware in the womb. But at some point, remaining in that Edenic condition becomes decidedly unhelpful, like a child refusing to actually grow up and think for itself.

To say it a little differently, in that primordial Edenic state those beings are simply operating on "God's programs," not on their own. Akin to the way a child is guided along a path determined by its parents, so it is with these beings who reside cocooned in the warm embrace of God's creation. For them to grow, they need to start initiating their own lives, taking charge of their own destinies—to start stepping outside of the Garden, as it were.

So how does change like that come about?

Well, once again suppose you're God. How do you encourage those beings nestled within your creation to start waking up and breaking free from your cosmic programming, to start developing *their own* free will and consciousness? You can't force anyone to awaken and grow; that's tantamount to interference. For it to really "stick," that awakening has to come from within. So how do you ignite that spark, and do so without forcing it on those beings?

There is a way, actually, but it involves a kind of "trick," a sort of reverse psychology. You see, by offering Adam and Eve a choice

So, What Am I Doing Here, Anyway?

that's virtually *guaranteed* to make them decide for themselves, in a way that contrasts markedly with Godly directives and programming, you help to light that spark of their own free will.

So you say to Adam and Eve, "I have this magnificent garden, and you are free to enjoy it—but *whatever you do, don't eat or touch that fruit from the tree in the middle of the garden! I'm warning you, stay far, far away from that tree, or you're in big trouble!!!*"

Framing it this way, of course, essentially *ensures* that they will want to taste that fruit—much in the same way that telling someone not to think of pink elephants will ensure they'll soon be thinking of nothing but.

And therein lies the beginning of the so-called "Fall," when the mini-gods engage in their very first act of free will, one that was

Adam and Eve with the serpent (from Michelangelo's mural in the Sistine Chapel).

truly initiated from within and not enforced from without. They can now start to exert free will, because you've given them a choice—*because without choice, there is no such thing as free will.*

And surprisingly enough, their ally in this process was the serpent in the garden. How is that? The serpent advises them to go ahead and eat of the fruit, at which point they will become as gods! Esoterically, the serpent symbolizes the divine energy within each of us, the inner God-voice, and is associated with the spinal energies—the proverbial "tree of life" inside us. The serpent was actually speaking truth to Adam and Eve by directing them to go against the God without and awaken the God-nature within. *In fact, the serpent and God were close allies in this awakening process, as if working hand-in-hand.*

But there is a catch. Yes, this act of seeming defiance was the beginning of spiritual awakening—the inauguration of free will and the first act of self-determination—yet this same act *sets into motion the domino effect of karma.*

You see, there is no such thing as "karma" without conscious choice or free will being involved. Even our secular judicial system thinks along these lines—i.e., gauging the consequences of actions by how old or mature the accused offender is. We don't punish a seven-year old for stealing something the same way we would a 30-year old doing the same thing. That's because we know there isn't full awareness or free will involved yet; the child is simply acting out of their biological programming, blindly. Similarly, we don't judge an animal as "evil" when doing something deadly, because we know there's no real free will or conscious intention involved there either; they, too, are acting out of pure instinct, deep hardwiring.

In that same way, karma doesn't start accumulating until we begin awakening, until we start employing our free will. As described in the Biblical story of the Fall, Adam and Eve now enter into a new era of suffering, desire, and decision-making, at which point we're told they take on "clothes"—that is, *bodies*. As a result of this cumulative karma, they become denser in vibration, weighed down by increasingly greater amounts of karma—and thus begins the descent from the astral realms above planet Earth down into embodiment on the surface of the planet.

The Return

But that is hardly the end of the story.

On its surface, this story may seem like a downward spiral from perfection to imperfection, a tragic fall into a realm of sin, suffering, and struggle. But that's only a microscopic view of a much greater narrative, the first stage in a multi-act drama. Perhaps the best exposition of that broader story I've come across is in the ancient tale *The Hymn of the Pearl*, which is a passage from the apocryphal Acts of Thomas. To my mind, this story provides some crucial clues into the meaning of our sojourn on this lonely planet, and here is how I summed it up (slightly reworded here) in my book *When the Stars Align*:

It tells the tale of a boy, the "son of the king of kings," who is sent down into Egypt to retrieve a pearl from a mysterious serpent. But while on his mission, he is seduced by Egypt and its ways, and consequently forgets his home country and family. A letter is then sent to him from the king to remind him of his background and royal heritage, at which point he remembers his mission, retrieves the pearl, and returns home.

In terms of symbolism, "Egypt" in that tale represents sensory, worldly existence itself, in which we can likewise easily become lost—and will forever remain lost until we receive that message from our Higher Self reminding us to complete our mission and return home again. One of the key points of the story is that our sojourn in this realm is not a waste of time, nor is it meaningless; there is a treasure to be gained from enduring this mortal existence, which is symbolized by the pearl.

That choice of symbols (as opposed to, say, a treasure chest, golden crown, or even a butterfly) is significant, when you consider that a pearl's beauty arises from the interaction of a rough irritant (like a grain of sand) with the surrounding oyster.

In a somewhat similar way, it is through our soul's interaction with this "rough" world and its hardships that something of great beauty arises. That's not to say that one should seek out hardships or suffering, because even the mystics say the wisest option is to learn without it, if at all possible. But as the Buddha himself pointed out, that's *not* always possible; suffering is, to some extent, part and parcel of mortal existence, with its rounds of life and death, beginnings and endings. [2]

In short, the so-called "Fall" is actually a key part of the overall awakening, with our time spent in the incarnational cycle being integrally connected to the emergence of that beautiful pearl.[3] As the mythologist Martin Shaw said, "To never leave Eden is to stay surrounded by spirit, but remain uninitiated by soul" [4] Yes, this Earth is a "rough" realm, where we necessarily encounter resistance and obstacles at every turn; our patience is tested, our dreams delayed or denied, and we're forced to deal with difficult people and temptations of every kind. Most painful of all, we have to contend with our *own* limitations and flaws.

But in the process of working on these outer challenges and inner flaws, we're being "initiated by soul"—and something of great worth and beauty emerges from that process. Resistance is key to this: by pushing up against life's obstacles, by developing self-discipline to control our consciousness and resist the lures of countless desires or impulses, we develop inner mastery and thereby gain a newfound sense of direction. In Homer's epic *Odyssey*, Ulysses must contend with an assortment of temptations and challenges on his way back from the chaos of war, but in the end finally prevails and reunites with his beloved in Ithaca—his own *personal* "Eden."

So, What Am I Doing Here, Anyway?

It is because of our sojourns through the mortal realms that we also learn to develop sensitivity, empathy, and compassion—qualities far harder to come by up in idyllic Eden. [5] In the end, it's through the young man's journey down into "Egypt" that his soul thereby becomes refined, his nature is transformed.

Our own story began when we first *cast ourselves* out of Eden through that original spark of awakening, but in the end we return there with new eyes—at which point we see that it is actually an *inner* Eden we are coming home to. T.S. Elliot said, "We shall not cease from exploration, and the end of all our exploring will be to arrive where we started and know the place for the first time." [6] He may as well have been speaking about Eden.

Notes

1. There are different variants on the Gnostic perspective, some of which are more malevolent in nature, where God is viewed as a more sinister being out to entrap us (these versions being generally labeled as belonging to the "Sethian" school); while some other variants are more benevolent in nature, where God is regarded in a considerably more positive light (these being generally labeled as belonging to the "Valentinian" school). What I'm drawing on here, inspired primarily by the teachings of Shelly Trimmer, clearly falls more into the latter camp.

2. As cited in my essay "Suffering and Soul Making on the Mean Streets of Planet Earth, in chapter 12 of *When the Stars Align.*

3. The idea that the "Fall" is actually an integral part of our evolutionary growth has naturally led many even within the mainstream church to regard humanity's original transgression in the Garden in a surprisingly different light. Mythologist Joseph Campbell often spoke about the Latin phrase employed in church liturgy, "O Felix Culpa"—which translates as "O Happy Fault!," though sometimes paraphrased as "O necessary sin of Adam!" Necessary!? This curious phrase speaks to the paradox of how Adam's "sin" in the Garden actually made possible the eventual salvation of humanity by Jesus, and was thus to be celebrated, not lamented.

4. Quoted from Martin Shaw's online essay, "The Fall and the Underworld," https://martinshaw.substack.com/p/the-fall-and-the-underworld.

5. Here again, see my essay "Suffering and Soul Making on the Mean Streets of Planet Earth," in *When the Stars Align*.

6. T.S. Eliot, from "Little Gidding," *Four Quartets* (Gardners Books; Main edition, April 30, 2001).

Acknowledgements

I want to express my gratitude to all those who provided feedback or support during the writing of this book. They include Judith Wiker, Laurence Hillman, Eric Klein, Devi Bliss, Ken and Kamala Lee, Swami Pranananda Mahaswami, Bill Hogan, Sharon Harms, Barbara Keller, Richard Smoley, Mia Feroleto, Thomas Tiernan, Al Paoletti, Jenn Zahrt, Dave Gunning, Gale Ahrens, Janet Berres, Noah Campbell, Claudette Baker, Freya Reeves, Dany Petrova, Colleen Mauro, Greg Bogart, Victor Olliver, Deborah Houlding, Victoria Martin, Trevor Grassi, Perry Fotopolous, Jeffrey Bruce Gold, Sheri Robin Hartstein, John Culp, Annette McKinney, Gary Lachman, Jane Wodening, Paul F. Newman, Kevin Moore, Fiona Bowring, and Karin Hoffman. Many thanks also to the folks at Urania Trust, and last but certainly not least, Margaret Cahill, whose keen editorial insight and encouragement guided this project to fruition. My deepest appreciation to you all!

About the Author

Ray Grasse is a writer, photographer, and astrologer living in the American Midwest. He is author of numerous books including *Under a Sacred Sky*, *An Infinity of Gods*, *StarGates*, *Urban Mystic*, *Signs of the Times*, and *When the Stars Align*. He worked on the editorial staffs of Quest Books and *The Quest Magazine* for 10 years, and has been associate editor of *The Mountain Astrologer* magazine for over 20 years. He received a degree in painting and filmmaking from the Art Institute of Chicago, the latter under independent filmmaker Stan Brakhage. He studied extensively under teachers in both the Kriya Yoga and Zen traditions. His websites are www.raygrasse.com and www.raygrassephotography.com.

www.ingramcontent.com/pod-product-compliance
Lightning Source LLC
Chambersburg PA
CBHW062004220426
43662CB00010B/1223